ROOM WITH PARIS VIEW

Jason

Phillip

Reeser

with

Jennifer Reeser

Other books by Jason Phillip Reeser

Jury Rig

The Lazaretto

Cities of the Dead

Lady in the Lazaretto
(coming Summer of 2013)

Other books by Jennifer Reeser

An Alabaster Flask

Winterproof

Sonnets from the Dark Lady
and other Poems

The LaLaurie Horror
(coming Fall of 2013)

ISBN: 978-0615773292

Saint James Infirmary Books
Westlake, Louisiana
editor@saintjamesinfirmarybooks.com

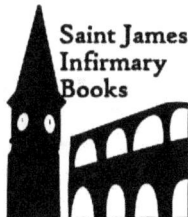

Saint James
Infirmary
Books

*Twilight of the Morning (*Le Crépuscule du soir*)*

The rising sun, within a dress of rose and green,
Advanced on the deserted Seine unhurriedly,
And somber Paris, eyes awakened by a rub,
Took up his tools, a man old and laborious.

Charles Baudelaire
Translated from the French by Jennifer Reeser

l'Menu

Photographs

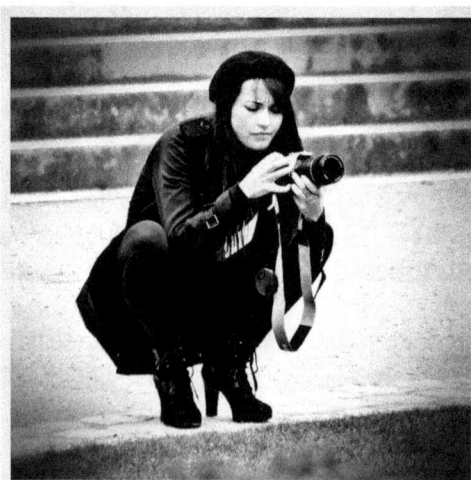

Authors' Note

The following text is not to be considered an expert's description of Paris. There are many far more accurate, knowledgeable, and well-researched books on one of the most documented cities in the world. A quick search at Amazon.com will uncover countless travelogues, blog collections, and historical tomes that will just about overwhelm you. Many are written by Americans or Brits who have been lucky enough to live in Paris for an extended time. While there, they learn the language, meet and befriend fascinating Parisians, and become experts in French food, French wine, French history, and French culture. All of this makes for interesting reading. It does not make up the basis of this book.

Our experience in Paris lasted only a short time; something that will be the case for most visitors. As we prepared for our trip, we often found that most of what is written for tourists is not very relevant beyond the usual *don't wear shorts to dinner* and *do not yell* Garcon! *at the waiters.* The bulk of what we found was more or less written for those who plan to spend months or years in France. It can be daunting to be told you need to learn the language and become an expert in French culture. It is tempting to forget the whole thing and visit London instead.

Our goal with this book is to encourage those who wish to visit Paris and let them know it is not as difficult as it is portrayed. It is also far more rewarding than you might ever imagine.

"He who contemplates the depths of Paris is seized with vertigo. Nothing is more fantastic. Nothing is more tragic. Nothing is more sublime."

— Victor Hugo

"A walk about Paris will provide lessons in history, beauty, and in the point of Life."

— Thomas Jefferson

"You belong to me and all Paris belongs to me and I belong to this notebook and this pencil."

— Ernest Hemingway

Paris is a hard place to leave, even when it rains incessantly and one coughs continually from the dampness.

— Willa Cather

Prologue

The story goes like this:

A boy from Illinois meets a girl from Louisiana in Oklahoma. They fall in love, marry, then move to Louisiana. He goes to work in a refinery. She stays at home to raise their five children. Somewhere along the way she says she wants to see Paris. He says okay, he'll take her. She doesn't believe him.

You have to have passports. Even I knew that. I insisted we do this early, the year before. I did not want any snafus to hold us up. We took the pictures ourselves, which did not turn out great but they did the job. Who cares what our pictures looked like? I had other things to worry about.

There was nothing about him to suggest he would ever take her to Paris. He was a romantic, she knew that much, but he was no world traveler. He liked to joke with their kids that since he'd never actually seen Europe, it might not really exist. Paris just didn't seem a real possibility.

She too was a romantic, and as she waited for Paris, unsure she would ever see it, she became a poet. And she waited some more, learning to substitute New Orleans for Paris.

I sat down at the computer one night, pulled up Google and typed in the following phrase: *take a vacation in Paris.* Do you have any idea how many companies want to sell you a package for a Paris Vacation? Bells were ringing all over cyberspace—*a guy in Louisiana wants to go to Paris! Line up fellas, there's money to be made off this one!*

I had a lot to learn.

He put a plan in motion without telling her. He knew she would worry. Knew she wouldn't like leaving the kids and flying across the ocean. Knew she wouldn't be able to say "no" once all the plans had been set. He put the plan in motion and patiently waited.

I determined to avoid hotels and tour-packages and anything that smacked of canned-tourism. I wasn't about to join a group that would require that we wear lime green shirts and follow the loud lady with the lime green flag on the end of a long stick.

No way.

So I bought every issue I could find of *France* magazine, a book entitled *The Unofficial Guide to Paris*, and I dug around on the Internet whenever I got the chance. It wasn't long until I knew what I wanted to do and how to go about doing it.

When he finally told her, she did not say much. She was not about to fall for a joke. And even if it was not a joke, she wasn't going to get her hopes up. Too many things could happen to cancel the trip. She had her own plan; she would wait and see.

Using an online vacation apartment service, I chose an apartment in the Latin Quarter and settled on a date (over a year in advance). Jennifer was not sure the apartment idea was a good one. I suggested that she ask her online friends what they thought about it. Almost immediately after posting the question, friends flooded her with encouragement. One friend, a native Frenchman, announced he was presently in that neighborhood, and it was a wonderful place to stay.

Cost wise, the apartment was comparable to a three or four-star hotel. I did my best to vet the agency; just to be sure I didn't send my money to some kid in Liverpool who made a living suckering dumb tourists into dumping their vacation nest eggs into his bank account. But everything checked out, and I reserved the apartment without any problems.

The agency was fairly helpful, and despite a few misunderstandings from their oddly worded instruction manual, and a slight disagreement at the end of our transactions over the deposit and what constitutes reasonable wear on the furnishings, I would eagerly say it was a successful venture. I will certainly rent an apartment again, steering clear of hotels, if our stay is longer than a few days.

She began to get excited when the passports came in the mail. It began to look as if his plan was actually going to materialize. It was a definite possibility; they just might be going to Paris. When she found the perfect shoes for strolling around Paris at a local thrift store, she knew it was meant to be.

My Internet advice short-circuited when I tried to determine what sort of electrical equipment we would need to power our chargers and computer; some said a simple adapter would work, others insisted we would need a converter. The first is only about three dollars. The second is ten times as much. This caused much trepidation for me, since I found many testimonials of fried laptops and digital cameras.

I settled on the adapters, after determining that our more modern equipment did not require the converters. However, just to be safe, I backed up all of the files on my hard drive, and held my breath the first time I plugged the laptop into the funny looking wall socket with my cheapo adapter. (As a spark shot from the wall—not a joke—I decided I could not have been a bigger idiot to go cheap on this decision. Sparks notwithstanding, I never had a problem with the many different cords and devices we used during our stay.)

And so on a sunny April morning, he loaded their bags into their car, she made sure she had the shoes and every other possible item they might need for two weeks in a foreign land, and they pulled out of the driveway and headed for Paris, France.

For Paris:
Merci Beaucoup

Chapter One: Arriving in Paris and other Sporting Events

The first time the AirFrance flight attendant spoke, I knew we'd made a mistake. Sure, I'd been able to understand the crew as we boarded, because every single one of them said *Bonjour!* as if they were filming a commercial. And when the announcements for the flight had been made in the terminal in that sensual French language by the cute brunette at the counter, she repeated herself in English, which seemed reasonable. But the flight attendant standing over me in my seat had added no such translation. Sure, it was an indication of the adventure that lay before us, but I had a feeling I was going to wish I'd taken French lessons.

Thank goodness I had Jennifer to save the day. She had learned French at an early age in Louisiana, where it is common for elementary school students to receive French lessons in the public schools, thanks in part to the CODIFIL legislation established in 1968. The Council for the Development of French in Louisiana has gone to great lengths to keep the French language and heritage alive in the state. And Jennifer had been quite active in the program, going so far as to compete at the State level in school.

Jennifer had also been dusting off her French skills as she translated a number of Charles Baudelaire's poems for national publication. Once she'd known we were actually going to visit Paris, she redoubled her efforts to hone her skills.

Despite my inability to order a glass of wine from the flight attendant without Jennifer's help, I was glad we'd decided to fly AirFrance. It was a great way to prepare us for Paris. Stepping from the terminal onto the plane was like stepping through a science-fiction portal that shot us five thousand miles across the planet and left us standing on the banks of the Seine.

It was also fun to listen to passengers around us. Many spoke French, as I had expected, but I could also hear German, and even a bit of British. (That's English, I know, but that accent mixed in with all of their colloquialisms leaves no doubt that it is a different language.)

I was intrigued by a couple across from us; they had two small children, and I overheard them say they were transferring to a flight in Paris that would take them to Beirut. I still think of the war-torn Beirut of the 1980's when I hear it spoken of, and it caught me off guard to think of taking children to a city that has seen so much grief.

We should not have been surprised that the wine served on AirFrance was superb. Of course it would be! And with this aid for relaxation, we pushed our seats back half an inch and watched the United States fade from our window view.

Most AirFrance flights leave the US in the afternoon, arriving in Paris in the morning. With the time difference (seven hours for those of us on Central Time), a nine-hour flight leaving at four-thirty in the afternoon will arrive at eight-thirty in the morning. And from that point on, you will not really be sure what time it is for about a full day.

Be sure to watch for the merry shores of England as you pass over them just after sunrise. We were justifiably moved as Great Britain slid under us, considering that it was the land of Shakespeare, Dickens, and Mr. Bean.

We passed through customs without any trouble and found a table next to a little coffee counter where we took a moment to catch our breath. It did not feel too different from being in the Houston airport, save for the fact that someone had played a joke and rewritten the signs with funny spellings.

If you are looking for travel tips, here's one I can confidently give: don't hesitate to use the AirFrance Shuttle to get into the city. It is easy to buy tickets (from a ticket machine that looks more like a soda-vending-machine), easy to board, and very clean and comfortable. The ride takes about forty-five minutes to an hour, depending on the traffic, and it was not crowded. It was also about a third of what a cab would cost.

Oddly enough, though we circled the city to approach Gare Montparnasse from the far side, we did not see more than a few faraway glimpses of the Eiffel Tower. However, once we left the *Périphérique* (the Parisian version of a loop expressway), we found our bus surrounded by the iconic image of the Paris streets—those slate-gray roofs and uniform facades so recently featured in that overblown film *Inception*.

My plan had been to step off the bus at Gare Montparnasse and catch a cab to the apartment, which would only be about a mile from the train station. It was a pretty good plan until we stood alongside Rue du Commandant René Mouchotte and were utterly perplexed to find no taxis on the street. Though the sun was shining, the wind blew hard and cold between the buildings. I could see that Jennifer was tiring quickly and I had to make something happen.

We had been told not to use the métro on our trip into the city. This was not a blanket prohibition but it was a warning aimed at protecting us from pickpockets. Since we would be carrying our luggage with us, we would be great big targets to the pickpocket population of Paris. It seems that pickpockets have been a problem.

Our apartment managers, in their wisdom, felt the need to warn us of a recently detected threat. In our packet of information that was sent to us by email, and which I dutifully printed out in accordance with their wishes, a last sheet was tacked on which warned that recent reports of pickpockets in the city were increasing. I believe we were supposed to be duly impressed, concerned, and take precautions. This was a common warning tossed about by the travel guides. One gets the idea that pickpockets are a Paris invention—something unheard of in the United States.

I'd read the novel. You know the one. That obscure little story by Victor Hugo. Something about a Hunchback? A reader of classic literature can hardly be unaware that Esmerelda's poet husband Pierre Gringoire had already discovered a vast network of pickpockets and beggars in the Court of Miracles. The warning actually went so far as to tell us that many pickpockets employ children to work for them. Now here I have to admit I'd never read *that* novel; I'd seen the movie *Oliver Twist*, but never read it. Still, I knew all about Fagan and his ilk. It seemed quite possible that our apartment managers were getting their information from Children's Illustrated Classics.

To be fair, I understood their concern. After all, we visit New Orleans on a regular basis. Keep the wallet in your front pocket. Be aware of who is close to you. The usual precautions are habit for me. I'd recently vacationed in Chicago, Philadelphia, and New York City. Pickpockets are not unheard of in these locations. I doubt the travel bureaus of those cities will complain much if I suggest you had better hold onto your wallet while walking around their streets. The United States is hardly a haven from pickpockets.

And so, in direct opposition to the warnings thrown our way, we entered Gare Montparnasse and descended the steps to the métro, our shoulders loaded with bags as we tugged on our rolling luggage. I was familiar with the métro line that ran from the station to our apartment at Saint-Sulpice. I had looked it over many times. Once the decision was made, I did not think we would have any trouble.

We stood in line to buy tickets, watching a young man asking questions of the métro attendant. The young man had to be about 18 or 19 years old. He was obviously American— he looked straight off the farm, maybe Iowa or Kansas—and did his best to speak French as he struggled to understand the man behind the glass partition. It was encouraging to see this kid alone in Paris, a backpack on his shoulder, making his way with his schoolroom knowledge of French. It was possible that our being there was not so strange. I was reminded that Americans had been coming to Paris for a very long time.

Our first obstacle to taking the métro was something fairly simple: the gates. We were loaded down; each of us carried a bag on both shoulders, Jennifer pulled a rolling suitcase, while I pulled two of them. I'm sure we looked like we came straight out of central casting. I had seen someone with a stroller enter the métro through a large swinging gate though I could not tell how they managed to make it open. So I opted to try and get us through the gates that split in the middle, like the swinging doors of an old western saloon.

I went first, so that Jennifer could see what she needed to do. Slip the ticket into the voracious ticket-taker. It eats it, then spits it out through another slot. After grabbing it (to verify you are in the métro legally, otherwise you will be fined) you have a short time to step through a turnstile and the now open saloon doors. I shouldered through them, yanking the two rolling luggage pieces off the ground. The gates swung shut and I turned to watch Jennifer pass through. Her rolling suitcase did not cooperate with her, or the swinging gates did not cooperate. In either case, her suitcase became trapped when the gates swung shut. Jennifer pulled to no avail. The bag was not going to be freed by force.

Well, we had been warned not to take the métro with our luggage.

Behind Jennifer, about to come through the gates, were three or four twenty-something guys who looked a little perplexed at her predicament. Most of them bailed out through another gate, avoiding her altogether. One of them, a good-looking, casually dressed young man, hesitated, thinking through the situation. I made no pretense that I spoke anything but English and asked him if he could use his ticket to open the gate. He nodded, but held out a hand in the universal gesture for *wait a minute*. He said in French-accented English "Quickly, quickly!" When he fed the ticket into the machine, I jerked the suitcase free and he dashed through the gate behind it.

The gates swung shut. I thanked him many times, in English and French. He just smiled, nodded, and caught up to his friends. Looking back at that little incident, I wondered about his admonition to do it "quickly." Would the gate have closed on him as it had on the suitcase? It seems odd to think so. I'm not sure if it would have. Safety precautions ought to prevent that. I did not ever test the gates again to see if such a thing would happen.

We began to move in the direction of our métro line. We would need Line 4, in the direction of Porte de Clignancourt. That wasn't hard to figure out. However, it turns out that from where we were, the Line 4 train was a pretty fair distance away. We walked through long tunnels, which always ended in stairs that sometimes went up and other times went down. At each of these, we had to sort of portage our way along, since by now, Jennifer was pretty worn down. After all, to us, is was about four-thirty in the morning, and we had been going since the morning before.

Still on alert regarding métro pickpockets, I dragged the bags up the first flight, set them down, and then told Jennifer to leave her bag and climb up the steps. It looked like some kind of absurd exchange where the good guy yells at the bad guy "send the girl first and I'll give myself up once I know she's free." Only in this case the bad guy was only a purple suitcase sitting at the base of the steps.

It wouldn't have been so bad if the stairs hadn't been so full of Parisians passing us in every direction. We portaged numerous times, and three times helpful individuals offered to carry Jennifer's suitcase for her. We declined their offers, unwilling to allow anyone else to take possession of our bags. It was our first day in Paris and we were still under the impression that Paris was as dangerous as New York City. Having learned what we have about Paris, I am sure the next time around we would have felt no compunctions about accepting their help.

We finally emerged onto the Line 4 platform with the station name tiled above our heads: *Montparnasse Bienvenue.* I liked that. It is something I am accustomed to seeing. Whenever we travel out of our home state, we always enjoy returning, where a large sign welcomes us with the words *Bienvenue en Louisiane.* Welcome to Louisiana. Here in Paris, we were being welcomed in the same way. (Later I learned that the station was merely the combination of two previous stations joined into one: Montparnasse and Bienvenue. But if you are traveling on this line you are free to imagine you are being officially welcomed here. And I know all about official welcomes. But that story comes later.)

The train quietly arrived on its rubber tires and I was no longer on edge about taking the métro. These beautiful trains, first introduced in 1963, were a retro-train lover's delight. Green and white, flat-nosed and square, they do not have the modern look of an aerodynamically designed carriage. I loved them immediately. And no matter what lines we took throughout our stay, many of which are serviced now by the newer, flashier trains, we always ended up on Line 4 as it sped us toward our apartment. It doesn't get much better than that. Oddly enough, this was a once in a lifetime experience. Just a week after we left, the official report on Line 4 was that nearly half of their rolling stock had been replaced by newer trains, with plans to scrap the last of them soon, though some of them will be used to spare Line 11.

By the time we boarded the train it was nearly noon on Sunday. There was plenty of space on board; we were not pressed on all sides by malevolent children with sticky fingers working their way into our pockets. The train lurched into motion and we sped off. I dropped a hand to my front pocket and felt the shape of my wallet. I scanned the few Parisians around us and could see that no one there paid any attention to our luggage. I glanced at Jennifer, who despite being tired, had perked up at the exhilaration of traveling the métro in Paris. We were only moments from our temporary home and I could tell she felt it.

For the first time I heard the male announcer say the name that would come to mean so much to me: Saint Sulpice. *San Soo-peece.* We gathered the sum of our belongings, pushed our way though the *sortie* gates, and found yet another stairway up which we had to portage our goods. But at the top…this was not simply another stairway. We came up into the most beautiful place in the world.

We had finally arrived in Paris.

It should not be difficult to describe a feeling that I will always remember the rest of my life. But I am afraid I will never be able to convey completely the joy, the relief, and the awe that came over us as we stepped up that last stair and stood along the Rue de Rennes. Even before we came out we could see the Haussmann-type roofs and windows of the buildings lining the avenue. We were tired and cold and that did not matter as we stood in the peaceful sunshine of that moment. Cars and motorbikes hurried by as wind blew hard enough to force us to widen our stances. Our luggage heaped atop the métro stairs. We still had to find the apartment and figure out how to get inside. But what did any of that matter?

We had finally arrived in Paris.

If I had not known how tired Jennifer had become, I could have stood there for an hour, soaking in that scene. In time, I would find places in Paris that would compete for the title of *favorite*, but that corner of Rue du Vieux Colombier would have been enough. It is often that way when you first encounter a city or a woman or a good book; you learn more about them, and fall in love with them the more you discover, but you will never quite match that moment when you first encountered them, knowing you had found something extraordinary and realizing how exciting it would be to explore the city or hold the woman in your arms or read the book to its very last page.

Jennifer felt it as well. She wasn't so tired that she ignored the magic of the moment. She insisted I take a picture and I did; our first glimpse of Paris with her surrounded by the pile of luggage at the top of the métro stairs.

We had seen the outskirts of Paris as the AirFrance shuttle circled the city from Charles DeGaulle Airport to Gare Montparnasse. But this had not been the Paris we had been seeking, though there were portions of that drive that included the Haussmann style rooftops. After following along Boulevard Périphérique and curling around Stade Sebastien

Charlety (an impressive soccer stadium whose field was dotted with young boys in bright uniforms that Sunday), and catching a beautiful glimpse of Parc Montsouris, we spied an early view of Paris' ordered beauty along Boulevard Jourdan and Avenue General du Clerc. But it had all been from behind the jolting view of bus windows accompanied by the sounds of TV commercials played on a flat screen television at the front of the bus.

Even at Gare Montparnasse I will admit that I had failed to look around and enjoy the fact that we were in Paris. I'd been too intent upon finding a cab and too perplexed when we were unable to locate one. At that point the wind had been cold and I was not in the mood to ignore it in exchange for beautiful scenery.

And so that first glimpse of Paris at the corner of Rue du Vieux Colombier and Avenue de Rennes stays with me always. Maybe the wind had died down, or the compass bearings of the avenue allowed the buildings to block the wind or perhaps it is truly possible for a beautiful city or a stunning woman or an exciting book to restore the warmth that the real world has drawn off our souls. I like to think it is possible. How much colder the world would be if it were not.

All of our weariness that had been building since the two and a half hour drive to Houston, the nearly three hour wait at Bush International, the ten hour flight across the black Atlantic night, and the three hours we spent getting through customs and busing into Montparnasse and failing to find a cab and trekking through the métro was gone as we crossed Avenue de Rennes and saw the double door entrance to our apartment on Rue du Vieux Colombier. Just half a block down, we entered our code and felt welcomed yet again as the oversized door swung inward and allowed us into the passage beyond.

We had to be in a fairy tale. This stone passage was part of a building that still housed the *Comédie-Française*, a one-hundred-year-old theater that not only performed plays by Molière, but whose acting troupe is descended from the players with whom Molière had performed and for whom Molière had written many of his plays. As we passed through we noticed a statue off to one side in a stairwell. I could not recall ever seeing such a large beautiful work of art sitting in such an ignominious location. Apparently in France, statues were common and not always considered to be noteworthy.

I would like to say that the fairy tale continued for the rest of the day. It did not. It ended right about the time we crossed the inner courtyard and approached our stairwell.

In that packet of papers the rental agency insisted I print was a simple declarative sentence describing how one went about entering the stairwell. It read thus: *Use digital key to unlock the door to the…* When I had read that line, back home, I wasn't sure what it meant. One of my sons wisely suggested I find out what it meant. I unwisely stated that I was sure it would be clear to me once we were on site. My son had it right. As for my idea, I discovered quickly that it was not clear whether I was on site or still back home where I had time to take my son's advice and email a question to the apartment managers.

A keypad with an LCD display stared out at me as I tried the most obvious solution and keyed in the same code as the first keypad. It was so obvious it did not work. I read the simple declarative sentence out loud from the packet in hopes that Jennifer might see what I was missing. This did not work either. As I tried pushing buttons and commenting on the rental agency's skill at writing *simple* declarative sentences, Jennifer sat down on the lip of the doorstep and rested her feet. I was a little worried. As a last effort I lifted the keychain up to the keypad, hoping some kind of proximity reader would kick in.

I had the local manager's phone number. But that was a bit of a problem. When we had learned that our cell phones would not work in Paris, we had to decide if we wanted to rent cell phones, buy disposable ones, or upgrade our cell phones. Jennifer was for taking one of those options. I considered a fourth option: don't carry cell phones. After all, people had been perfectly able to travel to places like Paris without cell phones for *centuries*. Why couldn't we? We would have email available in our apartment, as well as a landline that would allow free calls to the United States. Just how often would we need to use a cell phone? We would be together nearly all the time. I had trouble imagining any situation when we would need one.

Confounded by a simple declarative statement and a foreign keypad lock that kept speaking to me in French, I finally thought of a situation where I would need a cell phone.

I had a funny feeling this was one of those decisions that would come back to me in many arguments with my wife for the rest of our lives. I began to wonder how one asks a waiter for the use of his phone in French.

And then a funny thing happened. A man came down the stairs with a bag of trash in his hand and opened the door. He asked if we were the Reesers and added that his name was Karim. I knew that name. I had read it in the information packet.

Amidst our relief and thanks, Karim pointed out how to open the door. The keychain contained an RFID that had to be placed against a round plastic circle on the keypad. When they touched, the door would unlock. (I'd had the right idea, I just hadn't touched the one with the other.) The manager was happy to take us up to the apartment, and even offered to take one of the bags. He took Jennifer's suitcase and led Jennifer up a lovely wooden staircase that circled around itself and its continuous iron railing. I hitched up my two carry-on bags, lifted the two rolling suitcases, and gave chase.

At the second floor I heard Karim suggest that I leave one

of them and come back for it. I cheerfully discarded the suggestion. After all, I'd recently dropped some weight and had been walking/jogging 24 miles a week. Carrying some luggage up a stairway was not something that would kill me. I had to turn sideways to make it up the narrow stairs. It was a little harder than I had imagined it would be. By the third floor, I was lagging behind. The sounds of the others on the stairs above me were growing fainter. I have no idea what floor I was on when I ditched one of the suitcases. There were no floor designations, which seemed odd. But I imagine that one might have been tempted to despair if one knew how many floors were left. Besides, there was that whole European/American floor thing which at this point I was no longer feeling well enough to remember how it went.

A European apartment on the second floor is in fact on the third floor from an American's point of view. Europeans consider the ground floor something that should not be counted. The first floor is in fact the second floor. We had an apartment on the fifth floor, which was clearly on the sixth floor. We had been aware of this before we booked the room, and were actually glad about it. We had been promised a great view.

I heard somewhere above me—as if I were a mountain-climber who could hear voices above him in the clouds—the manager explaining how to unlock the door. I pushed on, with a great deal of pulling on as well, until I reached our door. I barreled into the apartment, dropped the suitcase I was carrying, let the carry-ons slide off both shoulders, and headed right back down for the abandoned luggage. I found it, grabbed it, and dragged it up the remaining flights of steps and dropped it next to the others.

With my head swimming I tried to focus on the scene in front of me. I was in the apartment. Off to my left I could see the promised view of the city. It was magnificent. We had finally made it. Our gamble had paid off. The apartment was perfect! My heart was beating so hard I actually put my hand to my chest and felt the poor thing trying to hammer a hole through my shirt. The manager was showing Jennifer how the washer/dryer combo worked and none of them noticed that even though I had made it to Paris I was going to die before I had even had a chance to sip some wine and bite a croissant.

I wasn't sure if 911 was an option in Paris. I felt bad that the ambulance crew would have to carry me down that eternal flight of stairs. I briefly wondered if Jennifer would feel as if she should return home immediately with my body or if she would stay and use the apartment since it was already paid for. I hated to think she would leave without using the apartment. It would seem like such a waste.

Listening to Karim explain a few more details, it occurred to me that he was speaking English. He was, in fact, speaking English with a British accent. At least it sounded like that to me. He was very helpful, extremely polite, and eager to show us everything he could. As my heart ceased attempting to chisel its way out of my chest, I thanked Karim for carrying that third suitcase up the stairs. It is quite possible I really could have killed myself if I'd made one more trip down, then up those stairs anytime soon. He was gracious and did not want to make a big deal of it. He also pointed out that climbing the stairs gave one the freedom to eat a crème brûlée. I was thinking more along the lines of eating three or four pizzas.

Once he was gone, and we were able to take a silent moment and collectively catch our breath, we both turned and looked out the floor-to-ceiling windows overlooking the courtyard. It was stunning. We were on the eastern side of a southern facing horseshoe. The right side of our view was the apartment building with its charming Parisian balcony and roof. To the left we could see rooftops below us as they fell away from our vantage point before climbing back up to create a horizon. Along this artificial ridge we could see a flagpole bearing a French flag, as if a heroic Frenchman had scaled that mountain of copper roofs and stone chimneys and planted the flag simply to provide us evidence that we were indeed in Paris, France.

We were unable to take our eyes off that view. As worn out as we were we just couldn't help but pull out the camera and take a few shots of the view with us in front of it, one at a time, before collapsing onto the loveseat. The rental agency, through Karim, had left a bottle of wine; a Medoc red, with which I was unfamiliar. I looked forward to sampling it until Jennifer pointed out that we had nothing to eat. It was close to one in the afternoon. We had not eaten since the light breakfast served on the plane around six that morning. Someone was going to have to venture out into the city and bring back some food.

And by out I mean *down*. And by back I mean *up*.

What were the chances I could get Chinese delivered to our *fifth* floor?

I had recovered enough to know that I wasn't going to go out into the city without my camera. I filled my bag with the camera, my travel journal (which contained the all-important door code as well as various European phone numbers for my bank and other significant contacts, without which I never left the apartment) and my small collection of Euro bills and coins. Jennifer insisted I take a French phrase book, though I had my doubts that it would do me much good. I promised my bride that I would return and began the easy task of climbing down the stairs.

From our landing I counted eighty stairs to the bottom. Not loaded down with luggage, and heading in the easier of the two directions that one can take on a stairway, I felt a great deal better. It was exhilarating to watch that front door swing open and to step out onto the Rue du Vieux Colombier. Paris lay at my feet. I'd been planning this for nearly three years. I wasn't anybody of importance, yet here I was walking along a street in Paris.

There was little chance I was going to seek out food immediately. Who needed food? I knew exactly where I was going. And as soon as I turned right out that front door and took just a few steps along the street I could see where I was going as well.

The Rue du Vieux Colombier is a short street that runs just a tenth of a mile from Place Saint-Sulpice to its terminus at Rue de Sévres. There is a slight bend in the street where Rue Madame crosses it just northwest of Saint-Sulpice. From our apartment, near the end of the street, you can look back along it, and the bend that pulls it to the left allows a view of one of the towers of Saint-Sulpice Cathedral. I had never heard of this church before researching the neighborhood around our apartment. (In fact I had, though I did not remember it. It plays a part in Dan Brown's *Da Vinci Code*, but I had not been impressed by the book and did not watch the movie so this bit of literary fiction slipped my mind.) Once I had begun to explore the neighborhood with Google Earth, a delightful new twist in travel preparation, I became enchanted with the square in front of it. As our visit drew ever closer, I became more and more eager to see it.

I no longer had to wait. I could see the north tower and I was not about to ignore it. I had a feeling Jennifer would understand. In fact, it was a safe bet she had already fallen asleep, so tired had she been. I had time to explore.

There is a funny feeling that comes with walking the streets of a foreign land. It doesn't matter that you are not attempting to communicate with anyone. You can walk block after block and never have reason to speak to another person, yet just the knowledge that if you had to stop in at the next shop and ask directions you would be met with a blank stare is enough to make you rethink your world. The parameters of that world are smaller. The ceiling is lowered. The horizon is pulled in closer. Your options are limited. Your prospects have been reduced to a few basic outcomes.

If you do not speak the language in this foreign land you can list the probable interactions you might have with the local population easily enough. You can stop the nearest local and pull out the phrase book your wife insisted you keep with you and then rather stupidly read incomprehensible French to said amused local. With hand gestures, and exaggerated phonetics, you should be able to say anything you want. (This doesn't mean your local will understand *anything* you say, but that shouldn't stop you from forging on ahead with your phrasebook French.) A second option is to stop the same local, take on an appropriately humble and pathetic expression, and launch into a slow, exaggerated English with plenty of hand gestures. This method, slightly different from the first method, should allow for the same results. Either way, you have a fifty-fifty chance that the person you stopped is an American who will be overjoyed to find someone else who speaks English, and he or she will promptly ask you whatever question it is he or she has been trying unsuccessfully to ask the locals for the last four days.

The remaining option, if you want to make a serious effort to communicate, is to learn a little of the French language so that you can make an honest effort to speak to them in their language. They will give you great leeway in your efforts and will also be willing to meet you halfway as they try to use what little English they have learned. It is simple courtesy. It requires the slightest of efforts and repays you with the greatest of dividends.

I had yet to learn this fact. As I crossed Avenue de

Rennes, passing by Café du Métro, which was oddly closed at such an early hour, I only knew that I was extremely isolated. It is a feeling with which I have always been accustomed. Having moved around countless times as a child, I began to think it was normal not to know anyone in town. It was the same here. Only, I also knew I could not communicate with them about the most basic of topics. So I drew on my experience as the new kid in a town: keep to yourself, say as little as possible, and figure things out on your own.

At the corner of the square, where Rue Saint-Sulpice becomes Rue du Vieux Colombier after crossing Rue Bonaparte, I saw the square for the first time. I had seen it on Google Earth before, yet here it was spread before me, the sound of the fountain overcoming the traffic in the same way the white clouds prevented my seeing the blue of the sky. The square was nearly empty save for one man in a camel coat sitting on a bench. Pigeons milled about the fountain as well. One of them was kind enough to take flight just as I was lining up a shot of the fountain with the south tower as a backdrop. It is a shot I was thrilled to capture.

I lingered only a little. I knew I had to find us something to eat. I had scouted a grocery store on Rennes during my virtual tours of the area. I snapped a few parting shots, knew that I would return to it many times, and went in search of dinner.

I should have paid more attention to that little item I had read about Sundays in Paris: most stores are closed on Sunday by law. One or two stores must be opened in a neighborhood for a few hours, but they are allowed to close early. I had assumed the grocery store would still be open. I had assumed wrong.

The grocery store was closed despite the fact it was only about three in the afternoon. Fortunately, at the sharply angled corner of rues Rennes and Cassette, the Café Cassette was open. This seemed like a pretty good prospect. It was a cheerful looking place, with heaters over the outdoor tables. Still unwilling to attempt what little French I knew, I gained the attention of a waiter and gave him my best wide-eyed face that should have clearly read *help!*

"English?" So much for wooing his favor with an attempt at his language. He just nodded and called to a young waitress passing by, pointed at me and said "English". This was obviously common practice. I ordered what I could read on the chalkboard menu in front of me. A club sandwich for me, and a club sandwich for Jennifer made with salmon. Jennifer loves salmon. Eats it all the time. I could not get that part wrong.

Well...

I waited at the bar. The bartender, who looked like the actor Liev Shreiber, paid no attention to me. One man at the bar kept offering the seat next to him. I politely declined. At least I hope I did. I expected the food to be ready any minute. That's when I had my first scare of the trip. A scare that involved money.

The bartender set down my sandwiches and fries and told me how much I owed him. In my attempt to look as if I fit in, I glibly handed him my Visa. It was to be the cornerstone of our purchasing power.

Back when I had determined that we would travel to France, I started a Visa travel account with a major bank. It was ready-made for travel in Europe: no transaction fees in Europe, just a straight exchange according to the exchange rate of the day of each transaction. I'd been using it for two years, building up points to use on travel expenses. So far so good. I was even diligent enough to call up the bank before the trip, verify their overseas policies, and activate the card for our travel dates.

And then the bartender tried my card, handed it back to me, and said their machines would not work with my type of card.

My *type* of card? That type of talk gave me a funny feeling in the pit of my stomach. Not the warm fuzzy feeling I had hoped to feel strolling the banks of the Seine with my sweetheart. He didn't exactly say *type*, since he wasn't using English. Whatever he actually said, I knew it wasn't good. He held up my card, looked at it with a shake of his head, then looked at me as if I knew what to do. I had a pretty good idea.

Panic.

I had a little cash on me in Euros. But I had intended to use my Visa for nearly everything, as I did at home. The bank had *assured* me the card would work and had been activated. I dug out my debit card, which was from the same bank, which I had also received assurances about, and watched the bartender carefully. To my semi-relief, it worked. Though this posed a different problem, since I had not transferred the main share of the money I had saved for the trip from my savings account at a different bank to the account for the debit card.

The wonders of Saint-Sulpice were fading quickly.

At least I had food for us. And so I carefully made my way back to the apartment without spilling the food. But I was still thinking about that credit card. I made it through the first door. I had remembered the code without looking it up in the book. But when I passed the digital key chain over the stairway entry box, I heard the click at the door, I heard the female voice say incomprehensible things in French, and I pulled on the door and found it was still locked.

Really? I still didn't have a phone to call Jennifer in the apartment. And I had no idea which apartment it was, since the call box had names, not numbers. I looked up at the balcony knowing it was too cold for Jennifer to leave those big windows open. Would she come looking for me? Of course not. She was most likely still asleep.

I tried the keychain again. Whatever the digital French chick was saying, I could not understand her. I pulled again and again on the door. No luck. Unless you count bad luck, as the song says.

Though it was scant comfort, at least I had the food with me. I wouldn't starve out there, though I might just freeze once the sun went down.

I made a half-hearted attempt at calling Jennifer's name. I knew that wasn't going to work. With my love of all things New Orleans I considered putting down the food, stripping down to my t-shirt, and yelling "Stella!" That would have been memorable for the local residents.

Speaking of which, one of the local residents miraculously appeared in the stairway and opened the door. I said "Merci, merci" many times, then explained that my keychain was not working.

"Yes, yes," the fit-looking Frenchman said to me with a simple but condescending smile. "Just place it like this, see? You hear the door unlock."

"I tried that," I said quickly, glad that he could speak

English. Sadly, I immediately felt this gave me the right to argue with the man who had saved the day. "It wasn't working."

"Just like this," he said again with that smile. He let the door close and took my keychain. He placed the black tag against the black circle and I heard the door unlatch and the French woman start up with her spiel again. I was about to point out that the darned door would not open as he expected it to when he reached out and *pushed* the door open.

Despite the fact that he understood English I did not feel compelled to explain that the tourist from the United States had been pulling when he should have been pushing. I was quick to say "merci, merci" and then grabbed my sandwiches and hurried up the stairs. I proudly entered our rooms with my first fresh kill on our adventure to a foreign land. My woman was going to be proud of me.

Fresh kill is an apt description.

I expected kudos for finding a club sandwich made from salmon. You don't see that anywhere in Louisiana. You might say it is *rare*. You wouldn't be wrong. It is even less frequent than rare. And if something is less than rare it is *raw*. So was the salmon.

I'm not a fan of salmon when it's cooked. I don't even think ham is eaten raw. Who eats raw meat? Well, the simple answer is the French. They eat salmon raw. So much for my ordering skills. Jennifer was gracious, and hungry, and gave it a try.

It turns out that raw salmon is pretty safe if you freeze it first. That seems to kill off the tapeworms. We soon discovered that the French love this stuff. Salmon was everywhere. It was in the grocery stores with the lunchmeats and it was on nearly every menu we read. We even found a pizza place with salmon pizza displayed. You learn something new every day. But that doesn't mean you have to eat it.

Tapeworm concerns notwithstanding, we felt better after eating something. We had regained some of the balance we had lost during the long flight and struggle with the bags. Travel is funny that way. Most of the time we had just been sitting down during the flight; an activity that is never as restful as it should be. Our minds were also still trying to adjust to the new time as well as the fact that we were in a new land. We had not just driven to a city in the States that we had never previously visited. We had traveled over an ocean, arrived on land that cannot be reached without actually leaving the land in which we had been born and raised. Perhaps most people don't see anything significant in this fact. So many people today engage in international travel it is perceived as normal. A non-event. Just another day-trip. But for a couple of provincials like us, this was something remarkable. We are fortunate that it is. I would hate to make such a thrilling voyage and discover that neither one of us thought it was special.

With food now in our slowly recovering systems we began to feel adventurous. Or maybe it would be better to say curious. We also began to require coffee. It is our one vice. We don't smoke. We don't drink more than the occasional glass of wine. Coffee is another matter. And we were in Paris, a city known the world over for its cafés. So we began our descent down those eighty steps. And I led Jennifer to the Café Cassette.

The bartender was waiting tables now. We took a table in the corner of the outer dining room, which was enclosed with glass walls, had no door, and where heaters glowed red above us. There was still a brisk wind chilling us, but the heaters did their job, and so did the waiter. He brought coffee and a piece of cheesecake. We laughed at my attempts to order in French. Jennifer coached me, pointing out the proper pronunciations. She also chided me for omitting "s'il vous plait". This was to be my common error. The French are more formal, and expect the same from everyone. I had no quarrel with them on that point. I just had so much trouble trying to speak French that I would forget to add the *please.*

Before long, I had us out of the café and heading toward Saint-Sulpice. We walked slowly, as I phonetically read aloud the signs we passed. Jennifer would correct me, or even confirm my attempts, then translate what I had read.

For all of you Dan Brown fans out there, I have little to say about Saint-Sulpice and the role it played in The Da Vinci Code. I had read the book long ago, forgotten most of it as soon as I read it, and only remembered the bit about the Rose-line and gnomon during some post-Paris reading on Saint-Sulpice. One French woman, when she heard we were in the Saint-Germain-des-Prés district, asked if we were De Vinci Code fans. I said no, and she nodded with approval. As far as the fictional claims in the book go, you can read up on them at several sites on the web. This was one literary connection that did not interest me.

The fountain and the cathedral were just as magnificent the second time around. There was still plenty of light even though the clouds had begun to darken. We circled around to the east end of the cathedral, along Rue Palatine, and I introduced Jennifer to one of the most beautiful spots in Paris. The east end is the older portion of Saint-Sulpice. Whereas the western end, with its towers and arches, has a classical flavor, like something from Venice, the eastern end looks decidedly medieval. Here, the apse ends with a turret-like formation. The walls are nearly flush with Rue Garancière, which only narrowly separates it from the buildings on the opposite side. This little spot is visually arresting as you turn the corner and catch a glimpse of it. During the next two weeks I passed this sight time and again and I was never able to do so without taking a moment to marvel at it. If a bench had been placed on that narrow sidewalk outside the shops looking toward Saint-Sulpice it might have been difficult to dislodge me from it.

Back at the fountain we saw other couples in the square snapping pictures of each other. It is one of the more common sights you'll find. This is not Disney World. Families of four and five do not tramp about like a troop of Boy Scouts. Yes, Paris is for lovers, but I suspect it is also expensive enough to discourage those who would usually bring the entire family. As much as I wanted to taste the romance of a vacation-for-two, I kept wishing we could have brought some or all of our children. I hated to think they were unable to see the wonders of this city.

But we were unable to bring them and so I was forced to suffer alone in Paris with my bride. We all must face the hardships of life with courage. Hemingway would have been proud of my fortitude.

We ventured into the church, though there was a service in progress. It was, after all, a Sunday evening. Other tourists circled around the nave, and I'm sure those attending the service were used to it, but we felt it would be better to come back later. After all, we had two weeks ahead of us. The interior was full of dark, beautiful artwork, and later we wanted to spend time taking it all in. This was to be one of the many dropped intentions of our trip. In truth, we never made it back inside. Like kids in a candy shop we had trouble knowing just what to taste. But we did not know this as we crept through the massive and ornate wooden doors.

By the time we made it back up the stairs we were thoroughly worn out. We had been on-the-go for nearly thirty-six hours. We are not the type to dance the night away. Even if we had been, it would not have been an option that night. We turned in early, excited about the days to come.

Room With No View *Excerpt, April 16, 2012:*

It has only taken me a day to learn a significant cultural difference between the United States and France. Despite the fact that the French are known for their coffee, they seem to have a problem pouring out more than a few ounces of it at a time.

It is one of the first phrases I tried out after we landed. *Je voudrais un café*. I was proud of that one. And the mademoiselle behind the airport coffee counter did not bat an eye. She turned her back to me, poured out, then handed me what looked like a free sample that we might see being offered outside a coffee shop. It was *not* free. It was very good, don't get me wrong. So I figured maybe it was just the fact that it was coffee from an airport—high-priced and a small amount. But after getting coffee in a local café, and then buying coffee in the early morning hours at a little *pâtisserie*, I was beginning to see a pattern. I'll be humble enough to accept the fact that we Americans are spoiled, and perhaps overindulgent. So I won't say the French are stingy with their coffee. I'll simply say we Americans drink *a lot* of coffee. And I wanted *a lot*.

We arrived on Sunday, which we had been warned about. Nearly everything is closed on Sunday. Which is sort of ironic, since the once puritan United States has abandoned its closed-on-Sunday routine. But here in France, the State has set Sunday as a no shopping day with only a few exceptions. In the tourist areas, a few types of stores are allowed to operate. Supermarkets are allowed to be opened until 1 pm. Here at St. Sulpice, by the time we were situated in our little home, everything was closed except one café. Most importantly, that meant we had no coffee of our own to brew! So, as I often do, I awoke early and was out on the street looking for coffee.

Looking.

Looking.

Okay, so Paris is not a morning city. Yes, there were a few people out and about. But nothing was open. It was seven in the morning and nothing was open. I walked all along Rennes Avenue, down to St. Germain Boulevard, and still nothing. I passed by the iconic cafés *Les Deux Magots* and *Café De Flore* and apparently Jean Paul Sartre had never been up early looking for coffee. So I tucked my chin into the cold morning wind and went looking for Rue du Dragon. I'd read about it in a history book, and really wanted to get a look at it. It is a beautiful little street and it was right where I expected to find it.

Turning into it, I forgot about the coffee and began to take pictures. It was a perfect little spot. I saw a glimmer of hope when I spied a little place called the PDG Restaurant, with the words *American Restaurant* in red neon. The lights inside were on. Coffee! These guys surely understood my need to have a big cup of coffee!

No. Not open. Still looking.

But what was this? A *pâtisserie*! Wonderful, glorious pastry shop! The little French *grand-mère* smiled at me. She was open! I grabbed the door and pulled. Locked! Now, I'm getting the idea that Paris is laughing at me. But then, along comes a dandy-looking elderly *monsieur* who said *bonjour* (of course!) and pushed on the door. It opened easily enough. The stupid *Americain* couldn't figure that one out. But I was in! I might still survive.

"*Bonjour*! *Je voudrais deux café, s'il-vous plait.*" (And hold up two fingers, just in case she doesn't recognize the word for two. Because, you know, she might be a beginner with this language too!)

Two sample cups coming right up.

She put tin foil over them so I could take them back to the apartment.

Well, it was a start.

I also ordered the *pavé suisse* and a *brioche*. The first looked like an egg and mushroom sandwich sort of deal, the second I knew was a sweet bread. Okay, we had the beginnings of a breakfast. (The *pavé suisse* turned out to be a sweet bread with cheese and chocolate, which was a surprise, and a happy one, to be sure.)

After carefully transporting the precious coffee back to our apartment, up the six flights (eighty stairs, yeah, I counted them), I arrived triumphantly with the coffee!

Jennifer looked at my two little cups and was not very impressed. Well, I did the only thing a husband could do, and let her have both of them.

But it was getting close to opening time for the local market. I went back down the stairs (80!) and back out into the cold wind. Around the corner back onto Rennes. The Franprix, the local equivalent of a Piggly Wiggly, was finally open. I hurried in, not caring what language they spoke, ready to battle whatever cultural barriers remained in order to buy coffee.

I could not have been more at home. One thing I know is how to shop. And this was as simple and as familiar as shopping at our local grocer. I grabbed a basket, and began collecting orange juice, milk, bananas, everything a man needs for breakfast. Just one more item to capture: coffee.

Looking.

Looking.

You're kidding me, right? Where the heck is the coffee? I searched every aisle. Nothing! Lots of wine. But where was the coffee? This is France! They must have coffee. Unless I was in the middle of a really bad nightmare, there had to be coffee.

Right?

Wait. A little staircase in the back corner led to a second floor. I heard angels singing. I saw the golden glow. There, on the second floor, tucked back in the corner, I finally saw the holy grail. Shelves of coffee. *Café Noir. Café Delicate. Café Intense. Café Nuit* (decaf). All sorts of coffee. Sailing through the checkout line, I was back to the apartment, back up the stairs (80!) and through the door.

The sound of a coffee machine never sounded so good.

Fortified with coffee, we set out on an extraordinary day at Père Lachaise Cemetery and Montmartre. I'll tell you all about it another time. For now, I'm going to have another cup of coffee.

Chapter Two: The Mountain of the Martyr

I had promised the readers of *Room With No View* that I would tell of that extraordinary day at another time. I finally get to fulfill that promise. I hope it was worth the wait.

For those who are not aware of the fact, I am something of a graveyard devotee. I have written many stories about the above-ground cemeteries of New Orleans. I have also amassed a rather extensive collection of photographs from those cemeteries. One of the goals of this trip to Paris was to add to that collection after visiting the three major cemeteries of Paris along with a trip underground to the fabled *l'empire de la mort*: the Paris Catacombs. I had been dying to see them.

Part of our preparations for this trip consisted of researching what we wanted to do once we arrived in the City of Light. There were times I nearly had a panic attack as I realized that it was possible to spend two weeks there and still miss parts of it that we would regret for the rest of our lives.

We were treating this realistically. We had no illusions that we would ever get back to Paris. This was a once in a lifetime shot. And if we arrived unprepared, and wasted time wondering what to do, we were going to miss too many things to imagine. So we read, researched, and made out our list.

Of the museums we intended to visit, the Louvre was the primary objective. But we did not want to start there. We wanted to be able to get our bearings a little before we tackled one of the most important museums in the history of the world. Our second choice for museums, the Musée d'Orsay, was closed on Mondays. I took this opportunity to promote a suggestion that was high on my list: Père Lachaise Cemetery.

Père Lachaise Cemetery is the largest cemetery in the city of Paris. At two hundred and eight years old, it is modestly aged, Saint Louis Number One in New Orleans is sixteen years older. As European cemeteries go it is a youngster, to be sure. However, it is one of the most visited cemeteries in the world. Among the historical French characters buried within its walls are such giants as the painters Corot, Ingres, Pissarro, Seurat, David and Delacroix, the actress Sarah Bernhardt, singer Edith Piaf, and the writers Balzac, Nerval and Apollinaire. Many famous residents there are not French, including Modigliani, Chopin, Gertrude Stein, Oscar Wilde, and the most visited resident within the walls—Jim Morrison. And that is just a sample of the artists found therein. A list of the politicians and soldiers and architects and mistresses and royals that are entombed there would be too long to add here.

I was aware of the two other cemeteries within Paris proper: Montparnasse and Montmartre. But very little was written about them. Everyone talks about Pere Lachaise. I became easily distracted when looking at it on Google Earth. Many photos have been uploaded there and I became quite enthralled with the offerings from my fellow devotees.

This was my target that first day. I wanted to go there

before anywhere else. As any good salesman would do, I packaged the deal with a suggestion that we visit Père Lachaise followed by a stroll up Montmartre to see Sacré Cœur and a final walk to Montmartre Cemetery. I knew that Jennifer was eager to get to the cemetery on Montmartre to conduct research for one of her poems. That was all she needed to hear. We quickly agreed on the first day's itinerary.

All of these locations were relatively close together. They were on the Right Bank—*la Rive Droite*—near the outer perimeter of Paris. Père Lachaise is in the 20th *arrondissement* and Montmartre is in the 18th *arrondissement*. Although it is nearly eight miles to travel from Saint-Sulpice to Montmartre Cemetery if you stop at Père Lachaise between them, it is relatively quick to do so, with the métro. A quick ride on Line 4 from Saint-Sulpice to Réaumur–Sébastopol with a connection to Line 3 in the direction of Gallieni and you can arrive at Gambetta station in under thirty minutes. There is a Père Lachaise station on Line 3 just before Gambetta, but I had seen suggestions that Gambetta was a better way to enter the walled cemetery.

Place Gambetta is a pleasant little hub of activity and an enjoyable area to walk. I had planned our course to the cemetery without regards to where the métro stairs came out of the earth. This was a problem on several occasions. When you come out at ground level and you find yourself on the edge of a traffic circle, it is difficult to know just where you are. Reading the street signs that are affixed to the walls of the surrounding buildings does not automatically help. At this particular circle, Avenue Gambetta comes in from the west and leaves heading northeast. Rue des Pyrénées comes in from the southeast and stays on that course as it leaves. Rue Belgrand and Rue Père Lachaise appear from the east and southwest respectively. The stairs from the métro leave you facing away from the circle down Rue Belgrand. It takes a little effort to get going in the right direction without a phone that has a GPS.

Approaching the cemetery, I was duly impressed with the walls that surrounded it. Iron spikes line the top of the stone wall. The gates are ten or twelve feet high. Grave robbers have a low probability of success here, which is a good thing, considering the works of art that fill this sacred ground.

A cold wind blew through the trees that stood guard over that ground. White fluffy clouds were scattered across a blue sky. There was no threat of rain, though the forecast said it would soon arrive. The air was colder than I expected. I didn't mind it so much. We were prepared for it. But it was cold enough that it was hard to stop thinking about it. I am more accustomed to walking the cemeteries of New Orleans in the extreme heat of a Louisiana summer. The cold seemed appropriate as we began our tour. Rain is overused in graveyard movie scenes. I was glad to forego that cliché. I had an umbrella but no hat to warm my head, which has far less natural cover than it once had.

I wasn't interested in Jim Morrison's grave. I find it absurd that so many people come to Père Lachaise and head straight for the site of the former Doors' lead man. Maybe if I liked their music I would join them. Probably not. I am a big fan of Edith Piaf's but I was not about to rush off in search of her grave. I was, however, interested in seeing Oscar Wilde's crypt, since it is considered one of the more remarkable memorials. I'm sure Wilde would have something witty to say about that. I'll leave it to him to do so.

Right away we were treated with something unusual in that august garden: weed killer. One of the sections in the northeast corner was taped off to visitors. Impressive warning signs told of highly poisonous toxins that were being utilized to kill off the weed populations. We saw four or five workers decked out in chemical suits with cartridge respirators strapped over the lower portions of their faces. They looked a little like the decon squad from *Monsters Inc.* It intrigued me that they were on their side of the red-and-white striped tape liberally spraying the ground all around, while we were on the other side of the tape watching them from a distance that could not have been greater than six feet. With the wind swirling in multiple directions, there was a better-than-slim chance we might be overcome by a toxic biocide that would make us the newest residents of Pere Lachaise.

This kind of thing shouldn't happen on your first full day in Paris. Poison me on the tenth or eleventh day, but not the first. That just makes the whole trip seem so pointless. To survive a trans-oceanic flight and a brush with raw salmon just to end up dying from the French version of Roundup is a little too much tragedy for me. Yeah, it might have made a good story, but I wouldn't have been the one who had the pleasure of telling it. And then there were the two all-day métro tickets I had purchased. We'd only taken one trip so far that day. What a waste of money it would have been.

The métro tickets were a bit of a sticky wicket for me. I like to plan, I like to budget, I like to think that I find the most clever approach to what everyone else takes for granted. The tourist advisories all say the same thing: buy a five-day métro pass for your week in Paris. It makes sense, I suppose. If you plan to stay in the center of Paris, in the first three zones of the métro, this will provide all the coverage you'll need to get around. With the exceptions of Versailles and a few of the big markets on the outskirts of the city, you will be able to reach any site you can think of with this pass. Logically, the five-day pass is the way to go.

Well, for a normal person, that would be true.

Okay, I had no trouble with the three-zone limitation. That was fine. I should have just bought it, in advance, even, and really I might have, and would have felt it was worth it, but for one little thing: the five-day stipulation had me a little confused. It makes sense if you are there for a week. You arrive on one day, begin to use the métro the next five days, and leave on that sixth day or the next. But we were going to be there for two weeks. I love math games, and I began to see that with two passes each, we would use it for ten days, leaving us three or four days without it. So then a three-day pass would need to be added. All of this added up to a pretty sizable amount of cash. I chewed on my lip about this for weeks, trying to decide if it would be worth it.

The image of the Paris tourist is one of a romantic couple zipping about the City of Light along the darkened tunnels of the métro. But just how often would it be used? Sure, I'd saved up a pretty nice sum of money for this trip, but I'd seen no reason to toss it around carelessly. This was one of those things I'd decided to play by ear.

That first morning, on our way to Pere Lachaise, we entered the domain of Paris' underground railroad by way of Saint-Sulpice station. These wide stairs, one on either side of Rue du Vieux Colombier, are the perfect wind tunnel for a spring morning. We wore our sweaters and jackets but the wind was a little more than exhilarating. To purchase tickets, we had to use a machine. The métro employee behind the Plexiglas did not dispense tickets. All she could do was point at the machine, which is not a bad job, really, since she was out of the wind. Thankfully, the machine spoke English, by way of touchscreen, and with a funny little rollerball which only rolled up and down, I navigated my way through the ticket buying process.

I was still stuck on that big five-day-pass price. It seemed more than it should be. So, with the wind harassing me, I made a quick decision and just bought us one-day passes. Or, I tried to. But again, my credit card did not work. Now I was pretty sure my bank had lied to me. I was in Paris without a working credit card. This was going to be fun. Glad that I'd obtained a few Euros before leaving the States, I bought the tickets and off we went on our first day's adventure.

One more note on that métro trip. As we came up at Gambetta, the station had the equivalent of a convenience store at the lower end of its stairway. Here you could buy newspapers, drinks, snacks, and other sundries. I realized that when stores are closed above ground, this might be the best chance to find something open. Our own Saint-Sulpice station had no store, but many of them did. Some of them even had coffee shops. It was something to keep in mind.

I eventually decided against the five-day pass. Our trip that day involved three trips on the métro. And that was a fairly extensive day. So had we used just single trip tickets, we would have used only six. To do a little math, the two one-day passes we bought were a little over 22€. The six single-use tickets (at 1,70€ each) would have cost 10,20€. Consider that if you use a multi-day pass, you must use them consecutively, which means that if you take a day off from sight-seeing, or your planned trip is within walking distance, you'll waste that day's allowance. I ended up buying ten tickets at a time then buying more as we needed them. At the end of the trip, I had two tickets left. We just didn't use the métro (or buses) that much. This is Paris, and you want to walk everywhere. It is a city made for walking.

But enough math. Back to Pere Lachaise.

The size and feel of Père Lachaise is something like a State Park. It is beautifully landscaped, with gently rolling hills as its foundation. Tall trees lined most of the paved lanes, their branches pruned high out of reach. On this day their leaves were green and full as if they had just been painted on by Van Gogh for the new Spring season. Sunlight hit this canopy and tumbled down over the gray, green-black stone shapes that filled the gardens. The wind stirred up dust and fallen seed pods (and weed-killer!), filling our view as well as our ears with that peculiar feeling one gets on a Spring day; the feeling that a new year waits to see what you can make of it.

I was intrigued that every engraving on those stones was in French. Anything written on any given memorial was French. I'm not saying I was surprised at this. It just took a little getting used to. Having spent my whole life in the United States, with the exception of one short trip to Cancun, I had not been any place where English was not the predominate language. Everywhere we saw the word *Famille*. That one was easy: Family. One even saw this a time or two down in New Orleans. New to me were such phrases as *ici repose* and *Dans le Seigneur*: here lies and *with the Lord*. Though it was just my first full day in France, with Jennifer's occasional instruction, I was quickly learning to read the memorial plaques.

Near the Gambetta entrance stand a number of memorials to the fallen from World War One. Several of these were dedicated to non-French nationalities like the Czechs and the Italians. One such memorial was to the Russians who had assisted the French Resistance in WWII. The memorial to the Czechoslovakians who died in the Great War is an elaborate, moving piece of a heroic warrior who is about to be embraced by a young maiden, while an old woman watches with hands nearly clasped in prayer, as a wounded soldier falls backwards into the warrior and maiden. This copper statute, of course, is covered with green and black verdigris, and it was the first time I realized what lay in store on this trip. As I would see again and again, there are works of art in this city that completely outshine anything I have seen on our side of the world, yet here, where great art can be seen every day, many amazing pieces go unnoticed.

We eventually spotted Oscar Wilde's rather silly looking tomb. I do not know if he designed it, though I hope he did not. It is an image of an Egyptian or Babylonian figure, stretched flat on its belly, suspended in air, with a jagged spot midway along its body where a portion of him once dangled. At some point in the past, someone had either taken a souvenir or they had made known their displeasure with Wilde's memorial. The grave is now surrounded by Plexiglas, where mourners (groupies?) write notes and leave lipstick kiss impressions on its surface.

I don't mind this kind of nonsense too much. But I will admit to being rather appalled at the fact that a very large group of tourists had bunched around this monument to poor taste, ignoring the wonderful, moving memorials that surrounded it. Just opposite Oscar's tomb is the carving of a woman who has thrown herself down across a fallen and broken column. The work is somewhat rough, it is not polished stone. The woman's eyes are closed and she seems only to be asleep. A delicate fabric has been draped over the lower half of her unclothed body, though some of her leg is uncovered. Her faithful vigil is made the more poignant by the crowds who ignore her. Nearby, two women, covered by stone robes spattered with moss, comfort each other, one face worn down by exposure to the weather, one face blackened by mold and time.

As we moved away from Oscar and his admirers, I began to realize that Père Lachaise would never win my heart like those New Orleans' Cities of the Dead. It was something I was able to recognize immediately. Père Lachaise seemed to lack the spiritual backdrop of old New Orleans. More than anything, it felt empty. Sure, it was a cemetery, populated with bodies that no longer contained life. But that is not my point.

I began to write my anthology of the Cities of the Dead after my first visit to one of them after Hurricane Katrina. By then, September of 2006, just shy of the one-year anniversary of that terrible disaster, the majority of the wreckage and debris had been removed from the high traffic areas of New Orleans.

Many of the hardest hit neighborhoods were still far from recovery, but places like the Garden District were well on their way to a return to normalcy. About the only evidence of their travails was the constant sound of electric saws and hammers ringing through that wealthy neighborhood. Into this atmosphere I came to visit Lafayette Cemetery Number One. I was easily overcome with the sense that within those walls were more than empty shells. It was easy to imagine that at night, those grassy lanes filled with the spirits of those who had been laid to rest above ground. It was true in the other cemeteries as well.

While I do not literally believe such spirits roam those stone gardens, I recognize that the history of the people who have gone before lingers over such a place. Perhaps I believe that the humid atmosphere holds this history in place, not allowing it to dissipate like it does most everywhere else, in the same way a plastic greenhouse traps the heat and moisture to aid whatever has been planted under its soil. I think mostly it has to do with the heavy decay that rots the very stone houses that become ovens for those who lie within. Even marble is not exempt from this deterioration. A man's tombstone is not sacred there; the memory of his basic statistics is as fleeting as the body he once filled. It is a humbling thing, indeed. The Bible tells us we are but vapors in this world. In New Orleans, we see the evidence of this *in flagrante*.

At Père Lachaise I could sense this was not the case. Nowhere did I see the kind of decay to which I had become accustomed. Steles, declaring the birthdates and death dates of those buried within, were still legible after nearly two centuries. About the only signs of age were the heavy stains of black mold; something that is not as prevalent in New Orleans. But I was not surprised at this. The world of Paris is wet and cold, and the heat is never close to what one finds in the Mississippi delta.

I could also sense the wealth that was on display. Not just material wealth, but I could see that this was where a city came to display its sorrow with the great wealth of artists available to them. The memorials, the statues, the tombs themselves, seemed the result of a desire to impress. A desire to impress the living, not a God above. Yes, Paris was predominately Catholic, but it was a more secular system than the one in New Orleans. The Catholics of Louisiana conduct themselves with more fervency, as if the passion of the American Evangelicals had infected them over time. This spiritual difference could be felt in Pere Lachaise.

For all its beauty, it just seemed to lack humility in the face of our mortality. Pride was stood in its place. This should not surprise anyone. Beauty is so often the springboard for pride, and is certainly an obstacle in the nurturing of humility.

This was all mere observation. We did not stay long enough to get to know the French well enough to make such judgments with authority. Maybe, if I were objective about it, I would realize that my view was clouded by the fact that most of the sepulchers, while shaped like the New Orleans tombs, are often fronted with glass doors, where one can see that they are empty, with elaborate stained-glass windows on three sides. This is not done in New Orleans, where bodies cannot be buried underground. But there, in Paris, the bodies were safely tucked underground, and so the stone "house" is empty, often with a bench inside available for loved ones to take a moment during their visit and pray for the deceased or simply sit in quiet reflection and remembrance.

With a cold wind hurrying us along the paths, I took as much time as I could to capture image after image of the gorgeous statues we encountered. It became Jennifer's belief that I was mostly drawn to the ones that portrayed women in distress. That made me sound creepy. I corrected her, insisting that it meant I felt most for those women weighed down with sorrow since one of my great virtues is my ability to cheer people up. At least I like to think so.

Near the end of our tour we came upon several memorials to the victims of the Holocaust: most memorable of these being the profound Auschwitz Memorial. It depicts four camp members accompanying a man who is pushing a wheelbarrow. In that wheelbarrow is a body which is lying in the corner, its head hanging back over the front of the wheelbarrow. All of the figures are stick figures who have a surreal resemblance to many of those poor souls rescued at the end of the war. One of the men walking in front of the wheelbarrow has dropped his head back, his mouth open as he gazes at the sky, his shoulders dropped as well, as if his hands have been tied behind him. I was sure I could hear his sigh of despair in the wind that blew through his spare frame.

Perhaps it was the Auschwitz Memorial, or just the cold wind that kept insisting we pay it attention; either way, we decided we had seen enough. We were also hungry.

After peering in the window of several cafés on the streets outside of Pere Lachaise, we were not quite sure we were brave enough to try out our French phrases or the French Cuisine. There was a certain wariness that I could feel at the doors of these restaurants. Maybe I had read too much about them and their formal attitudes. But really, in reading the menus, there did not seem to be much we desired. We are not big eaters, at least not when it comes to steak and fish. Added to this reluctance for the finer establishments, we really had not eaten much since we'd arrived twenty-four hours before.

When we are this hungry there is often only one solution: a good ol' hamburger. And we found that back at Place Gambetta. I had remarked on it when we were first there. It now stood out like a bright beacon on the living shores of the River Styx: Indiana.

The *Indiana Café* had a great black awning decorated with

what would almost pass for the Pontiac (as in automobile) symbol. Bold red chairs were lined up under this alluring cover, and a few English words beckoned us with the promise of *Brunch* and *Cocktails*. I wasn't too interested in a drink right then, nor did I want brunch, but the fact that English was in use was a good sign. It seemed we were not quite ready to go completely native. This was a welcome sight.

It almost felt like we were entering a Chili's. After the salmon incident, this was not a bad feeling. The hostess at the door immediately asked *English?* even before we spoke. (My response—*oui*—did not seem to confuse the hostess.) I didn't mind that she had pegged us so easily. We both nodded happily and a young blonde waitress showed up with a smile and said *Bonjour*. She switched effortlessly between English and French as needed, and before we knew it we were seated in a corner table under a collection of very colorful Indian figures.

We were happy to see the menu was in English. Perhaps the waitress had menus for both languages. We ordered, then took in our surroundings.

What hit me right away was the fact that the name of the café was *Indiana*, and yet whoever had come up with this theme obviously knew little about the word Indiana. I'm a former Hoosier, I did a few years in that wonderful state back when I was a kid. What I had never seen until that moment in Paris was the assumption that the name Indiana had anything to do with Indians. Yet there, in that café, were scores of eight-by-ten photographs of Indian Chiefs, the kind we saw in the Time-Life Cowboys and Indians set when we were kids. Yes, there is an Indian heritage that goes back to pre-statehood days in that state, but there isn't much once it became a state. The café should have been called *Wyoming* or *Colorado*. But it was cute and we played along.

The burger I ordered was very close to an American

burger. The fries were not far off either. We did not dawdle over our food. It was just what we needed.

The waitress, Gabrielle, was very friendly, and her English was great, without a hint of a French accent. I figured she was an exchange student and asked her where she had grown up, sure it would be someplace other than France.

"Here, in France," she said, nodding as if that were the only possible answer. "Not Paris, but a small town outside it."

"I'm surprised at that," I said, "when you slip into English you have no accent whatsoever."

"Oh, well," she confessed, "I spent a year in Australia. And that's where I learned English so well."

As she spoke more about the Land Down Under, she allowed herself to slip into a pronounced Australian accent. She was very good. I pointed out to her that most French actresses couldn't hide their French accent. (I was thinking specifically of Juliette Binoche. She's a favorite of mine, but she can't hide that sexy accent, and why would she want to?) Gabrielle laughed and thanked me for the compliment. She was possibly the most relaxed Frenchwoman we encountered on our entire trip.

We could have stayed all day, especially knowing that cold wind was still blowing outside. But we had places to go. And that place was Montmartre.

Back down into the métro. This time we took only a short hop from Gambetta back to Père Lachaise station, to catch Line 2. From Pere Lachaise, we swayed through eight stations on our way to Anvers, passing the scene of a horrific fire that overwhelmed the Couronnes station in 1903. Seventy-Five people died at Couronnes, seven at Ménilmontant. Whether we are in a cemetery or not, it seems the dead are all around us. Not up on my Paris métro history at that time, we shushed through this landmark unaware of any ghosts that still feared smoke in those tunnels as we climbed to Montmartre.

My fancy gets the better of me sometimes, but I do not think such fancies are nonsensical. I am always sobered by the layers of man that have been woven over a geographical point. And Paris is a place where you should never ignore these layers. How can you walk streets that are eight hundred years old and not think about those who once walked them when we were just an intangible thought in the future? It would be wrong to do it. As wrong as shouldering our way through a group of old men, pushing them aside, never recognizing how hard such men have worked to pave the way for our present generation. As if we truly believed we are all that exists and none ever existed before us.

It is easy to do this at home in the States. We tear down buildings that are twenty years old. We reroute roads that do not fit our needs. We dig out lakes and fill them in. The world is our canvas and we paint, repaint, tear it up and start over again. It all depends on what we need and want at the present time. When we do recognize the past, we make an amusement park of it, or at least a shopping mall. We air-condition it, stamp a cute logo on it, and sell the hell out of it. If you can't do that, we don't bother to save it.

I have kids who are not yet out of their teens who say, "remember that (fill-in-the-blank-store-name) that used to be right on that corner? And I say "Yeah, and I remember when they built it the year you were born." Permanence means nothing to us. We think Denny's is ancient.

But each day we were in Paris, I began to look around me with a new awareness of this historical atmosphere that seemed to cling to the walls of the houses like multiple layers of thick, dripping paint. The streets were alive with it. My mind wanted to keep taking each view and refocusing it until I could see it as a washed-out and faded post card from 1900. You can do that in New York City, too, but the trick in Paris is that you can then refocus again, until you see the 1600s. Then further back again. Kings and queens, lords and dukes rode through these streets as they gathered to *joust*, for Pete's sake.

And you don't have to picture these things as portrayed in the movies. In this same city, hanging on the walls of the Hôtel De Cluny, you can see tapestries from the late fifteenth century that depict these ancient times. The sheer number of people who have lived and loved and fought and died in Paris astounds me. There are older cities, by far, but few that have been as populated at Paris, for so long. Few that have been visited by so many, for so long. Maybe Rome would be the exception.

You could stand on a corner on the Isle de le Cite or along the Rue de Rivoli and imagine who has walked at that very corner throughout the history of the world and you would not be able to imagine them all if you stood there for a year. And since it is a literary city, we have an incalculable quantity of written accounts of these men and women, including accounts of their deaths. Couronnes station is just another example of this. You would always do well to keep an eye out for ghosts. They are there and they might just appreciate it if you acknowledge them with a look or even a tip of your hat.

The little métro ride from Père Lachaise to Anvers, at the foot of Montmartre, actually slips above ground just outside of Place du Colonel Fabien. You get a chance to see the rather large and popular discount store *Tati* (an upscale Wal-Mart, from what I have heard) on Boulevard Rochechouart just before the train slips back under the streets. The day we passed it there was a great deal of foot traffic all around, and plenty of pink Tati bags to go around.

As we climbed the steps of the Anvers station, its view framed by the famous Guinard Art Deco ironwork (which resembles a Steampunk garden entrance from Alice in Wonderland), I was not sure what to expect. I had seen pictures of Montmartre, and its brilliant white cathedral, but I knew little about it. I had read about Picasso, and Toulouse-Lautrec. And I knew the basic story of the Moulin Rouge. But I had never been able to piece it all together into a cohesive image in my mind. I had an idea we would like it, but beyond that I couldn't say.

We stepped up into a carnival.

Montmartre is a small mountain (or a big hill, depending on how you look at these things) that overlooks Paris. It began as a village outside of Paris, and over time became a haven for artists and writers. The original estates were farms, including the oldest one, where Pierre August Renoir once made his studio.

It was also on Montmartre that Pablo Picasso began his forays into cubism. He, along with Modigliani and other artists, made *le Bateau-Lavoir* known the world over.

Sitting atop the mount is the *Basilique du Sacré Cœur.* Though its construction began in 1875, it was not finished until 1914, less than one hundred years ago, making it a new cathedral by European standards. Made of calcium-rich travertine, it cleans itself every time it rains, thereby saving its caretakers the effort of cleaning the exterior. The cathedral has an Eastern appearance, with a large central dome fronted by two smaller domes. A great cascade of steps rolls down the side of Montmartre to a retaining wall, where two smaller sets of steps continue below. At the base of these is another retaining wall, below which is a beautifully decorated carousel in Square Louise Michel. Originally, this was Square Willette, named for the artist Adolphe Willette. Times have changed. Michel was a revolutionary of the *Communards* and it seems this is more honorable than the life of a Montmartre artist.

Unable to see any of this yet, we emerged from the métro at the base of Rue de Steinkerque. There, amidst the milling noontime crowd, we took a few minutes to browse the souvenir kiosks that looked very much like the type we had seen in New York City the year before. Watching over us was a large relief sculpture in the façade of the nearby Élysée Montmartre, a theater built in 1807, of a dancing girl, decked out in a dancehall dress, smiling down from under the cover of a great fishing net. It was a rather odd image, but it lent a bit of weight to the carnival atmosphere around us. Here, unlike at Père Lachaise or Saint-Sulpice, the crowds were more vibrant, noisy, restless, and certainly souvenir happy. All along the narrow street leading to the summit of Montmartre there were shops with many different names selling the exact same trifles.

It would be tempting to say the knick-knacks offered there were tacky or cheap. Some of them were, I suppose, but the nice thing about Paris is that no matter how cheap the souvenirs are, they are still from Paris, and that adds a substantial significance to them. Sure, the shops have really creative names like *Galeries des Souvenirs*, and signs rife with catchy words like *Bijoux, Bazar, Gadgets, Fantaisie*, but it all serves its purpose. When you need to buy a baby bib with the Eiffel Tower on it, or a postcard with an old black and white photo of a topless dancer on it, it is not hard to figure out where to go even if you don't know the language.

The store that did catch my eye was *Sympa*, the designer-seconds bargain store where you can buy t-shirts and all things unmentionable at basement prices. (There is something about buying lingerie "seconds" at basement prices that just sounds really wrong.) This place was overrun with women who were elbowing their way to a spot near the square bins which were loaded with piles of unfolded, colorful...*laundry* seems the most appropriate word. That's no joke. Some of the piles were actually in laundry baskets. Dig in and get you some.

But all of this funhouse activity disappeared once we climbed up the street far enough to catch a glimpse of Sacré

Cœur. Framed by the two sides of the upward sloping street, we could see two great trees beneath that magnificent Basilica of the Sacred Heart. There, above the gaudy street scene, it stood out serenely, as if the cheap spectacle below had as little effect on it as the dirty rain upon that chalk-white stone. We no longer stopped to browse the last few shops. We ignored the French version of a hot dog stand on the corner. We simply made our way to the base of that breathtaking green slope and took a moment to partake of the view.

The carnival atmosphere could still be felt. The carousel was spinning around, its music mixing with the sounds of cars passing along Place Saint-Pierre, various spoken languages that were not French or English, and our own voices as we put our first impressions into words.

Instead of forging into the Square, or bending left with the crowds that headed toward the main stairs leading up the slope as well as the Funicular incline railway, I guided Jennifer to the right, and we skirted the base of the slope in the direction of our first off-the-tourist-map destination. This little location involved Meg Ryan and Kevin Kline.

If you've ever seen the movie *French Kiss*, then you'll have an idea of what I'm talking about. If you haven't, just play along. It will all make sense. During an early scene in the movie, Ryan and Kline are arguing as they walk along a street. They come to an intersection where two streets make an acute angle. The street they had been on rises up a slope, while the street that connects at the intersection drops away. It is visually stunning. The first time I saw the movie I mentioned it to Jennifer. And once I began planning our trip, I had every intention of finding it.

With the aid of Google Earth, and a few helpful hints from movie fans on the Internet, I eventually pinpointed this location. Looking at it on the street-level view of Google Earth, I knew I was in the right spot and began to look around to see what else was in the vicinity. Just a few steps away, I discovered that I was at the base of Rue Maurice Utrillo, which is not a street at all, but actually a set of stairs that leads to Sacré Cœur. What luck to discover I could visit this spot without any excessive deviation from the normal routes.

We found a pleasant walk along Rues Ronsard and Paul Albert, the latter being a set of stairs as well. It was here that we saw a group of artists, toiling half-way up the steps with their canvases on their laps, sitting outside Number 4's red door. I suspect they were only tourists who had signed up for an art class. Behind them, on the wall, was a black hand-painted image of Marilyn Monroe, toting a big machine-gun yelling "Follow Me!" It must have been scribbled on recently. There is not much graffiti in the tourist areas of Paris. It must be painted over regularly.

Atop Paul Albert's steps, I found my movie site. That little oblique corner might have been one of the most perfect spots I ever found in Paris. There is a café directly across the street from it—*Soleil de la Butte* (The Sun of the Mountain), and I would have liked to sit there for most of the afternoon. But of course, we had just eaten, and time was limited.

As I lingered at the corner, taking photographs, Jennifer began the ascent up Maurice Utrillo. I finally gave in to the constraints of our schedule, and followed. As I began to climb, I was interrupted by three ladies with heavy Spanish accents, asking if I could help them find their hotel. They had a general map of the city that did not begin to show them what they needed to locate it. I did my best to help. It was obvious they were on the wrong side of the Cathedral. They were carrying shopping bags, which suggests they went shopping before they even found their hotel. To paraphrase the title of a Twilight Zone episode—Women are alike all over.

My shrewd wife was attentive enough to know that three rather good-looking, stylishly dressed women had ambushed her husband. She took a picture, which clearly makes me look like I know what I'm doing. I doubt my directions were of much help. But I doubt they had any trouble finding other men to assist them in their quest for their hotel.

At the top of the stairs, as we marveled at the view over the city, I was approached yet again, this time by a couple speaking English with a Spanish accent that was not so pronounced. The man smiled at me and held up his camera.

"Would you please take our picture?" He gestured at the basilica, then at his wife.

"*Absolument!*" I quickly replied in my best French imitation, a broad smile on my face.

"*Absolument!*" he mocked me, a wry smile on his lips. "I heard you speaking English."

It was a great ice-breaker, and we traded favors, snapping pictures of each couple. In what would become a tradition for us, we asked from where they hailed, and told them of our own hometown. We found it was easiest to say New Orleans. It seems that the French have heard of it. Most of the time, it did no good to say Louisiana. Even Americans aren't always sure where that is. But for the French, or the other non-American tourists, I can understand their lack of recognition. If they had told me they were from Toulouse, I would have nodded since I had heard the name, but I would have had no mental picture of any geographical location whatsoever. I'm not even sure I could give you a decent description of the shape of France. And I'm a history buff who at least knows where it is because the Germans kept overrunning it.

Rue du Cardinal Dubois runs along the front of Sacré Cœur. Though somewhat crowded with visitors, it is still a peaceful summit, with plenty of space to lean on a railing and gaze out over the city of Paris. Right away you'll see the Church of St. Vincent de Paul, Gare du Nord, Montparnasse Tower, the Louvre…the list is enormous. About the only things you cannot see from this point are the Eiffel Tower and the Arc de Triomphe. The western view is blocked by trees and the castle-like Montmartre Reservoir. But this is not anything to worry over. The rest of the view is spectacular.

I have looked out over New York City from the top of Rockefeller Plaza. It just does not compare. There is a distinctive blue-gray color, as if the top of Paris, in a series of swells across the horizon, is actually an ocean just before a storm. Cathedrals like Madeleine and St. Vincent de Paul float like ships, their blunt prows pushing hard through the waters, while we stand on shore, watching expectantly for the swells to grow and toss the ships high out of the water.

As Jennifer sat down with her journal to write, I could not stop looking *out* there.

Up and down the steps, groups and couples wandered around, either taking pictures of the landmarks or pictures of themselves, hands outstretched with iPhones at the end of them. Several street performers vied for our attention. A man dressed all in white—skin painted white as well—did his best to look like a statue of a monk. I thought he looked too much like Uncle Fester. The most entertaining performer we saw was a man with a soccer ball, keeping it off the ground without touching it with his hands as he stood up on one of the stone fence endposts. With a boom box playing a simple rhythm, he worked the ball, bouncing it off his head, his chest, his feet, his shoulder, and everything else but his hands. Once he had drawn a big enough crowd, he began to climb a nearby lamp-post, always keeping the ball moving. Near the top, he used his remarkable strength to horizontally flatten out his body while holding the ball between his foot and his lower leg.

It was about this time that I snapped a few pictures of Jennifer as she sat against a fence, writing in her journal. A pigeon walked by as I did so. I only mention this because later she posted the picture on Facebook and all her friends raved about it. It was great fun to be able to shoot Paris and then share the pictures with friends and family that same night. It felt like we were not alone in the city; a special feeling of community that would not have been possible twenty years ago.

The interior of the basilica is impressive. I thought it was a level above Notre Dame, though Jennifer did not agree. Her attachment to Notre Dame would be obvious just a week later. But for that first Monday, we removed our hats, refrained from taking photographs as requested, and made the circuit inside the sanctuary. Of particular interest to me was the plaque thanking the Heavenly Father for sparing the basilica during bombing raids in World War II. It was a moving tribute, describing the Bishop who stayed to pray for God's mercy. I was surprised that I read the rather lengthy inscription despite the fact that it was in French. I had only been there two days and I was learning more than I realized.

Back outside, we strolled up the western side of the basilica as I snapped shot after shot of my first gargoyles. I was almost surprised to see them, as if the only gargoyles in Paris would be on Notre Dame. The two are so intermingled in our psyche that I had to take a moment to recall that gargoyles are found outside of Quasimodo's realm. There on Montmartre, I found monkeys, hyenas, griffins, and oddly enough, some little guy stuck in a corner who looked a lot like Quasimodo. Considering the cornerstone of Sacré Cœur had been laid forty years after *The Hunchback of Notre Dame* had been published, it was all too possible that the figure was indeed that sad, abused, yet heroic man.

The rest of the afternoon was spent walking (climbing might be a better way to describe what one does on the vertical streets of Montmartre) through the streets that inspired the world's greatest painters: Renoir, Van Gogh, Modigliani, Pissarro, Monet, Toulouse-Lautrec, and many others (including the forgotten Willette). Take a short walk west of Sacré Cœur, passing the shops full of wonderful little paintings (buy at least three of them like we did), turn right on Rue de Mont Cenis, then down to the turn onto Rue Cortot. It's here you'll find the *Musée de Montmartre*, where you'll get to see Renoir's studio, and the oldest house on Montmartre, the *Maison de Rosimond*, built in the 1600's. The museum is full of posters and other paraphernalia from the turn of the twentieth century, when Toulouse-Lautrec, Theophile Steinlen (of Le Chat Noir fame), Adolphe Willette (you should remember him by now), and other great artists captured the *joie de vivre* of Montmartre at that time. There is also a model of the old village created by famed sculptor Georges Folmer.

This museum was a quick add-on to our tour. I read about it only that morning while surfing the web for information on Montmartre. We had bought the tickets with only about forty minutes left before it closed. I wish we had made the effort to return and explore it. We enjoyed it more than many of the other museums.

The great part about the last half of this Montmartre journey was the fact that we were walking downhill. We sloped past Le Maison Rose Café, Au Lapin Agile Cabaret (the historic Nimble Rabbit cabaret frequented by Picasso, Apollinaire, and Modigliani), and eventually ended up on Rue Caulaincourt where we stopped for a cappuccino outside a little pâtisserie overlooking the steps of Rue de Saules. There we rested our feet, and did our best not to annoy the waiter, who seemed a little unhappy to have customers outside. It was one of the rare times we felt a French waiter was being rude, but it did not seem like anything more than we would find back home. It just seemed like he was tired and ready to go home.

After jotting down a few notes in our journals, we headed off for our last destination of the day: Montmartre Cemetery.

After a charming walk through this more modern-looking business district, we finally found the cemetery. To our dismay, it had already closed. However, we were quite tired by this time, and going home seemed like a good idea. Jennifer made me promise we would come back. Not at all sure that we would, I promised, and we walked off in search of the métro.

By then, it had been hours since we'd eaten. We stopped in at a small grocery store (*Superette du Sacré Cœur*) and bought a few bags of food to take home. We also bought a baguette, which I was not sure we would be able to safely get through the métro. But we gave it a shot.

Turning down the famous Boulevard de Clichy, we kept walking, almost too tired to pay much attention to the red windmill on our left. It was, of course, La Revue du Moulin Rouge. It was not quite seven in the evening and people were already lining up to get a seat. We trudged on, happy to slip down into the Blanche metro station, and catch a ride home.

By this time the métro was crowded, and we had to stand in very close quarters. I did my best to keep Jennifer from getting shoved around. It was very tight. No one was pushing maliciously. It was just too full to enable everyone to be polite. We made it to the second stop, Barbès–Rochechouart, switched to our home line Number 4 after descending its elevated station steps, and took an equally crowded métro train all the way back to Saint-Sulpice.

The day had been long, exhausting, exhilarating, and magical. We could hardly believe we still had twelve days ahead of us. We ate well that night, drank French wine (medoc for me, riesling for Jennifer), and slept hard.

We had stood atop Paris and gazed upon her in wonder and delight. Tomorrow we would crack open one of her most popular, prized possessions: the Orsay Museum.

Journal Entry, April 16, afternoon

--The streets of Montmartre are far more quaint than the Left Bank...stunning in their beauty. How could artists not flock to such a site?

We have walked where Renoir walked, where Toulouse-Lautrec hurried along on his short legs. We have worn out our calves where Picasso climbed, painted, then climbed down again...We go now, in search of the Montmartre dead. We will not disturb them. Merely pass by, nod by way of acknowledging that we understand we must join their list one day, and move along while we still draw breath.

Chapter Three: Breaking French Law

There was little question where we wanted to go on that second day of sightseeing. After waking to a cold yet coffee-rich morning (Jennifer had the coffee brewed by the time I awoke), we ate a hearty breakfast from the items we had carefully transported on that crowded métro the night before: sliced bread (*Americain* proudly stamped on the package), with eggs and slices of turkey and cheese. All of this I did in a skillet on the stove, as if I were a real chef. I rarely do this at home, but it seemed right while in Paris. I usually just nuke my food, but I felt a desire to slow down and actually take the time to create something wonderful to eat. Besides, we were heading off to one of my most anticipated venues: *Le Musée d'Orsay*.

As I mentioned in the last chapter, we tend to tear down buildings in the States that should never be destroyed. In France, this is almost never a problem. However, after World

War II, a debate raged regarding the future of an unbelievably beautiful former palace. Gare d'Orsay, a train station that served the southern railways of France, operated out of the former *Palais d'Orsay*, once the home of France's Council of State, a quasi-Supreme Court for administrative law. A fire gutted the palace in 1871. It opened as a railway station and hotel in 1900. By the end of World War II, last used as a reception center for returning prisoners of war in 1945, it was obsolete. Sitting on prime real estate opposite the Louvre, officials spoke of tearing it down.

Wisely, it was ultimately decided to renovate it and turn it into a museum. It became the showplace for *impressionist* and *post-impressionist* art. If you want to see paintings by Cézanne, Monet, Degas, Pissarro, Manet, Renoir, Gaugin, Van Gogh, etc…this is the place to go. You could spend days at the Orsay without ever seeing it all. And since I am a big fan of *post-impressionism*, I could not wait to see it.

I had actually never heard of the Orsay before my research of Paris began. I knew of the Louvre, and had just assumed that most of the collections of the painters listed above that were found in Paris would be at the Louvre. It turns out this was true until the Orsay opened.

That sounded great to me. No need to wade through all the older style of art that did not appeal to me. It sounded too good to be true. A perfect museum.

And so, unable to visit it Monday (closed every Monday), I planned a full day for this one, highly anticipated art playground.

We were in no hurry. Though we anticipated a long line, we had no other plans for that day. We would just take our time strolling the galleries, taking in the view.

As I did each morning, I planned out our travel route. A bus could easily take us on a ten-minute trip on the 68 RATP catching it at the Rennes-Raspail stop, and drop us off right at the museum. However, I decided that seemed just a little too easy. We would be inside most of the day, and the rain looked to be in a holding pattern, so I took a different approach.

Since the museum was only 1.3 kilometers from our front door, we had the opportunity to walk the route, through some beautiful streets around the Saint-Germain-des-Prés area. Jennifer was kind enough to trust me in this, and we set off late in the morning with a cold wind blowing through my green windbreaker. I knew we would be inside most of the day so I took a chance and left the heavy coat at the apartment.

Just outside our door, and to the left, is the funny little intersection Place Michel Debré, where Rue de Sèvres meets up with Rues du Dragon, du Four, du Cherche-Midi and du Vieux Colombier. It is a charming little spot that is almost always quiet and deserted. An oddball statue of a centaur by César stands guard between Sèvres and Du Cherche-Midi, his tail made up of what looks to be farm implements. We ignored this as I steered Jennifer toward the adventurously named Rue du Dragon.

This was the scene of my coffee purchase the morning before. It is a lovely walk, and short, at just one-tenth of a mile. I had read about the old Cour de Dragon that connected Rue de Rennes with Rue du Dragon. This *passage*, once a manufacturing center for wrought iron, had a dragon carved over its entrance. The *passage* was demolished in the 1920's, and the dragon was barely saved and is now at the Louvre. This was a great place to start our walk.

We then turned onto the broad St. Germain Boulevard and crossed over it to catch Rue des Saints-Pères, passing by an enticing *pâtisserie*, as well as the University René Descartes where groups of students smoked cigarettes clustered around the entrance.

A recent new city ordinance outlawed smoking inside, and so everywhere we went, people were huddled outside the front doors of the buildings, puffing away. It sort of made Paris look like a den of nicotine freaks. I haven't smelled that much smoke since eating at a Denny's when I was a kid. It also gave the Paris streets an older, film noir quality that I didn't mind at all.

We were supposed to turn left on l'Université, but I did not realize that Rue Jacob, on the right, became Rue de l'Université on the left. This was something I never adjusted to. We do not have many streets that change names at an intersection. At least not in the many places I have lived. In Paris, one sees this all the time. Some street names are only a block long. So we passed up our turn and kept going, I gave up looking for the streets on my handwritten route—I could see the main drag alongside the Seine ahead of us. I knew we only needed to reach it and we could walk along it until we came to the museum. A few sprinkles were beginning to drop on us. There were many scaffolds erected in this area, and we had to duck in and out of them as we made our way along, avoiding many others who had the same idea.

Still, no matter who we nearly ran into, we continued to hear *Bonjour* without exception.

It was our first look at the Seine. We had never been out of the narrow streets of the Left Bank. The cold wind, with a few raindrops, only served to add to our exhilaration as we crossed Quai Malaquais and looked out over the river to the Louvre.

Big. It is hard to be more eloquent than that. Everything looked so big. I've never been to Moscow, so I realize that those who have will laugh at my comparison, but it reminded me of those massive buildings on the Moskva. This might be in part due to the narrow width of the Seine, and the crowded banks. The long Louvre, along with the Orsay opposite it overwhelm the scene. They are not tall, but they are just too solid to ignore. Their highly decorated stone facades will not allow you to look elsewhere. Palaces are built to impress. These were built correctly.

With great discipline, we did not walk across the Pont du Carrousel, we did not seek out the Mona Lisa or the Venus di Milo, and we did not give in to the lure of Egyptian mummies scratching at the lids of their sarcophagi. It would wait. That was not to be for another week. Instead, we turned west and took in the view of what used to be a train station.

The Orsay may be the only train station that was built as a palace. I don't know that for sure, but I'm not even going to Google this one. The odds are pretty low that anyone else but the French turned a palace into a transit depot. We strolled along the northern side of the museum, marveling at the artwork that sits atop its stone walls. It was shaping up to be the perfect museum day.

At the northwestern corner of the building we came upon the *queue*. Now to be fair, we had dawdled away the morning, and did not arrive until about 11 am. So we were not too surprised to find a massive snake-tail line at the entranceway. Having expected this to some degree, we walked all the way around the group and finally took our place in line and settled in for a moderate wait.

Like the métro-pass math games I had played before, I had done the same with the Paris Museum pass. Anyone who even thinks about going to Paris is suddenly inundated with advertisements for—as well as personal counsel that will lead you to believe you need to buy—the ubiquitous Paris Museum Pass. You will become convinced it is the greatest thing since the sliced baguette. Just listen to the pitch:

With the Paris Museum Pass, you get *free* entry into over 60 museums and monuments. You even get to skip the lines, getting fast-tracked into such crowded venues as the Louvre and the Orsay. What a deal, right? You have the choice of a two-day, four-day, or six-day pass. Each one becomes progressively more economically wise, starting at 39€, then 54€, and finally just 69€ for the six-day pass. Considering you can visit 60 venues, it's a steal!

And really, you might just want to do this. It depends on your plans. I could see right away, however, that I was not about to try and run myself through sixty museums and monuments. It just wouldn't happen. And that consecutive day deal tripped me up again. I knew we wanted to take a few days off now and then. With this pass you can't do it. To get your money's worth, you gotta go, go, go. Move, keep it going, onward and upward, make it worth your while!

You must see where I'm going with this. I did a lot of homework, checking out the prices of the individual museums that we actually intended to see. Even if we had made it to every one of them, it just wasn't going to cost anywhere near the price of the Museum Pass. First of all, there are only so many places you can see in one day. Places like the Orsay and the Louvre can take a full day. This quickly begins to fall apart as an option. To have this pass for the two weeks would have cost us about 280€ each. I knew that just didn't carry the least bit of logic. One day at the Orsay only cost 18€ for the both of us.

Now, I really had to think about the fast-track system. Standing in line can be a real pain in the neck, literally if you are carrying a backpack full of camera equipment, so it might have been worth the money to stay out of the lines. I rolled the dice on this one. I had no idea what to expect in the area of wasted time standing in line.

The Orsay was our first test of this gamble. And as soon as I saw that twisting line, I knew we were gonna wish we'd had the pass. Sure enough, the total amount of time in line was about an hour. And yeah, it did start to rain a bit while we were in line. But the people were easy-going, and at least it wasn't hot. Just two little things made it annoying. Just two.

That's not bad.

First off, there were no posts with nylon straps designed to keep you in line. We did our best to snake back and forth, but the ebb and flow of the crowd really seemed to warp the shape of those lines. We did our best to stay in the most orderly line we could form. This did not always work. Instead of a snake twisting and turning its way along, we were more like a possum, waddling blindly from side to side. Once in a while a museum official would show up in an attempt to stretch us back out into the proper lines, but once they left, it all collapsed again. I was getting my first look at French efficiency.

Now the next little hiccup was comical from this side of memory. It was funny when it happened, just not nearly as much as it is now. Here's how it went down. And downhill is the best way to describe it.

As we were standing in line, moving along slowly, hitting a switchback in the line from time to time, I suddenly noticed a young girl, maybe fifteen years old, with a brightly colored backpack that looked more like a pack for a ten-year-old, who had appeared just ahead of us. She had not been there before, but like magic she had appeared. I gave her a good stare, trying to decide what she was up to. She had a wonderfully sad and lonely appearance, and she kept her head down, as if she had become lost and was too timid to look around and confirm the fact. I should have felt sorry for her and not bothered to pay her any more attention. Could she have come to the museum all alone? I doubted it.

To confirm my suspicions, a second girl appeared. She was a dead ringer for the little brat Kimmy who was best friends with one of those girls on Full House. If you've got children who watched the show, you know who I mean: the girl you always wanted the Dad to throw out. Well anyway, Kimmy did not look so lost. She began chatting away, happy as could be. The first girl, no longer alone, did the same. Both were talking away like a couple of the old biddies from The Music Man. (Pic-a-little-talk-a-little...) I knew we'd been had.

"See how this works?" I asked Jennifer a little too loudly. "These two girls are just the tip of the iceberg. They're the advance scouts for a whole crew who wants to cut in line."

Okay, I admit it. I was getting grumpy, actually more along the lines of grouchy, and to top it off, I was bored.

Jennifer shushed me. "Wow," I added, "someone must really want to get into the museum."

The French girls ignored me. I don't doubt they understood me. I know most of the schools teach English. In fact, judging by their insistence on looking away from me, I would have bet money they knew what I was saying and knew I was saying it about *them*.

Well, I wasn't going to cause an international incident over a few spots in line, so I examined the rooftops around us.

Enter the mother.

When she popped into sight, I laughed aloud. It seems this wasn't the plan of a few schools girls out on a lark. This was a family plan. I wondered how many more would arrive.

I did not have to wait long. Youngest daughter suddenly turned up at mom's side. All of them seemed very interested in whatever the heck they were gossiping about. They were certainly disinterested in the tall American man making snide comments.

By the time the dad showed up, I was all out of steam. The serene Frenchman, fresh from his passive-aggressive line-cutting victory, stood surrounded by his female warriors, his thin hair slicked back, his small glasses framing his pensive eyes, all the while refusing to make eye contact. *Fait accompli.*

As rudeness goes, it was about the most direct form of it we'd seen from the French. Perhaps they hated the fact that all these foreigners were in their way, blocking their quick access to their French National Treasures. Maybe they just had to hurry up because their train was leaving in the early afternoon. Or maybe they were trying to see all sixty sites with their Paris Museum Pass in two days. (No, scratch that, they'd have been able to skip the line altogether.) Well, whatever their reason, it seemed to tarnish the day just a little. But the increasing sprinkles finally stopped, the line kept moving, and there were no more members of *La Famille Buttinsky*.

Before we knew it, we were ushered into the museum.

After the hustle and bustle of getting through the metal detectors, and buying the tickets, and finding the right entrance, we came out into the main floor of the museum. Bathed in the white light of the expansive skylights above, we looked out across what used to be the main terminal of the station. Instead of tracks and trains lining the long open gallery, we saw many statues spaced out across it, flanked by the walls of galleries, stacked on top of one another three floors high.

This central atrium, so wide open and airy, felt quite modern. Unfortunately, the map that was given to us was a bit confusing. I did the best I could to decipher it, and we set off into the galleries. The galleries there were small, which added to the congestion. We found a few of the earlier pieces that we liked, including an incredible portrait of a girl, her arm outstretched in supplication, one shining tear rolling down her cheek. It was hard to believe it was only done with paint. You felt as if you could reach out and wipe the tear away.

Not far from the girl was a large painting of William Bouguereau's *Dante et Virgile*, a disturbing image of a man being eaten alive by a demon. It is from Dante's Inferno, and my youngest son, when he saw the picture of it I had taken, immediately knew which scene was being portrayed.

And that brings us up to the subject of cameras. As we came into the museum, I had my rather large, DSL Nikon around my neck. I removed it to go through the scanner, then put it back around my neck. None of the attendants said a word to me. So once inside, I took a few pictures here and there. I'd been to museums like the Art Institute of Chicago and the New Orleans Museum of Art, as well as many others that did not mind photographs, as long as the flashes were turned off. Too much exposure to flashes can actually damage many of the paintings.

Now at the Orsay, there are many no signs (red circles and slashes) to remind you food and drinks are not allowed in the galleries. This also includes a picture of a camera. It seemed likely that it was simply prohibiting flash photography. I wondered if it meant no cameras at all, but all around me, people were snapping pictures willy-nilly, some even with flashes. So I felt confident that my assumption was correct.

Enter the mean museum lady.

Now let me set the stage. I'm just your average middle-aged Fred MacMurray type, pockets full of maps, pocket journals, and a bag full of cameras. I'm wearing a hat that looks like it was stolen from my grandfather's closet, and I wear glasses. So when you see me taking

pictures, you gotta think I'm harmless, right? And when there is a room full of tourists taking pictures, I really shouldn't stand out.

Perhaps it was the fact that I was taking a picture of a sculpture of a nude woman taking a bath. I dunno. Anyway, this rather angry looking lady of Asian descent (I only mention it to give you an idea how bizarre this all seemed to me) came at me pointing her finger. In what must be very good French, she told me no photographs.

"Pardon?" I asked, my tone clearly giving her a chance to back off and admit she had made a mistake.

"No photo!" she said, pointing all around then back at me and my camera.

"No flash." I nodded, to assure her I had no intention of wearing down the marble artwork with a flashbulb.

"No, no photo," now making signs that clearly mean she despises my camera.

"Everyone else seems to be taking pictures," I foolishly pointed out.

"Museum policy," she added in English. "No camera."

No camera? Why had they let me walk in with it hanging around my neck?

"Are you gonna tell everyone else?" This seemed like a reasonable question.

She pointed at my camera, and stared me down until I tucked it inside my bag. I looked around at everyone else, as if to make sure she noticed what was happening around her.

I am not kidding you. She walked off, never saying a word to everyone who had their hands in the air waving iPhones around. She could not be so outside the mainstream culture that she only thought my DSL camera, which *looks* like a camera, was the only one there. She had to know all those phones clicking away were cameras as well.

Then I got to thinking about this policy. Who would run a

museum of famous paintings and tell everyone they couldn't take a picture? It's not like the pieces there are well-kept secrets that people pay to see. You can find most of them on Wikipedia, for pity's sake. I usually prefer to take shots in a museum of Jennifer in front of a piece she particularly likes. Sort of a proof that she was there kind of deal.

Well, I didn't want to run afoul of the French Authorities, and so I honored their rather harsh request. With my camera firmly packed in the bag, we continued our tour.

Lunch became a problem, since the only place to eat in the museum was a tiny little sandwich counter in the basement. That line was long and not moving. We decided to keep looking and head out earlier than we had planned.

After about an hour at the Orsay, the close quarters in the small, overcrowded galleries were beginning to wear on us. We found the Van Gogh gallery, and I enjoyed it somewhat. He is my favorite painter, and anything he does should be seen in person. The gobs of paint he slapped on defy logic. With just a dab here and what appears to be a random glob there he suddenly makes you see things you never thought possible in art. It almost looks more lucky than skillful, yet he did so many paintings of this quality it could only have been skill.

We rode the elevator to the fifth floor gallery where we were looking for the impressionists. Along the way, we continued to see canvas after canvas of nudes. It is something that stands out here. It was in this era that the nude became something different than an element in a history or mythology. It became an object of its own. Divorced from moral context. More importantly, it became a subject of commonality, not exalted beauty. Effort was made to portray whores and loose women as merely neutral subjects. At the same time sensuality overtook beauty. This is quite evident when you are standing in the center of it all.

I'll sound like a prudish American here, and that's okay.

It's just the way our country developed. France developed differently. At any street corner you are likely to find a statue of a nude woman, or a man. It is so pervasive no one pays it any attention. It is considered natural, and it may be a reflection of the French attitude that allows the age of consent to be fifteen.

Jennifer is as big a fan of Monet as I am of Van Gogh. Yet, as we neared the Monets, Jennifer decided she was ready to go. She was finally beginning to tire a bit, we had not eaten, and the crowded, grouchy atmosphere of the museum was too much. I could hardly disagree with her. We were able to catch a quick look at Fantin-Latour's painting *Hommage à Delacroix* which includes Charles Baudelaire in the crowded scene. But that really was enough for us. We did our best to make a hasty retreat.

Despite the fact that it was raining as we left, the cool air revived us and we headed back toward Rue des Saints-Pères where we had seen a little lunch counter across from the University Descartes: Lina's Sandwiches. We collapsed our umbrellas, ducked into the shop, and ordered. Jennifer had still not completely caught up to the French spoken by the counter girls, so she thought we were suppose to choose which cheese we wanted with our sandwiches. Once we sat down with it, it turned out not to be cheese but yogurt. We got exactly what Jennifer asked for, *blanche* yogurt. Plain as day.

A little note for those who might be eating in Paris. There are a great many places serving some British potato chips (crisps). They look great, like they would be a nice change from French food. They are not. They are greasy and full of black pepper. It was just something I would need time to get used to, and I wasn't going to do it while in Paris.

Once we'd finished eating, we stopped in that pâtisserie we'd seen earlier at 36 Rue des Saints-Pères. The shopkeepers were friendly, easy to practice our French with, and their *pain au chocolat* (bread with chocolate chips) was delicious. I wish we had found a reason to go back into that neighborhood. When I finally did, on our last Saturday, it was closed all day. If you ever get over there, check it out. As with most places like that, the sign simply read *Boulanger Patissier.* We left with our arms full of bread and treats and retraced our steps to the apartment.

The poor experience at the Orsay threatened to finish our day right there. We trudged up the steps and felt relieved to be back at the apartment. Perhaps we were just tired and needed a break. And so we relaxed, ate a few goodies, and watched the intermittent rain wet our balcony's ironwork.

Journal Entry, April 17

--I should be happy for Vincent that so many people crowd into the gallery at Musée d'Orsay where his works are displayed. I should be but I cannot be. So many people push in to see them, but simply stare at them, eyes blinking, as if they are checking off a task on a list. They have been told that the portrait of Doctor Gachet is a great work of art, so they make sure to see it, never recognizing the look on Gachet's face, never seeing his worn, tired eyes. Then I hear a man speaking in English, lecturing a friend on Van Gogh's use of color. He sounds as if he is reciting something from a textbook. I feel pretty sure he is. I am not impressed.

I felt drained from the Orsay experience. One little speed bump had really cut down my enthusiasm. In my younger days I could be an extremist, going from exuberance to despair at the turn of a switch. I don't do it as often anymore, but the threat can arise without warning. It would have been a shame to let it happen while I was in Paris. We'd been planning for this trip too long to spend any of it in a blue funk. Fortunately, when you're married, you have a partner to keep you balanced.

Jennifer spent the afternoon writing and resting, and by six, she managed to convince me to head out the door with her in search of Saint-Germain-des-Prés Église. We'd seen Saint-Sulpice but we had not yet been to the other local church.

"It's still raining," I said, looking for a reason to stay indoors. "I won't be able to shoot pictures."

"We'll just go for a little while," she countered.

So off we went, back down those stairs.

Despite the disappointments of the earlier half of the day, once we stepped out those great oak doors on the street, none of that mattered. We turned right and walked down to Rennes, which heads straight toward Saint-Germain-des-Prés. Rain still fell, though it was very light rain, but it was enough to encourage me to keep my camera tucked safely away in my backpack.

The old church at Saint-Germain has a more medieval look to it. But it should. In fact, the Abbey of Saint-Germain-des-Prés was founded one thousand five hundred years ago. This makes Notre Dame seem very young. There are kings buried at Saint-Germain from the sixth and seventh centuries. These were Merovingian rulers from what was then Neustria. Guys like Childebert, Clothar, and Childeric, all of which sounds like it is straight out of a Tolkien epic. Which, in a sense, they were, when you consider that Tolkien gleaned much of his background work from ancient European history. So maybe it is safe to say that Paris is the Osgiliath of Europe.

I am not sure how old the structure is, though if I understand correctly, the tower and nave are original. It seemed appropriate to enter such an old, stone church as rain fell from the sky. I half expected the nave to be full of peasants, taking refuge from the storm, candles and oil lamps trailing black smoke from flames that danced in the draft from the open door.

The interior was certainly dark, though not candle-lit. The nave was not full of peasants from the sixth century, but it was not empty either. Parishioners were scattered throughout the rows of chairs. A sort of bible study could be heard in the apse as we rounded the ambulatory. (I had to look that up to get the terms right.) We walked around the sanctuary, reading what inscriptions we could. Some in French, some in Latin. We snapped a few pictures, though I am always uncomfortable doing so in churches. I don't think I would mind someone coming into my church and taking pictures, though it is hardly remarkable enough to do so. However, I feel sure that I am degrading a sacred site by snapping away inside cathedrals like Saint-Germain-des-Prés. Of course, if you are going to do this in a church, these are precisely the churches in which you should do this. They are dazzling to behold. But they are also dark, and require either flashes or a steady hand for slower shutter speeds.

The small chapels that lined the walls were full of ancient artwork that could have rivaled museums throughout the United States. Yet most of these sit in the shadows, rarely seen by the world. I would love to spend a week in such a place, with one of the elder priests, discovering the significance of all those treasures. It was not to be for that day. We moved along.

Once again, with all of my research in the previous months, I missed yet another ghost. René Descartes is buried in one of the side chapels. We never saw him, nor the kings of old who have become his companions. It was probably for the best. I know little about him and would have embarrassed myself if we had talked.

The atmosphere inside the church went a long way to washing away the disappointments of the Orsay. Even better, as we stepped through the door and back out of the Middle Ages we found sunlight filling Place Saint-Germain-des-Prés. Able to pull out my Nikon, I was happy again, as we strolled around the outside of the church, watching the pigeons perched in the ancient brickwork of the old bell-tower.

The church stands just yards away from the famous cafés Les Deux Magots and de Flore, made famous by such writers as Sartre, Bouvoir and Camille. If you want a real tourist notch in your belt, check these out. We didn't. Instead, we went in the opposite direction on Boulevard Saint-Germain and set out with no real plan.

It was our first spontaneous exploration.

This section of the Latin Quarter is noisier than the Saint-Sulpice neighborhood. It is hopping with traffic, people, and electronic signs. Spinning kiosks display the latest movies; newsstands splash the latest headlines under Plexiglas. Buses wade through the mass of tiny cars while motorcycles incessantly buzz around on the rain soaked pavement.

Though I had not learned much about the specifics of the old Abbey, I read Leonard Pitt's book *Walks Through Lost Paris*, which went into great detail on the redesign of the Latin Quarter as started by Baron Georges-Eugéne Haussmann. This left me with a pretty good mental picture of the area and so I felt certain that I could create a walking tour from the hip, so to speak.

We soaked in the energy of that broad boulevard and made it to Rue de l'Odéon. From there we could have turned away from the old quarter and headed toward the Luxembourg Gardens, but I knew we were getting hungry, so I steered us toward the Seine. Not only had I read up on this area, but I'd "strolled" these streets on Google Earth, and so I knew there were small places to eat on Rue de l'Ancienne Comédie, which was the continuation of Rue de l'Odéon. This was tourist country, and the streets were full of couples that looked a lot like we did, as well as sandwich shops, Chinese (and Japanese) restaurants, brasseries, boulangeries, and hotels. There also seemed to be an inordinate amount of cell phone stores.

We forgot to eat, enchanted by the storefronts we found as Rue de l'Ancienne Comédie becomes Rue Mazarine. At number 41 we found a wonderful old bookstore, *F. Chanut Livres Anciens* it reads above the door. The lights were on, but we did not go in. These were not books you could find on Amazon. There were dozens of these little shops dotted throughout the Quarter. Many of them had multiple volumes of Jules Verne novels, richly decorated with gold leaf and brilliantly colored artwork.

Drawn by the great dome of the *Institut de France* at the end of the street, we kept moving, eventually slipping into the side street Rue Guenegaud which delivered us to Quai de Conti, along the Seine. We were back out on the river.

Now that we had left all the little eateries behind, we started to get hungry. And while this part of the river was picturesque, there did not seem to be many places to eat. But I realized that we could go ahead and walk up to Notre Dame. I knew how much Jennifer wanted to see it, and could see how Saint-Germain-des-Prés had affected her, so though we had not planned to do so, I steered in the direction of Quasimodo's old hangout.

If you ever go this way, check out the entrance to Rue de Nevers. Opposite Pont Neuf, it has an arched entrance, which creates the coolest little spot. There is a bar just inside it, The Highlander, which might have been worth exploring but by then I had the idea we would eat in sight of Notre Dame. So we pushed on.

We finally found a great little pizzeria in sight of Notre Dame just before Place Saint-Michel. Appropriately named Saint-Michel, this Italian restaurant was just what we needed. I had read warnings about the little pizzerias sprinkled throughout Paris like parmesan on a pizza pie. They are everywhere, and according to many travel-wags, they offer really bad pizza. Now one thing I'd learned about reading reviews, people love to gripe. About everything. So I tend to ignore much of it. I decided to use my own instincts, and they were telling me that it is almost impossible to mess up pizza.

The place was very small. There might have been six tables in it. It looked surprisingly like any number of pizzerias you'd find in small towns in the American Midwest. A table along the right wall was occupied by two young French girls who were chatting merrily away. An old man with a head of white hair shuffled over from the counter and muttered *bonjour* in response to our own French greeting. He looked at us, then at the tables around us as if to say "pick something, I don't care" and so we chose the table at the window, with Jennifer facing the towers of Notre Dame.

Not a bad way to eat dinner.

The old man, wearing a white shirt, worn, dark pants and old dress shoes—all of which looked just a little too big for him, as if he'd recently shrunke—handed us menus. We'd only tried a few words in French and he had already pegged us as tourists. He pointed at a few things on the menu, acknowledged our requests for coffee, then shuffled away.

I watched the girls at the other table, trying to catch any of their words. I don't think I recognized one in ten words they spit out. Looking around the rest of the little dining room, I decided that it really did look like pizzerias back home, and not counting the obvious difference in language upon the signs, the only difference I saw was the many wine bottles on display.

Most of your Midwesterners don't consume much wine with their pizza. Instead of wine, you'd more likely find beer.

We chose our dinners, practicing our French before the old man returned. It was tempting to let Jennifer order, but I was determined to speak when I could. And ordering food seemed like something that any four-year-old could do, so I figured I should at least be able to get beyond the toddler stage.

By the time he'd returned with our coffee, I had picked out pizza for myself and Jennifer went with spaghetti and chicken. As she began to order in French, the old man raised his brows and patted her menu with the back of his hand, adding a shrug to his shoulders. She pointed at the item on the menu and he nodded, looked at me, and I pointed at the pizza I wanted. Nodding a second time, he turned away.

Having seen all those bottles of wine on a shelf over the opening to the kitchen, I decided to add wine to my order.

"Monsieur!" I called. "Pardon, Monsieur!"

He continued shuffling away. The third time I called was pretty loud and still he did not hear. I gave up.

"I think he's deaf," I said.

"That would explain his pointing at the menu," Jennifer added. "But he heard us order the coffee."

"I suppose he reads lips. We'll have to speak clearly for him."

And so we enjoyed our coffee. When he came back to set out plates for us I caught his attention and as I spoke slowly, and clearly, I pointed at the menu and indicated I wanted some Rosé. He pointed at my options, bottle or glass, and I chose the glass.

Soon he was back, my Rosé in a small carafe. So small I mistook it for an odd shaped glass. Nothing like letting the waiter know you're both a tourist and an idiot all in one sip. No matter, the wine was excellent.

Setting our food in front of us, he grabbed a red pepper dispenser from another table and asked Jennifer if she wanted it by way of holding it up in front of her. She nodded, and he held it out to her, playfully pulled it away when she reached for it, then finally allowed her to take it. After this, our hearing-impaired *restaurateur* stepped outside the glass door to smoke a cigarette. The two girls at the table, mostly finished with their dinners, stepped outside to join him. All three of them lit up and began to talk.

The old man suddenly looked about ten years younger. He stood straighter, his bored face now more keen and shrewd. To top it off, he began regaling the girls with all sorts of entertaining conversation, often turning away from them and eyeing the traffic on Quai des Grand Augustins. He had fooled me for a short time, but I could see now that his hearing was just fine.

"Watch the waiter," I tilted my head toward the window. Jennifer casually turned to spy on him from the corner of her eye.

"He hears just fine. In fact, he's quite a character."

"Oh yeah, he's a rounder," she added.

At this point, as a tourist, I could have simply blown him off as a nut, another example of the rude waiters that we'd been told to expect in Paris. But as we discussed it, we decided that there was a pretty simple reason for all the pointing and shrugging and his deaf act. We had been in Paris long enough to hear dozens of languages on the street and we had an idea that maybe he just did not want to put forth the effort to understand all the tourists and their butchered attempts at French. Cut down the chitchat, point at what you want, and let's get this over with. Something like that.

Instead of being offended, we were amused, and even a little impressed. It made a great deal of sense. If I had been alone, I would have just left it at that. But Jennifer had a different plan. When he came back inside, she drew his attention.

"Pardon, Monsieur," she began, speaking easily, knowing full well he could understand her.

I could see he had returned to his old man posture. It was subtle, but effective.

In French, Jennifer told him how much she enjoyed her dinner. He smiled and nodded in that way that made me think she could have told him the place was on fire and his response would have been just the same. But Jennifer wasn't going to let him off the hook so easily. She continued on in French. I was surprised to discover I was able to keep up with their conversation pretty easily.

"We are from Louisiana…" she began. He interrupted.

"Louisiana? Oh, it is beautiful there."

"Yes, it is," she smiled big, knowing she had won him over, "and they have very good *café au lait*. Yours is just as good."

"Thank you," he said, straightening his posture, his old man charade now tossed aside. "I would like to visit Louisiana."

"Well, it is very hot there, it's much nicer here in Paris," she advised him.

"Oh no, this is cold, too wet." He pulled his shoulders in and shivered as if a great wind had just blown through him. "It is not nice at all."

"We are enjoying it very much," Jennifer assured him.

He made a face, obviously amused at her viewpoint.

Jennifer had most certainly won him over. He no longer shuffled, and no longer seemed disinterested in us. After many *mercis* and *c'est bons*, and smiles and nods, he bid us *bonsoir* and we reluctantly left his pizzeria.

"That was the best pizza I've had in a long time," I said as we walked the last stretch of the Quai and came upon Place

Saint-Michel. "We will have to go back there at least one more time, if not more."

We did not know that we would never make it back that trip. Maybe it is for the best that we didn't. If it was only a once-in-a-lifetime event, that would be okay. Some events like that don't need to be repeated. It makes them all the more special.

It was now about six in the evening, and though the day had been cold and rainy, the sun was now shining through scattered cloud cover and the air had warmed considerably. We would come to rely on this. The afternoons in Paris, that April, were always warmer and more pleasant than the mornings. It was as if Paris knew her children did not like to venture out until the afternoon, and so spilled her rain early to allow for picture-perfect afternoons.

Full of good food, as well as that Rosé, we turned and viewed what would become one of the more familiar sights for us: *Place Saint-Michel*.

At the conjunction of Boulevard Saint-Michel, Rue Danton and Pont Saint-Michel stands the busy little intersection highlighted by Gabriel Davioud's *Fountaine Saint-Michel*, a grand façade built into the exposed end of the buildings on the north end of Saint-Michel Boulevard. Set above the fountain is a statue of the Archangel Michael standing astride his adversary Satan. Two dragons sit on either side of the fountain, spitting water instead of fire. Four beautiful red marble columns give the monument an added flavor.

This is the heart of the tourist section. From here, you can head out across the Saint-Michel bridge onto the Île de la Cité, in search of Marie Antoinette's prison cell, or the islands lesser known cathedral *Saint-Chappelle*. Go in the opposite direction, and you enter the Latin Quarter, heading either southeast along Saint-Michel Boulevard toward the Sorbonne, the Pantheon, and the Luxembourg Gardens, or you can veer southwest on Rue Danton and find the exciting Odeon neighborhood as you head toward Saint-Germain-des-Prés and Montparnasse further on. Follow the river to the east and you'll have your choice of cafés and souvenir shops as you close in on Notre Dame. Or you can head west, back from where we had come, and search out the Orsay, the Louvre, and eventually the Eiffel Tower.

It is a fun and lively crossroad.

Before making our choice, Jennifer ducked into a souvenir shop on the corner as I inspected and photographed the fountain. When I'd finished, I found her with a handful of postcards, taking her time as she inspected all the little trinkets displayed on the crowded shelves.

Once she'd finished looking around we placed our souvenirs on the counter and unexpectedly met a man who we would forever remember with great fondness.

The clerk spoke immaculate French, slowly, with careful diction. I would say his accent was African, though I could not be more specific than that. He had a great big smile that lit up his entire face. He eagerly chatted with Jennifer in French as if he had known us for many years.

When he found out we were from Louisiana, he was quick to tell us that New Orleans had great jazz. I nodded in agreement, still not confident enough with my elementary French to join in the conversation. Jennifer kept up her end of the discussion quite well. I could tell she was gaining confidence with each new *tête-à-tête*.

When Jennifer explained that she was a poet, the clerk nodded, happy to hear it. At this point he began rhapsodizing on how so many people passed through his shop, buying the trinkets, spending their time drinking, partying, but never stopping to think, to look around and pay attention to life. I did not catch most of this, though I could see a great passion come over him.

Jennifer later told me most of what he said. She responded to him that he must be a poet too. His vociferous protestations notwithstanding, I have the feeling she was right. Here was a man who watched tourists day in and day out as they wandered mindlessly through what should be an inspirational city, more interested in drinking and grabbing the cheapest baubles they could find. His very evident passion on this subject, which was based in wonder, not anger, will always stand out in my mind.

We thanked him for talking with us, then decided to head back toward Saint-Sulpice and home. Though we could see Notre Dame, Jennifer decided she wanted to wait until we had more time in the day to experience it.

We made our way down Rue Danton, crossed to Rue de l'Odéon, passing the original address of Sylvia Beach's Shakespeare and Company, circled around the impressive *Odéon-Théâtre de l'Europe*, then walked along the front of the Luxembourg Palace, bidding *bonsoir* to both *gendarmerie* guarding its entrance. The sun was finally going down, and as twilight began to darken the streets, I realized that we were completely alone. I had no idea how safe it was to be wandering these neighborhoods at night. So we slipped under the arched entrance to Rue Garancière and walked until it ran into Saint-Sulpice.

Jennifer stepped into our local Franprix while I waited outside holding our bag of souvenirs. From there I watched a man who stands outside the entrance every night. He is something of a mix between a beggar and a Wal-Mart greeter. He greets everyone entering and leaving with the same phrase. "*Bonsoir, Monsieur/Madame*," he says with a nod of his round, kind face. His hair is closely cropped and white. He does not hold out his hand. He is, in fact, holding a small bundle of magazines of some kind. At first, I thought he was selling them. But as I watched the people pass him, I saw them occasionally give him a few coins. *"Merci, merci beaucoup."* He did not hand them a magazine. A few of the older ladies stop and ask him how he is. He is quick to reply, always with a big smile. I am surprised by the more professional looking Parisians, dressed smartly as they are coming home from work. Many of them, young and looking like the types who would disdain being bothered by the door-greeter, upon hearing his words of greeting, turn and look at him, smile, and return the greeting, as if speaking with an old friend. Some of them even slip him some coins. Under all of his friendliness, however, I can see just a hint of wariness. He keeps his head tilted just so. His eyes often look up through his brows, to scan the street. When another man who, by his appearance, must be homeless, stops at the entrance, my greeter speaks quickly to him, as if to shoo him away. I imagine he is saying to move on, this spot is taken, or perhaps he is telling him his appearance is bad for business. The interloper gets the same message and moves along.

Not long after Jennifer went into the store, I witnessed a fun action sequence. I heard running on the street, loud enough to overcome the general din of the busy intersection of Rue Cassette and Rue de Rennes. I looked up in time to see two girls, perhaps nearly twenty years old, giggling and running my way. They were quite excited about something. After they passed, I looked back in the direction from which they had come and I saw our waiter from the Café Cassette (from just the other day) charging down the street after them. He was not amused. He was in fact...*in earnest*...to put it mildly. His head tucked in, his elbows also tucked in, he ran in the perfect sprinters form. Still wearing his apron, tied low around his waist, and unhindered by it, he blew past me, making up ground on the girls, who had no chance to match his speed. Before losing them at the corner of Rue du Vieux Colombier, just at the entrance to the Saint-Sulpice métro station, he grabbed the taller of the girls by her arm. She yelled at him but did not put up much of a fight. He spun her around and began to drag her back to the café. She smacked at him with her purse but this was only for show. She seemed amused more than alarmed. As they passed, she pulled out her phone, calling someone, perhaps someone who could get her out of the tangled mess she was in. The waiter was not too concerned with her civil rights. It was best not to attempt to skip out on this guy.

Jennifer appeared shortly after, arms laden with groceries, and we made our way back to the apartment in the dark, amazed at how our little trip to Saint-Germain-des-Prés Église had turned into such a wonderfully perfect evening.

Chapter Four: Rain, Baudelaire, and the Dead of Paris

Refreshed from our adventure to Saint-Michel the night before, we dressed warm for the coming day. Temperatures were still not rising above 55 and the rain kept falling off and on. But we were not about to be bullied into staying indoors.

We were starting off in a cemetery again. But this time it wasn't my fault. Jennifer had been asking to go to Montparnasse Cemetery since we'd arrived. It was the resting place of Charles Baudelaire, and she was doing her best to be patient. She would have to wait no longer.

Most of the sites of Paris were north, east or west of us. The exceptions to this were Versailles, which was about 10 miles to the southwest of us, and Montparnasse, which was just a mile to the south of us. Versailles was on our list, but it was to be one of our last excursions, later in the second week. Montparnasse, however, had several sites that I knew we could combine into one day. We would start at Baudelaire's grave, take the subterranean tour of the catacombs, and after lunch at the literary mecca *La Rotunde*, we would wander through the Luxembourg gardens and end up at the Pantheon.

I had spent some time plotting this one out back home. I knew how to get around Montparnasse, since our Number 4 métro line serviced Montparnasse quite thoroughly. The only hitch had been getting over to the Luxembourg Gardens. There was no direct métro line linking them, and I had some trouble visualizing the best way to get from one to the other.

As was becoming my habit, I spent the morning on Bing's map site, working out the best route. Jotting down notes from this into my travel journal, I strapped it shut and stuck it in my pocket. I had it all worked out.

Getting to Montparnasse Cemetery was simple. A quick métro ride south and we hopped off at Raspail. This time, I'd made sure to look over the area from the satellite shots to know where the métro exit would point us, and we quickly traversed Boulevard Edgar Quinet until we came to the cemetery's entrance.

Built in 1824, Montparnasse is best known for its residents Jean-Paul Sartre and Simone de Beauvoir. But that is not who we were looking for when we stopped in at the guard's shack to ask for a map. Incredibly, once Jennifer asked for a map (in flawless French, I thought) the guard handed her an Italian map. We only noticed this after we'd walked away, but Baudelaire is spelled the same in Italian as it is in French and English so we were able to work out where we needed to go.

Montparnasse has a more intimate feel than Pere Lachaise. The majority of the memorials are less ostentatious and it feels like a cemetery one might find in a smaller city. The rain held off while we were there and it did not take us long to find the grave of one of France's greatest poets.

Tucked in behind a row of gravestones facing Avenue de l'Ouest close to where it intersects with Avenue du Nord, a slim cream-colored headstone marks the grave of Charles Pierre Baudelaire; poet, translator, art critic, and the man who coined the term *modernity*. The grave is marked with métro tickets left by admirers, though this turns out to be a mistaken ritual that should actually be done for the French songwriter/poet Serge Gainsbourg, also buried at Montparnasse, whose popular song *Le Poinçonneur des Lilas* told the story of a Paris métro ticket puncher. More appropriately, several folded and unfolded scraps of paper containing either bits of Baudelaire's verse or verse from his adherents had been left on Baudelaire's grave.

There was much to see that day, it was cold, rain threatened from a very active sky; we needed to push on. Maybe try and find the abused Alfred Dreyfus, the oddball Man Ray, or the designer of the Paris Opera House, Charles Garnier. Sometimes a husband needs to know when to quit worrying about the schedule or the weather and just back off a little. So I wandered the nearby sections, taking pictures, giving Jennifer time with one of her favorite poets. Was he there with her, scowling at her as she dared to interrupt his rest? I doubted it. He never showed up in the pictures, though I don't think ghosts are as easily captured with digital photography as they once were on film. I'm not much of an expert on Baudelaire, but from what I can tell, he doesn't seem the type to slink around his tomb, watching his admirers carefully put a pebble on their métro tickets. If he did, he'd likely end up scaring them off, cursing them for their idiocy.

The top of his headstone tells of Jacques Aupick, a General, Senator, and Ambassador to Constantinople and Madrid. Below the date of his death, the inscription reads: *Charles Baudelaire, Son Beau Fils, Décédé À Paris.*

Charles Baudelaire, his stepson, who died in Paris. Nothing on it tells us that he was a poet.

Elsewhere in the cemetery is a cenotaph in his memory. It

is one of the many sites of which we were unaware and left without seeing. It is quite moving; Baudelaire is laid out, wrapped from neck down as if he were an Egyptian mummy. Perhaps it is better that we did not come upon it. I might not have been able to get Jennifer to leave.

The shrouded sun did nothing to warm our morning, and so we finally hurried on, passing up most of the sites at Montparnasse. We slipped out the south entrance onto the tree lined Rue Froidevaux and found ourselves in a very quiet, upscale neighborhood. It felt more modern here, as if we were walking along a street just off Chicago's Lake Shore Drive.

After a brisk walk, we arrived at Place Denfert-Rochereau, and circled it to the right, charmed by the sight of very young school children lined up at the *Cinema Le Denfert*, which was about to play a Chaplin movie. Disappointed that I could not join them, we found the oddly placed entrance to *Les Catacombes* in the center of Square de l'Abbe Migne.

Having become accustomed, already, to the large structures like the Louvre and the Orsay museum, it is disconcerting to approach the entrance to the Parisian catacombs. The entrance is a door in a dark little structure that has been tacked onto a modest stone house sitting by itself on the square. There are no large signs signifying the fact. I don't remember seeing any signs except for the odd paddle-shaped historic marker sign. (These canoe-paddle historical markers can be found all over Paris. It seems the origin of the name Paris has a vague tie-in to river canoes, and so when the historical markers were designed, someone thought canoe-paddle. Not the best choice, in my opinion. But they did not check with me, so I'll cut them some slack.)

We knew we had the right place, however, because there was a long line of people circling around the north side of the square. We trotted across the street, heads tucked to ward off the cold wind, and staked our place in line. Because only a limited number of people are allowed in the old mining tunnels at a time, this line moved very slowly. And while we were in line, the rain continued to fall sporadically.

Fortunately, we were entertained by the French family in front of us comprised of a mother and her two children. One was a very young boy, maybe four or five, who never said a word. The other was a darling little girl who must have been about eight or nine. She was not discouraged by the cold, prattling on about who-knows-what, her mother happy to chime in whenever the girl stopped to catch her breath. I could never catch what they were saying, but the tones and pacing were universally playful.

I did understand it when they joked about the fact that no one came back out of the catacombs. We had also observed this, and it is an easy joke to make. Is that where all the bones came from? Are they simply collecting the bones of all the tourists? The girl laughed gaily at the idea.

If you're in line at the Catacombs, be sure to check out the staid lion in the center of the Denfer-Rochereau traffic circle. This proud guy memorializes those who fought in defense of the nation in 1870 and 1871. As we stood staring at him, I could not help thinking he looked more British than French. My apologies to the defenders of France. I mean no offense.

The couple behind us, mostly hidden under hoods and an umbrella, turned out to be from Washington D.C. Once we'd braved the wind enough to allow our necks to rise out of our collars and extend to full length, it became possible to interact with our fellow Americans. They had only been in Paris for a day, had about four days ahead of them, and it was her second time, his first. She was not happy about the weather.

"I was here last year at this time," she said in between sips of her McDonalds coffee, "and the weather was great, then. So I brought my husband this year, and this is crazy!"

"Well, I'm glad to hear you say that," I said, trying not to be angry that she had slipped from the line earlier, bought coffee around the corner at Micky-D's, and never thought to buy some for all of us, "I meticulously watched the weather in Paris a year ago and concluded it would be cool, but not bad at all. I was beginning to think I'd been watching the weather in the wrong city."

It was easy to chat with them, English had become something to enjoy in and of itself. We were still feeling a bit isolated, despite Jennifer's growing confidence in speaking the local language.

Finally we were allowed to enter the unmarked doorway. Inside, a sweet little lady took our Euros, and pointed at a spiral staircase. It was made of stone, and spiraled tightly down for about one hundred feet. It was a rapid, unsteady, deliciously ominous descent.

Once we'd spun ourselves to the bottom, we found a little museum that tells the tale of the catacombs. We skipped most of that, choosing instead to begin our trek along a low tunnel that forced me to walk like an arthritic old man. The passage seemed to go on endlessly with nothing of much interest to see. Eventually, we came upon some wonderful rock carvings by Decure, one of the first workers in the Quarry Inspections. His models of the Port-Mahon Palace were sculpted by memory from 1777-1782. It is said he died from a cave-in while trying to build a stairway that would provide easy access to his models. This set the mood nicely. Not long after this, we came upon that wonderful, macabre, and foreboding sign which reads: *Arrête! C'est ici l'empire de la Mort.* Or, as the English would say: Stop! This is the Empire of Death.

Oh, the dramatic French!

What, after all, is the big deal? We'd only entered a once abandoned mine where the bones of six million dead had been stored. Once inside, I realized I hadn't seen this many femurs and skulls since I'd seen that photo shoot from last year's

● ● ●

Room With No View *Excerpt, April 18, 2012:*

...an unexpected visitor can improve a picture. Down in the Paris Catacombs, I was having trouble taking pictures, since flash photography was prohibited. My camera would take the pictures, but with slow shutter speed to compensate for the lack of light, and I have never had a steady hand for that kind of work. Finally, I found a better-than-average lit area where I could get a decent shot. Just then, a little boy came over and began playing with the single spotlight behind us. I was tempted to become annoyed, but then I saw his shadow-puppets and I wanted to capture at least one of them. I did, but I had to act quickly. He moved pretty fast--nearly as fast as the French words that trilled from his lips.

● ● ●

supermodel convention.

There have been so many articles and books written about the Paris Catacombs, I won't make any attempt to fill in details on this massive subterranean memorial. Yes, gravesites such as *des Cimetière des Innocents,* now the site of the underground mall Les Halles, were once bursting with bodies. In these earlier days, before the 18th century, most people were buried in common graves. Only the very wealthy were buried individually. A pit was dug, and bodies were tossed into it (with the deepest respect, I'm sure) until it became full. Then, lime and topsoil were added, and a new pit begun. But as the number of pits grew, and the city built up around the cemeteries, heavy rains helped the pits swell to overflowing.

The great network of limestone mines that supplied the materials for so many of Paris's major structures became the answer to this deluge of the dead. The removal and storage of six million bodies was carried out with far more care and pomp than you might imagine. The bones were only moved at night, with clergy accompanying the carts and liturgies and masses said along the way. The bones were carefully stacked according to which cemetery they belonged—into walls of femurs and skulls, with all the others tossed in behind.

The effect is impressive. As you move along the narrow walkways, scrunching wet gravel under your shoes, you can read the names and dates of the cemeteries from which each section of bones was taken. Often times you will see scripture verses or select lines from poetry that help to add a sacred or profound touch to the scene. I had expected the tour to evoke a great deal of feeling, especially with Jennifer, whose poet's heart can be particularly sensitive. I did not ever sense such emotion, despite the presence of *so many dead*. As the poet R.S. Gwynn said to me later, this was something so overwhelming it left you numb. He was right, though I would also add that there was no tragedy involved here save for the human tragedy that we all experience. These were the physical remains of millions who had lived and died in that most common of pursuits—life.

I tried to imagine the skulls as Parisians from the tenth, twelfth, or fourteenth century. I had trouble doing so. This should have been right up my alley. At least it would have fit in with my comedic short story *A Night in the City of the Dead*, a story of the residents of a New Orleans cemetery, all of whom are now just skeletons, à la an old Disney movie. I may eventually be able to combine such a theme with the catacombs, but while we were there it just didn't work. It was the stacks that peeled back the skin of reality. It looked more like a bone factory, where skulls and femurs were mass-produced for next October's Halloween festivities.

This lighter mood prevailed even more near the end of the tour, where the workers seemed to have grown bored with stacking the bones and had made little artistic jokes, stacking skulls in the shapes of hearts, crosses, and other cutesy shapes. I began to wonder if the gift shop would sell little skull and femur packs to be used like legos. My kids would have loved them.

Once we'd passed through this mile-plus walking tour, we ascended yet another stone spiral stair and came out in a little room that funneled us into a small side street. We were nowhere near our entry point. Across the narrow street was a little souvenir shop that sold pretty tacky catacomb-themed junk. As much as we liked this kind of tour, we were disappointed in what we found in the shop. There wasn't even a decent coffee cup. All of the knick-knacks were covered with silly skeleton cartoons, which just looked too Disney for us. It saved us some money, since we walked out without buying anything.

This was the first time I would lose track of our whereabouts in the city. There is a certain mystery about where the catacombs disgorge their guests. I'd not found any definite address online as I had researched it, but I had an idea that it would be somewhere along Boulevard Saint-Jacques. So as we left the souvenir shop, I guided us confidently toward our next destination.

This mystery about the catacombs' exit still rather baffles me. Once back home in the states, I took some time to map out the area around Denfert-Rochereau as a way of recreating our walk from that day. Using online searches, online maps, and our photographs and videos from that day, I had serious trouble pinpointing the address where catacomb visitors pop out. The official site does not tell you, and various bloggers and travel guides give either the wrong address or extremely vague descriptions. Using a few of my pictures, I had to cross-reference them with pictures from other travelers who had posted them to sites like *flickr* and *tripadvisor*. I was finally able to get a bearing on this using one picture in particular, which matched up with one of mine but included a partially legible blue Parisian street sign in my original photo. From that, I went to the online map and finally concluded that the exit is on Rue Remy Dumoncel. (I wonder if I'm breaking some sort of travel writer's rule in disclosing this information. But I give it here to help those who want to know where they are once they return from the Empire of Death.)

I was only carrying a very sketchy tourists' map of Paris which had been provided by the managers of our apartment rental service. This map was carried by every tourist wandering the crazy streets of Paris. Oddly enough, it barely listed the main boulevards, and was not very useful as a navigation tool. But I felt pretty sure I knew where we were, so I routed us to the first main drag I could find, assumed we were northeast of our last location, and promptly stopped at a Starbucks for a very tall cup of coffee.

It was still very cold, though noon had come and gone. Starbucks was a compromise we had never meant to make. We had originally scoffed at the idea of stepping into a Starbucks while in Paris. Why would we? We were in the world's most famous café location. On any street corner you could see the most charming coffee shops ever built. We were not about to betray the sanctity of French cafés by darkening the door of the over-commercialized Starbucks. For one thing, we don't particularly like Starbucks coffee. We tend to drink it when there are no alternatives. So once we were out of the protective and relative warmth of the catacombs, we stood on the wind-swept Avenue du General Leclerc and both perked up at the sight of the green and white mermaid.

Mostly, we were tired of the little cups of French coffee we'd been stuck with, and the idea of a Grande cup of Joe was too good to pass up. So like all good Americans, we proudly crashed the Starbucks. Much to our surprise, it was not just full of tourists. There were plenty of French customers as well. Fortified with our luxurious American-sized coffees, we felt refreshed and ready to get on with our day. It was the best tasting Starbucks coffee we'd ever had.

A further note on Starbucks in Paris: according to one

American blogger living in Paris, Starbucks is thriving due to the fact that French cafés are known everywhere as purveyors of bad coffee. Sure the atmosphere is to die for, but the coffee is notoriously bad. If I had known this beforehand, we wouldn't have felt so bad abandoning the cafés for Starbucks on just our fourth day there. For those of you who make it to Paris, don't dither around about this. Go to the Parisian cafés for atmosphere and romance, and go ahead and order the coffee, since it is part of the experience. But when you really need some coffee, go straight to Starbucks. There's no shame in it, baby.

Now I knew I wanted to get us to *La Rotunde*, which is an Art Deco café in the center of Montparnasse. This famed eatery is known the world over as the former hangout of such artistic icons as Henry Miller, Picasso, Modigliani and most notably, Earnest Hemingway. I'm not the biggest fan of such writers, but this café looked perfect. We walked up the street (heading in the wrong direction) and finally descended into the métro at Alesia station. From there it was a quick jump to Vavin station, where we came out of the métro just a few dozen yards from the café.

Our budget allowed for the occasional trip into the pricier cafés , and this was one I was looking forward to patronizing. Impressed by its Art Deco façade, we crossed the street and began to read the menu. Every eatery in Paris displays its menu out front. We were used to this in New Orleans, and it is a great convenience. It will save you the embarrassment of leaving a restaurant after you've been seated and discovered that the menu does not have anything you are remotely interested in, or anything you can remotely afford. This happened to us once in New York City, and it was only easy to walk out because I knew we'd never be back and so I didn't care what the waiters thought of us.

The problem with French cafés, which are really more like

sit-down restaurants in the United States, is that they pretty much have the same food in them. It is all chicken and pork with some seafood. *Jambon et legumes* is gonna be everywhere. There is little variety. At this point, we were cold, hungry, and in need of chow, not in need of a fine meal. So as much as I wanted to eat at Hemingway's old hangout, hoping that some of his literary genius might rub off on me, we decided to find something less formal and more common.

Across the street I'd seen a pâtisserie. As we were learning, this was more in line with our tastes. And once we stepped under their awning, I knew we had the right idea. They have pizza, quiche, soups, hotdogs, and something I'd once heard about but not yet experienced: *le croque monsieur*.

Our kids have had French class in elementary school and middle school. It is part of the Louisiana heritage to give kids this foundation in French. Just before we left for Paris, I'd been reading a Paris phrase book aloud, which gave my kids plenty of opportunity to laugh. (Being an old Yankee, I'd been taught German by my schoolteachers, and that wonderful, harsh Germanic language has nothing to do with the romance languages like Italian and French.) While reading food items aloud, I came across *le croque monsieur*. My youngest son Simon, an amateur chef who would thrive in Paris, immediately let me know all about it. His French teacher had made them for her class. It is like a grilled cheese sandwich with ham. Change the name to *croque madame*, and you have the same sandwich with a fried egg on it. (Get it? You see, a woman has…never mind.)

A spunky French lady behind the counter was more than happy to take our order, patiently amused as I tried out my toddler-like French. She was most encouraging as I added a *torte normande* to my order. I had no idea what it was but it looked too darned good to pass up.

Squeezed into a high, corner table, we very quickly consumed our *bourgeois* meals and I discovered that the *torte normande* was in fact an apple pie sort of deal that even now, months later, I can still happily taste. (The *normande* bit comes from the use of Normandy apples.) I was convinced, and so was Jennifer: the pâtisseries were the way to go. And from here on out, I knew that if I needed to grab a bite, *le croque monsieur* was the thing to grab.

Still unsure of where we had been after leaving the underworld, I knew that our next objective, the Luxembourg Gardens, was a pretty far piece to walk. That was how it looked online, anyway. So I was still trying to find a way to get there by métro. Our line, the number 4, ran parallel to the gardens, and so we either had to ride back down to Saint-Sulpice, where we could then walk over to the north side of the palace, or we could ride in the other direction back to Denfert-Rochereau where we could catch the RER B train which would angle over toward the south end of the gardens, which is where I was really trying to go. There is a very large fountain on that end that I wanted Jennifer to see. At no time did I consider walking there, since from a bird's eye view on the map it looked too far.

I put us back on the métro and back to Denfert-Rochereau. Up and out of the station, we took a few more shots of our French Lion at the traffic circle, then, with my mind still looking at the world from the wrong viewpoint as set by the catacombs exit, we set off down the road. It wasn't exactly the right road, but it was close.

What we did was retrace our route that we had just taken on the métro; only we were now above ground. Now, keep in mind that we were walking in Paris, so at no time is a walk in the wrong direction an unpleasant excursion. Unfortunately, rain began to fall, and so we ducked under our umbrellas, enjoying our walk, but not getting where we wanted to go.

Despite my cock-eyed internal compass, I had a feeling that things weren't quite right so I began to look for ways to steer in a more right-ly direction. We slipped down a few side streets, smiling at the groups of students and solitary working-class men and women who eyed us with curiosity but who were not quite forward enough to just tell us we were obviously in the wrong place. A few of them certainly looked as if they were considering such a plan. We just kept moving as I puzzled out where we were on our sketchy little map.

After a few turns, we eventually came out at an intersection where Jennifer pointed to a statue that turned out to be Marshal Ney, one of Napoleon's generals with whom I was familiar. She suggested I stand beside him for a picture, but I passed on the opportunity, since I was still trying to make sure I could find the fountain I was seeking.

I wish I had listened to her. Though I knew of Hemingway's connection to *La Rotunde*, I did not learn until the next week, as I read more of Hemingway's *A Moveable Feast*, that this was one of Papa's favorite spots in Paris. Ney stands near the entrance to *des Lilas*, which Papa mentioned many times. I missed my chance for the photo-op, but was pleasantly surprised we'd finally found the fountain.

For anyone who would like to visit these wonderful places, let me give you a hint. *La Rotunde* is not quite a half-mile walk from *des Lilas*, which we could have done as soon as we had finished my *torte normande*. What I was still learning was the fact that so much of Paris is packed closely together. Don't ever think you can't walk to where you need to go. This was a perfect example. We rode the métro backwards, trying to make a connection that we ended up dismissing as we walked down unnecessary streets and eventually found our way simply because I'd overestimated the walking distance between two neighborhoods. This is precisely why I think the big métro pass is not such a good deal. Unless you are of an age that walking is prohibitive, you should take advantage of this city's layout. It is designed so that you can comfortably walk from one monument to the next. And with all the *pâtisseries*, *brasseries*, *salon de thés*, and *cafés* thrown in along the way, you really have no worries as you move along.

Approaching *Fontaine de l'Observatoire* from the south was well worth the walk. This extravagant fountain has the whole of the Luxembourg gardens as a backdrop. It is a smaller version of Versailles, and that is a reflection on its size, not the quality of the workmanship. Eight turtles, with rather powerful lungs, blow water up onto six horses as four not-so-clothed women hold an iron globe above them. A few fish spit water back at the turtles. The image is not as silly as it sounds, though one does have the impression that the animals are just a heartbeat away from breaking into a Disney song.

This fountain was built between 1867 and 1874 as part of Baron Haussmann's city renovations. The project, overseen by Gabriel Davioud, was meant to link the *Observatoire de Paris* and the *Palais de Luxembourg*. The fountain itself was designed by sculptor Jean-Baptiste Carpeaux. Like many monuments in Paris, the initial reactions to it were quite hostile. Critic Jules Clarétie described the four women above the fountain as "a group of wild, vulgar and wrinkled dancers." Everyone's a critic.

Though the rain had been falling for most of our walk, and I had been keeping the cameras sheltered in my pack and under the umbrella, I just had to pull out the Nikon here. If you're in Paris, be sure to take in this view. It is one of those places that you stand in front of, and realize that every effort and dollar spent getting to Paris was absolutely worth it.

We took our time crossing the plaza as we headed toward the Luxembourg Palace. The rain kept turning off then turning back on, but despite this, the temperature was finally warming up enough that we could ignore the fact that we were getting wet.

Because it was still early in the year, most of the gardens

were bare. As I was trying to get a picture of Jennifer with the palace behind her, I had to work around the small trucks and tractors that were buzzing around the gardens. I managed to get the shots I wanted, using monument bases to block the view of the trucks, but I was a little annoyed at their presence. What I didn't realize was that the grounds crew was just beginning to bring in the flowers. Though the gardens were bare and gray that rainy day, just ten days later, on our last day in Paris, I was to find a completely different *Jardin de Luxembourg*. It was a delightful surprise, and I cannot give enough credit to the hardworking grounds crew.

Our extended trek through Montparnasse left us with little time to dally in the gardens. We passed through, heading off toward the Pantheon. This was easier to do, since you can catch a grand view of it from the main pool in the gardens. We slipped out at the side gate onto Boulevard Saint-Michel and made our way through a few maze-like streets and turns until we came out at France's magnificent memorial to the greatest Frenchmen who ever lived.

Here, at what was originally intended to be a cathedral to honor Saint-Geneviéve, the patron saint of Paris, the people of France, after the revolution, set the Pantheon up as a site where Frenchmen and Frenchwomen of various professions and scientific disciplines are interred. It is, quite frankly, a massive, secular shrine to France.

To say it celebrates the greatness of France is not an exaggeration. The overriding atmosphere within those massive walls is one of gaiety and playfulness. You would not guess that it was a mausoleum. The central hub of this memorial would please M.C. Escher. Be sure to stand under the dome and look up at the dizzying array of arches and angles. With daylight steaming in through a myriad of checkerboard panes, you'll just want to stand still and enjoy the complex view.

Extraordinary murals tell the story of Saint-Geneviéve, as well as one that depicts the beheading of Saint-Denis, as he is about to retrieve his head. The legend says that Saint-Denis picked up his head and walked ten miles preaching the gospel before he finally died. Denis is also a patron saint of Paris. This rather detailed mural is just to the left of the entrance, where you'll see not only Denis, but also two other beheaded figures. It sure lets you know you have just entered no ordinary, boring monument. Joan of Arc is also featured in the north wing.

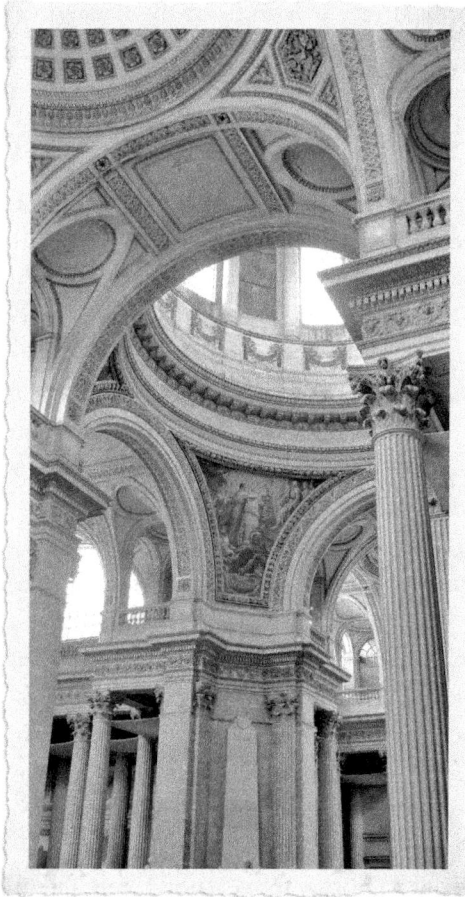

Since the Pantheon was secularized after the revolution, several large sculptures were added that paid homage to the heroes of the revolution. One looks like a 3D rendering of Delacroix's *Liberty at the Barricade*, though it is not an actual depiction of that famous painting. Across the aisle from it is another busy conglomerate of revolutionaries. This one caught my eye because of the two men near the top who are straining themselves as they work on a piece of the sculpture. At first, I thought they were supposed to depict how some statues are made. But it made no sense. One man has lain down on one part of the statue that extends into the air. This first man has reached around the stone, and is holding his buddy around the waist, who is wielding a hammer and chisel. Surely, I thought, there's a better way to carve a statue than to hang out on it so precariously. It was only after much study of the image that I realized these two men were *defacing* the statue. It was, in fact, meant to show us how the revolutionaries climbed out onto many of the beautiful works of art in this city and mutilated them.

When one hears stories of how the heads of the kings on the west façade of Notre Dame were busted off during the revolution, you begin to wonder that Paris has anything left to offer the world. There was much anger and resentment burning within the people of Paris, and much of it was taken out on the art work, since so much of it was designed to praise either the Royals or the Church. How ironic it would have been if this destruction had gone unchecked, and France had been left without its tourist trade.

Down in the crypt, you can find Molière on the left and Rousseau on the right, facing each other. Further in you can find a room with the entombed bodies of Alexander Dumas, Victor Hugo, and Emile Zola. It is a profound room for a writer; quite the exclusive book club.

Even down in the crypt, that festive mood was pervasive. Schoolchildren ran back and forth, shouting and laughing, ignored by their elders. Profound or not, we did not stay in the crypt. The noise was just a little too much. We returned to the first floor, and I had a photographer's holiday as Jennifer found a quiet spot to sit and write. I knew she was tiring out, and we still had a bit of walking ahead of us before we made it home. I hoped to make one more stop before we did, so I left her alone, knowing that she was reenergizing as she blocked out the noise around her and sat staring at the Saint-Geneviéve murals. (Geneviéve is, if you haven't realized it already, the French form of Jennifer.)

Eventually, we were ready to leave. We stepped outside and found that the sun was shining. Much like the day before, Paris had warmed up and the clouds had pulled back as the afternoon drew close to evening. One more surprise awaited us. From the steps of the Pantheon, we could see the Eiffel Tower. Aside from a quick glance of it through the trees on Montmartre, we hadn't seen it since we'd ridden the AirFrance shuttle into the city. I'd almost forgotten it was in the city.

"So are we going home?" Jennifer asked, with a heavy helping of hope.

"Well, there's a little surprise I have for you, if you can make it. It is just a small walk, right around the corner."

"If it isn't far," she said bravely, apprehension plainly visible in her eyes.

"Around here," I pointed to the left of the massive shrine. Buoyed by the warmth of the sun, Jennifer faithfully followed me as I showed her a little church catty-corner to the Pantheon across Place du Pantheon: *Église Saint-Etienne du Mont*. This was a spot I'd been eager to find.

We had planned this trip to Paris several years prior to our departure date. Even before that, we'd always talked about going one day. Oddly enough, just half a year before we left, Woody Allen released a movie entitled *Midnight in Paris*, which would become his most commercially successful movie up to that point. One day in November of 2011, while the kids were in school, Jennifer and I sat in our local theater and were overwhelmed by Allen's beautifully filmed, hilariously written nostalgic romp through Paris. As much as I had researched about Paris, I would have missed so much of it had I not seen *Midnight in Paris* first. Not only did I learn a great deal about the city itself, but I also learned much of the literary history therein.

This kind of a happy coincidence is called serendipity, and that is exactly what this was. We fell in love with the film, and made sure all the kids watched it at Christmas.

Central to the story is a magical portal that sends the main character back in time to the Paris of the 1920s. This portal was a set of steps on the side of a church. I had learned only days before we left where to find those steps. They were on the Rue de la Montagne Sainte-Geneviéve entrance to *Saint-Etienne du Mont*. It did not take Jennifer long to recognize it. And she was kind enough to take a picture of me sitting on the steps. It was my second movie location that week. I loved it. The streets around that site are very narrow, they bend and twist, which is not usual for Parisian streets, and the brasseries and cafés are terribly charming. This is the backside of the Sorbonne, and students can be seen in groups all around.

Yet again, Paris had beguiled us, with just a turn at a corner. We descended this wonderful street as I planned our route home.

Though Jennifer was, by now, exhausted, I had one more item on our agenda if she did not demand to be taken straight home. The nearest métro station was about five minutes away, and we were only about fifteen minutes from home if we just decided to walk the whole way. I steered us in the direction I wanted to go, hoping that she would make it. I knew I was pushing her toward her physical limit, but we also planned on taking a day off the next day.

I was looking for a bar. And I wasn't looking for a French bar. This bar was Canadian: the Moose Bar.

Passing through the University district, I pulled out my travel journal and checked the notes I'd made on the location of the Moose Bar. Able to get my bearings better than I had earlier in the day (hmmm, which might tell you what I was really interested in) we made it to the Moose just as Jennifer was assuring me she had gone about as far as she could. It was now six in the evening, the weather was perfect, of course, and we were starving.

Enter the Moose—literally.

This great little hole in the wall was given high praise by a magazine that had top ten lists on many different categories for each *arrondissement*. The Moose is run by Canadians, has split tree trunks as its wall décor and the base of its bar, and also displays multiple flat-screen TVs with any number of sporting events being displayed at one time. When we walked in, Nadal was playing a clay court match on the nearest screen and I knew I was gonna love it.

Jennifer was more than happy to order a meal, and so while I had a Mooseburger (just beef, not Moose meat, but still delicious) Jennifer ate a plate of stir-fry and we enjoyed a little tennis in the heart of the Latin Quarter. We weren't the only ones in the place that early, but nearly so. This made for a peaceful, quiet dinner. The waitress, though definitely French, spoke passable English (better than I spoke French). She was not too chatty, and eventually we realized it was the end of her shift. She bid goodbye to the barman and left just ahead of us. Her weary walk, aided by a cigarette, hinted at a long, hard day waiting tables.

Our own day had been long and hard, though full of amazing sights and unforgettable memories. Our dinner fueled us for that last stretch with which we were becoming familiar: Odeon, Saint-Sulpice, Rue du Vieux Colombier, and eighty steps to our room with a view.

Chapter Five: Madeleine, the Opera, and a New Orleans
Monster in Paris

One fantastic consequence of wearing ourselves out on the streets of Paris was that sleeping was easy. Back home in the States, we do not always sleep too well, especially with my shift work. We often are awake early in the morning. We do not sleep in as a habit. But Paris was both exciting and wearying, and so we slept well and we slept late. We always seemed to awake refreshed.

Feeling that refreshed makes it difficult to take a day off.

Part of the reason we'd decided to dedicate two weeks to this adventure was our expectation that we'd need to take a few days of rest scattered amongst the other days of sightseeing. The morning after our trip to Montparnasse, we fully intended to do nothing. That was part of the allure of Paris. To sit in a café, a journal in front of us, drinking coffee and letting Paris speak to us. That was the plan and it was a pretty good one.

But to our own surprise, we were in no mood for that. A good night's rest can be deceptive, and so Jennifer pretty much insisted that we head out and find the former residence of Madame LaLaurie. That was not unreasonable. But then I started to think. If we were going to head in that direction, which was just north of the Madeleine District, we might as well go ahead and see Place de la Concorde, and then we could stop by and check out the Opera Garnier on our way home. Piece of cake.

This plan was impossible to turn down. The sky was almost clear, and temperatures were already warmer than we'd seen them. This was one of those no-brainers you hear about.

So let's get going. Ignore the fact that we'd walked four or five miles the day before. And the day before that. And the one before that. Who needs to rest? We're in Paris!

With all that sunshine, it was a pleasant surprise that we did not need the métro for this first part of the trip. We were to pick up the number 84 bus at Michel Debré, the bus stop right outside our door, and ride it to Place de la Concorde. We stood and waited for our bus, as every other bus slid by—the 39, the 70, the 63—this just happens. You come to expect it. As we waited, a young lady with her nine or ten-year-old son joined us. Finally, as I kept watching and reading bus numbers with each approaching bus, the little boy bent forward, eyed the next bus, and told his mother "*domage, domage, un mini-bus.*" He was disappointed that they would not get to ride one of the double-long accordion style buses. I understood his disappointment. Accordian buses are cool.

The buses used the same tickets as the métro, and so we fed them into the machine, retrieved them after the machine spit them back out, and picked out our seats. The bus spun back onto the Rue de Four, and snaked its way onto Boulevard Saint-Germain, eventually crossing the Seine at Pont de la

Concorde. On the far side of the square, we jumped off the bus and into the bustling excitement of Concorde.

It seems that every day we said the same thing: *now* we are seeing the real Paris. And this was no exception. Once off the bus, we stood at the foot of Rue Royale, on the north edge of the Place de la Concorde, and felt overwhelmed by the array of buildings and artwork surrounding us. It was almost too much to take in.

The *place*, a large square, lies like this: in the center is the Luxor Obelisk, a 3,300-year-old artifact that once stood at the entrance to the Luxor Temple. This gift from an Egyptian leader from 1829 to the people of France stands not far from the infamous site of *le guillotine*. To the north and south of this lie two identical fountains, filled with mermaids, river-gods (and goddesses) and fish. These fountains spring to life every few minutes, shooting water from the mouths of the fish. Traffic, laced with tourist buses, motorcycles, and delivery trucks, circled the fountains and the obelisk in a roar.

If a Cirque du Soleil acrobat could clamber up the obelisk and hold himself up on the tip of it by his hands, he would be privy to a spectacular and very deliberate view. Beginning by facing south, he would look across the Pont de la Concorde and see the twelve columned façade of the National Assembly. Carefully flipping to the north, our nimble tourist-acrobat would stare down Rue Royale and behold the eight columns of the Madeleine Cathedral, which looks as if it had been stolen straight out of ancient Greece. (And with the pedigree of some of the artwork found in the local museums, this is not as impossible as it sounds.) With a little spin to his right, now facing east, our intrepid sightseer would behold the beauties of the Tuileries Gardens, and at the far side of them, the Louvre Carousel Arch is lined up with I.M. Pei's glass Pyramid, with the Louvre itself as the background. Before his arms give out, our overzealous voyeur would need to make one more precarious flip, after which he would be able to gaze down the Champs-Élysées, through the Arc de Triomphe, all the way to François Mitterand's ultra-modern Grande Arche at *La Défense*, the modern business center of Paris.

At this point, the acrobat had best let himself slip back to earth as gracefully as possible before a gendarme comes along and arrests him for a monumental violation.

These pinpoint views were designed on a scale that boggles the mind. Washington D.C. achieves this visual craftsmanship, and does so on a large scale as well. However, D.C.'s mall was designed with the city; all of it was designed and built at once. Place de la Concorde is in the center of a city that was already there, and the monuments and views were added after the fact. It is impressive to imagine and more so to behold.

We took our time, filming, shooting, and just staring at the sights. You can also see the Eiffel Tower from here, with great photo opportunities combining the fountains, obelisk, and the tower. We were able to find a friendly tourist-couple who took our picture for us. I offered to take their picture first, which is the best way to obtain a photographer.

If we had not already planned out our day, I believe we might have stood at that central point and been unable to make any kind of decision as to where we would go next. This was one of those dots on the map that I'd paid little attention to and only added to our itinerary because it was convenient and it was often mentioned on the usual lists. Now I understand why.

The square had a few performers in it, including one who was dressed as a swaddled King Tut. He never moved, unless you dropped a Euro in his bowl. Then he would stiffly bow for you. Not much of a payoff, but his costume was pretty decent.

One historical note really made me think: *la Guillotine* was very busy on this site, back in the early 1800's. It was here that Marie Antionette and Louis the XVI were beheaded. If you look up early woodcuttings of this event, you'll see the columns of the buildings that line the square to the north. Researching this later that night, it was hard to believe that we had just been standing in that very place, our picture taken with those same columns filling the background. Where we stood, and our friendly photographer stood, crowds had jammed into that space many times, cheering the bloody murder of thousands of the rich and powerful (and the poor and innocent as well).

It was something to pause and consider. Back home, our present leader knows full well the ease with which one can lead a mob against the rich. He is doing his best to use this to his political advantage. It is a cowardly way to gain votes, as this little lesson in French history warns us that it is no big deal to incite normal people to commit atrocities far worse than stripping the rich of their wealth through exaggerated taxes. It is not impossible to push such a crowd to the point that they cheer and egg on men with bloody machines that slice the heads off men, women and children. And all of this in a country that is overcome with artistic culture and philosophy.

We finally turned away from this site of monstrous public-sponsored behavior and prepared to search out a private monster that once made her home in Paris.

We headed out the north side of the *place*, dodging traffic and fellow tourists, as we made our way up Rue Royale, passing the world famous Maxim's restaurant, and eyeing the grand, solid façade of *L'eglise Sainte-Marie-Madeleine*.

I hate to admit this, but despite the massive and impressive structure that stands at the end of Rue Royale, we ignored it. There is too much to do in Paris, and this was one of those times we had to say *no*. Keep moving. I did take a few pictures of it, as we skirted the eastern side of it. And maybe one day we'll make it back and take a peek inside. But for that day, we simply walked on by. There are, after all, over one hundred churches in Paris, and many of them would outshine most churches you'll find in the States.

So we slipped around it, stepped onto Rue Tronchet, and enjoyed a nearly warm, sunny walk through the Madeleine district. It was here I discovered *Paul.* I love Paul. Paul is awesome. Paul is delicious.

Paul is the name of a chain of bakeries that are often mobile (small carts along the street), full of crêpes, bread, croissants, quiches, tarts, and everything else tasty. It was here I met Monsieur Lapin au chocolat. The chocolate rabbit. This sweet bread, shaped like a rabbit, has its ears and feet dipped in chocolate. Just the right thing to snack on while shopping in the Madeleine district. It is just right for us fast-food Americans. Quick, easy, and not fussy.

Since we were in such a prestigious shopping locale, we did take the time to do a little hunting for family gifts in a few shops. Girls, if you're in Paris, just drag your male traveling companion to Rue Tronchet and find Bonnie Doon. You'll be glad you did. And that traveling companion might be glad as well.

Our goal, as we angled onto Rue du Havre, was not Gare Saint-Lazare, though we could clearly see it at the end of the street. (Again, we passed this one, despite knowing that Monet had been impressed enough with this train station to paint it and we had been impressed enough with the painting to hang a print in our master bath.) A little street to the left was our goal: Rue de l'isly.

We entered this short street because a monster once lived on it. This monster was not a native of Paris. She (yes, the monster was a *she*) was from New Orleans.

In 1834, the same year Edgar Degas was born in Paris to a Creole mother from New Orleans, the people of that French-

American city discovered their local socialite Marie Delphine LaLaurie was actually a serial killer who had tortured and murdered a great many of her own slaves. Fleeing Louisiana, LaLaurie came to Paris, where she lived until her death in 1842. The details of her crimes, while heinous, are also too numerous and contradictory to allow us to determine which of them are true and which ones are apocryphal, but historians generally agree that she was guilty of extreme, grotesque violence of a kind we tend to associate with modern serial killers.

Jennifer had just begun writing a series of cantos retelling this story. It was a unique chance to see the exterior of Madame LaLaurie's Paris home. Rue de I'isly is something of an awkward street, covering four hundred feet between Rue de Rome and Rue du Havre. This peaceful little neighborhood is just a two-minute walk away from the second-busiest train station in all of Europe: Gare Saint-Lazare. Saint-Lazare was actually built while LaLaurie lived at Rue de I'isly, in 1837.

Jennifer photographed number eight's set of jade green, wooden doors, which remained firmly closed while we were there. I wandered up and down this little street watching the people and the motorcycles and anything else that caught my fancy. It was odd to think of a killer like Delphine

Paris, take-outs are called *Traiteurs*, an old term for a culinary guild that specialized in preparing catered meals. We had a Traiteur just a few steps from our building's door. They are like a deli. In Louisiana, a *Traiteur* is a Cajun faith-healer/herbalist. Sounds like the makings for a great short-story: a Lebanese-Cajun faith-healer who runs into Madame LaLaurie's ghost.

freely engaged in Parisian High Society. It was just as bizarre to see that the bottom floor of Number Eight now housed a cell-phone store on one side of the doors and a Lebanese take-out on the other side.

Word of that day's good weather was getting around. The streets in that area were coming alive. We finally bade farewell to our New Orleans *femme fatale* Delphine, and headed down Rue Auber, stopping to buy trinkets while Jennifer made yet another friend behind the counter. He was more than happy to chat with Jennifer, and so I stood by, admiring the posters, playing cards, and crystal Eiffel Towers. The man complained that young people today do not appreciate the 18th century figurines and designs as they once did. Now they just want the modern icons like the Eiffel Tower and the Chat Noir trinkets.

Jennifer assured him that our daughter would enjoy the older designs. He was not convinced.

Our souvenirs purchased, we made our way to yet another major landmark: the Opera Garnier. Until we began to plan for this trip, I had no idea that there was more than just one Paris Opera House. In truth, the Paris Opera was officially renamed the Palais Garnier after the opening of the new Opera Bastille in 1989. It is still often referred to as the Paris Opera, people just like to think of it in this way. Its historical and architectural importance is unmatched. In my mind, there is no other opera than the theater that sits at the head of the Avenue de l'Opera. (Which sort of makes sense, you know?)

We came at it sideways, ducking through the side doors to buy our tickets and learned that we had only fifteen minutes to see the performance hall before they closed it for rehearsal. This was something I regret, and we never did anything to fix it. We had just a few moments to step into an opera box, glance up at the Marc Chagall painting on the ceiling (done in 1963, full of color and whacked images that let you know it was definitely done in 1963), see the stage (open as performers began to arrive on stage for practice), then get shooed out by the cute French lady. We only caught a glimpse, and it was not enough. (I'm talking about the performance hall, not the cute lady.)

The good news was that the theater is not the only remarkable part of the tour. First of all, I should point out that we did not take the guided tour, but merely wandered around enjoying the sights. Also, I was glad I was carrying cash, since they did not take credit cards. Keep this in mind if you decide to check out the Garnier.

And you really should. Even with the abbreviated view of the theater, it was well worth it. You simply have to see the grand staircase (*le grand escalier*) and the grand foyer (*le grand foyer et ses salons*). This is every bit as beautiful as Versailles. The grand foyer is shockingly dazzling. It is nearly as impressive as Versailles's Hall of Mirrors; every little corner, every square inch is part of a painting or a thick and golden creamy relief sculpture. Nothing has been left bare. And while that might sound as if it is too much, it is not. The total effect is overpowering, to be sure, but it works. Stand in the center of it and you are surrounded by cupids and goddesses and winged horses and warriors and bathing beauties and angels.

Golden light floods the staircase, as scores of candelabras shine off the caramel-colored marble columns and shining marble railings. What a vision! I could only guess at how magical it would appear full of the Belle Epoch's finest ladies and gentlemen. The gowns, the top hats, the cream of Parisian society crowding into this magnificent space, ascending the

staircase as they anticipated seeing the latest performance by the Ballets Russes; Stravinsky's music pouring out of the theater, Nijinsky and Pavlova waiting in the wings, Picasso's groundbreaking sets covered by the curtain, waiting to be revealed.

But did those crowds even stop to look at the wonder of the Grand Staircase? Did they ascend to the top of it, and instead of entering the theater, turn to their left, circle around the open balcony, and turn into the anteroom of the Grand Foyer? How many of them noticed that in this little room, when one looks up at the chandelier hanging in the center of the ceiling, you can see bats and owls swirling around its base amidst a backdrop of golden stars?

Take the time to notice this. Such little things make you realize how much effort is put into places like the Opera Garnier. Marvel at this, take a picture for your family back home, then turn to your left and step into what might be the most beautiful room in the world.

The Grand Foyer must not be missed on a trip to Paris. If you have only one day in Paris, there are only two other places you will need to see: Notre Dame, and Versailles' Hall of Mirrors. And if you cannot make it out to Versailles in that one day, don't worry, the Grand Foyer will suffice.

When I think of a foyer, I think of a room that no one notices. You open a door, enter a house, stand in the foyer and take off your coat, and pass through to the living room or dining room where you begin to notice how nice or not so nice the house is. Yet at the Opera Garnier, the Grand Foyer is really a gallery that is designed to allow opera-goers a chance to stretch their legs during intermissions. A place to stroll with your partner. To see and be seen. And why not do this surrounded by glorious artwork?

I'm not much into French gilded-crusty-gaudy décor. (Not an official term, but this describes what I've always thought of French Royal tastes.) Well, I didn't think I was. But when I walked into the Grand Foyer, I'll admit they won me over. Perhaps I never liked it because I'd never stood in the center of something so grand. Maybe it was the strong sunshine pouring in those great windows, cutting bright swaths across that perfectly waxed marble floor. Maybe I've just been spending too much of my time surrounded by ordinariness. At any rate, I really can't describe how much I was floored by that sight. Perhaps I'm just a peasant who is easily impressed. (Though I doubt the designers and artisans who worked on the Grand Foyer would suggest that impression before me was easy to create!)

If you're looking for a technical, academic description of the designs and décor found in Paris, this is not the book for you. I've no training in such things, and I'm not about to become a specialist in order to write more of what has already been written about Paris. There are hundreds of books available that you can order to educate you on all the important features and specs. Where I can I'll add a few details. But my goal here is to encourage everyone to get to Paris, and if you can't, then you can at least read how it has inspired me. And technical architectural terms don't inspire me. Bats and owls painted on a ceiling inspire me.

Tucked into a corner, just as you enter the foyer, you'll see this fantastic light fixture. It's a peculiar blend of Medusa, the robot chick from Metropolis, and a candelabrum. Made of a dark red marble, this Amazonian woman has a candelabrum rising out of her head like the coils of Medusa's hair. Her torso is squared-off, with black iron points jutting out from her shoulders, as if she were a robot whose arms have been removed for repair. A wire coil necklace runs from her back, over her shoulders, and attaches to wire spools partly sunk into her décolletage. I have no idea what these lamps are supposed to be. There are four of them, in each corner of the foyer.

They would seem out of place; except they are so elegantly designed they fit in. To be frank, they're just cool.

Realizing that we couldn't stand there all day gaping, yet again we turned away from glorious splendor and stepped out into brilliant wonder. (I realize you'll think I'm just thunking down over-the-top adjectives here, but I'm not. When you finally decide to take this trip, you'll see I was being almost modest in my choice of words.) From the Grand Foyer, you step out onto the exterior balcony.

The balcony itself is resplendent in marble and polished stone, with painted ceilings and iron light fixtures. The tiling on the floor has red, black, and caramelized marble. We had arrived just in time to see the afternoon sun fill the space with golden streaks, sharp shadows and warmth.

As with most things in Paris, we marveled at the artistry around us, then shifted our gaze to the outward view. Emerging from between the marble columns, we stood on the edge of the balcony and looked down upon Place de l'Opera. What a busy hub of Paris life! Buses shuttle around and around, affording tourists a chance to snap pictures of the Opera house from their open tops, as countless other tourists on foot stand all around snapping the same pictures. I wonder how many of them have pictures of us standing on the balcony looking down upon them all?

Here you can see Haussmann and all his glory. The iconic, five-story Haussmann design fills your view. The slate gray roofs crown this traffic circle with their small rotundas sticking up like diadems. Straight out from the balcony you can see the Avenue de l'Opéra stretching out to meet the Hotel du Louvre, and behind it, the rotunda of the Louvre itself. What fun it is to lean on the balcony railing and watch *la vie de Paris*.

Here again we had to pass up another famous location. From the balcony, you can see a street angling off to the right. This is Rue de la Paix, and it will lead you to Place Vendôme, two short blocks away, with its Vendôme Column in its center. Napoleon Bonaparte had it erected in honor of his victory at Austerlitz. The Paris Commune had it torn down in honor of their penchant for destroying things, and it was resurrected in honor of rubbing the Communards noses in their defeat.

Still at the opera, we finished our tour and slipped out the east side through the gift shop. Crossing out to the center of the traffic circle, we admired the impressive façade of the Opera Garnier, watched an old man sitting on a three legged stool ink in his technically accurate rendering of the Opera House (an architect could not have drawn it as perfectly), and then entered the métro.

Here again, we found a Paul bakery, and stopped for refreshment. The Opera métro station had a small shopping mall in it. We drank coffee, ate *pain au chocolat*, and Jennifer was ready to head home. I, of course, had my daily surprise prepared for her.

I'd been reading about a little out-of-the-way spot that should have been perfect for Jennifer. Paris has a handful of little covered alleys called *passages*. Historically, when two streets were joined by an alley, an effort was made to cover them, and then the passage was cleaned up and used as a sort of old-fashioned shopping mall. Over time, some of them developed into more extravagant affairs, with beautiful artwork added. The *Galeries Vivienne* and *Colbert* are two of the more prominent passages in Paris.

Having worked out a plan on how to find them, I put us on the Number 3 line and we rode just a few stations to the east, arriving at Bourse station. We popped up out of the métro and I looked to my trusty travel journal for guidance.

I'd written it all down, plain and simple: *rue de la Banque, rue la Feuillade (right), Colbert and Vivienne. Then cross to Palais-Royal.* Simple.

Remember how I said a métro exit can leave you

disoriented? Well, I am still not sure how it happened. But once we came out into the sun—yes, it had become a perfect, sunny day—we stood beside the stolid, overbearing Bourse, unable to determine our next move. Usually street signs are located on the walls of the corner buildings, about fifteen feet in the air, in easy to see blue. But with all squares like the one at which we found ourselves, the signs tell you the name of the *place*: *Place de la Bourse.* That's not helpful. You cannot see the names of the streets standing in the center. You have to leave the square, enter each adjoining street, and look for the sign around the corner.

Unable to guess which side of the Bourse we were on, I led us around it, the wrong way. All the time, I was looking for Rue de la Banque. Walking three sides of the Bourse, which is just a big Greek classical columned building that looks like the Supreme Court at half scale, I began to lose faith in my notes. Put simply, I lost my way.

So far, I'd been pretty good about Paris streets. I'd heard plenty of stories about how confusing Paris can be, about getting lost in its labyrinth. True, I'd been a little turned around in Montparnasse, but I eventually found what I was looking for. So I felt confident I would never be completely lost.

So I did not insist on finding rue de la Banque. Instead, I saw Rue Vivienne, which made sense. Shouldn't I find Galerie Vivienne on Rue Vivienne? So off we went. In much the same way, we came upon Rue Colbert, and I knew I was looking for Galerie Colbert. So I made a left turn. (Keep this left turn in mind. We'll reference it later.) This led to the Lavois Fountain, which is a cute little fountain in a little park the size of a small police station, which would have been more helpful than a fountain and some trees. Be that as it may, we walked around the park, enjoying the sight of two little boys playing kickball in the street as a doorman berated them for playing near the entrance to his building on rue Lulli. I discreetly cheered them on as the man kept grumbling at them. He managed to make French sound as acerbic as German.

Now just for fun, I'll let you know that the *Galeries* were southeast of the Lavois Fountain. Painfully unaware of this, I turned left on Rue Rameau and headed west. Fortunately Rameau quickly dead ended at Rue Saint-Anne, which I liked the sound of, probably because I'm familiar with Saint Ann Street down in the French Quarter in New Orleans. Jennifer was thrilled because we'd found the Baudelaire Hotel. She asked if that was the surprise. I should have just said yes and called it a day. But heck no, onward and upward.

"Where are we going?" Jennifer kept asking.

"It's a surprise," I kept answering. Each answer spoken with less confidence.

Turning south, simply because I knew I was lost and turning right continually will only lead in circles, we came across Rue des Petits Champs, which was one of the few streets that showed up on my tiny little tourist map. Well and good. I knew we had to turn left again. This should do the trick. The really good news was that Rue des Petits Champs was full of eateries: Sushi, Italian, Chinese, even a Subway sandwich shop. Since Jennifer's energy was sapped, we were ready to eat. As much as Subway tempted us, we happened upon a little Chinese place with scrumptious looking displays in the window. *Palais Cristal* was a nice little shop that was run by a very polite Asian couple. We filled up on egg rolls and rice and chicken, and I was fascinated to hear (and watch) Asians speaking French with a heavy Chinese accent.

Full of food and tired of looking for *Galerie Vivienne*, we walked to the next corner and saw construction scaffolds and tarps over a large portion of the next block. Written all over the tarps were the words *Galerie Vivienne*. From what I could tell, the entrances were blocked. It appeared to be under renovation. I had to admit defeat. I told Jennifer of her now useless surprise, which as I described it, did not sound like it was worth all the walking, and then we turned down Rue de Richelieu (a familiar name, since I knew he looked a lot like Charleton Heston). To salvage the trip, I told Jennifer we were heading to the Palais-Royal. She was wearing out by then, the effects of the previous days beginning to add up, but she liked the idea of seeing the Palais-Royal. A brown street sign pointed out it was somewhere down Richelieu.

A nice unexpected appearance by Molière brightened our walk. At the point where Rue Molière angles into Rue de Richelieu, there is a statue of the playwright seated as if upon a throne. True, he looks exactly like Frank Finlay's portrayal of Porthos in Richard Lester's *The Three Musketeers*, but it is always a nice surprise to see a statue of a man with a book in one hand and pen in the other.

Now before we walk any farther, let me back up and let you in on the big secret of this *marché folle*.

First of all, if I had just walked around one more side of the Bourse, nearly completing the entire perimeter of it, I would have found Rue de la Banque, and my written directions would have led us to the *passage* in about five minutes. However, once I had taken us down Rue de Vivienne, if I had not taken the left at Colbert (that left I told you to remember), I would have found one of the *passages* entrances just about thirty feet further down the street. Even after we ate at the Chinese restaurant, when we stood observing the scaffolds and tarps (which covered the *Cabinet des Medailles*, part of the *Bibliothéque Nationale de France*, a lesser known Parisian museum), we could have walked straight down Rue des Petits Champs and found the entrance to the galleries in about a minute and a half.

And just to add salt to the wound, if we had wanted to see the Palais-Royal, we should have kept going straight anyway, since its entrance is right across from the entrance to the *Galleries*. Walking down Rue de Richelieu simply bypasses the Palais-Royal, which was to the left as we walked along blissfully unaware of its close proximity.

You might enjoy the little fountain at Place André Malraux at the end of Richelieu. We did eventually find the southern end of the Palais-Royal, where we entered to find a courtyard that contains the *Colonnes de Buren*, a failed attempt at modern art that essentially looks like a grid of stone blocks that are missing whatever artwork should have been standing on them.

Tired, watching clouds gather in a very threatening manner, and still not sure if we were in the right place, we turned around and sought out the Louvre métro station. As we began to descend its stairs, rain poured from the sky with shocking speed. We had just missed being drenched.

To our delight, as we navigated the corridors of the métro in search of the Number 7 line, we began to hear very loud music. It was, in fact, Pachelbel's *Canon in D*. I thought, wow, pretty cool, they're piping classical music into the métro. But as we rounded a corner, we found a nine-piece orchestra playing for tips. The sound resonated in those concrete tunnels with overwhelming beauty. People were rushing by, and others were standing still, as the five violinists and four cellists brought tears to our eyes. Suddenly, the need to catch our train was not as great as it first seemed. At the conclusion of the song, we tossed a few Euros in the open Cello case, clapped enthusiastically, and caught the next train.

We had missed out on the beauty of the *Galleries* as well as the Palais-Royal, but had been emotionally overtaken by nine men and women who had offered their skills with one of the most beautiful pieces of music ever written in a busy little corner of a city transit station. That's a pretty good way to end a walk that began at the edge of the Tuileries Gardens, passed through the most famous Opera House in the world, and meandered through the sun-dappled streets of the Vivienne district.

After some rest, as the sun began to drop in the west, we ate a light dinner at the apartment. Jennifer was through. Worn out. *Fini.* I sat down, as she curled up with her journal, and began to play a computer game. But as I did, it occurred to me that I was in one of the most beautiful cities in the world. I could not sit and play a computer game in good conscience. I needed to get back outside and explore.

I had also been hoping to check out a jazz club that night. Oddly enough, I'd read about it in a guidebook that was dispensing advice on where to find free bathrooms. One suggestion was to enter the Hotel d'Aubusson as if you belong there, turn right, and use the restrooms in the back of the Café Laurent. A side note on this mentioned that live jazz is played on Thursday, Friday and Saturday nights. I paid more attention to the side note and planned to look it up.

Assuring Jennifer that I would be okay on my own (and ignoring the fact that I'd essentially been lost in Paris twice already) I took her small camera, left behind my tourist backpack, tugged on my heavy leather coat, and headed out for my first real solo adventure.

No métro for me. I was only too happy to wander the streets. I first headed out for a little bar called Birdland on Rue Guisarde, just around the corner from Saint-Sulpice. I wasn't looking for a drink, I was looking for more jazz. Birdland Café is a historical club that has hosted the likes of Chet Baker and Miles Davis. At least that was what I'd read on it. Information was sketchy, and some of it mixed up with the famous Birdland in New York. But I wanted to check out Birdland Café just in case I might find some good music there. It was early in the evening, and the bar was open, but no one was playing. I decided I'd come back later.

I walked down Rue Dauphine, searching for Café Laurent. It was right where it was supposed to be, but no one was playing there yet either. I'd expected this. It wasn't supposed to start until 8pm. I had time to wander. So off I wandered. And I wandered toward the Île de la Cité.

A cold wind had started blowing along the Seine, and I was glad I'd worn the heavy coat. At Pont Neuf, on the tip of the island, I walked down the steps and enjoyed the view of the river from the Square du Vert-Galant. A crowd of tourists was waiting to ride the Batobus, a playfully named river boat bus. (*Bateau* being the French word for boat.) After watching this rowdy bunch climb aboard, I found a little stairway tucked inside the stone *quai* that led up to the base of the King Henry IV equestrian statue. This statue was erected almost four hundred years ago. It stood for one hundred and fifty years (give or take) and was torn down during the French Redecoration. (I mean Revolution.) Some twenty years later it was recast from the same mold and put back in place. (Now, *stop tearing down things!*)

Up on Pont Neuf, I watched the sun set, getting a perfect shot of it setting over the rooftops of the Left Bank. I did not know this would be the only sunset I would see in Paris.

As twilight engulfed the island, I walked along the Right Bank side, alone in Paris. No one else was on the street. Quai de l'Horloge runs past the Palais de Justice, with its grand façade and stone plates high on the corner paying homage to Napoleon. (*Code Napoleon* it says, something with which we Louisianans are familiar.)

I really couldn't believe I had the island to myself. It was a Thursday night, and the place was empty. It was about seven-thirty at night. I began to wonder why no one was around. I had not yet become accustomed to Paris at night, and I was not sure if it was safe to wander around alone. But surely, I reasoned, this was the heart of the tourist section; it had to be safe.

I saw a lone figure heading toward me. I was alongside the *Conciergerie*, the infamous site of Maria Antoinette's prison cell. Just behind it was *La Sainte-Chapelle*, the one-time home of the crown of thorns—*the* crown of thorns, or so they said. I had trouble believing that I shouldn't be walking there alone.

The lone man approached, I eyed him with some casual attentiveness, and was relieved to see in the gloomy light that he was only an exercise nut, out stretching his legs before a run. Behind him appeared a small crowd of teenagers, joking and laughing with each other. I felt somewhat silly after that, worrying about the safety of Paris at night. I just decided that while I would remain careful, I would also relax enough to enjoy myself. Paris was no New York City.

Crossing in front of the east gate of the Palais du Justice, I entered *Place Luis Lepine*, the square that separates the Hôtel Dieu (a hospital) and the Palais du Justice. Here you can find the *Marché aux Fleurs*. This market, which some say has been around since 1860, is transformed into the *Marché aux Oiseaux*, a bird market, on Sundays. You can also find the Metropolitan entrance to Cité Station. I found several boys playing soccer in the nearly empty square. It must have been a day for soccer playing. I hurried along, the wind sweeping through the square growing colder.

Finally, after almost a full week, I came upon Notre Dame. I felt a little guilty that I was approaching it without Jennifer, but the square in front of it had only a few tourists left and it was too peaceful to pass up. I walked around a little, wishing I'd brought my better camera. I did not stay long. The cold was beginning to penetrate my leather coat.

I made my way around the backside of Notre Dame, over the Pont de l'Archevêché, stopped to view the oldest tree in Paris at Square René Viviani, walked around the churches Saint-Julien-de-Pauvre and Saint-Séverin, and discovered jewels like Rue Galande and Rue de la Huchette. The first is an isolated little street that has a slight bend in it, something rare in Paris, while the second is a jumping hub of noise and tacky-looking tourist bars that made me think of Bourbon Street without the strippers.

Checking my watch, I picked up my pace, hurried past Saint-Michel fountain, and kept to the open Quai until I found my way back on Rue Dauphine heading toward the Café Laurent.

You should know that my experience in bars is pretty limited. My puritan upbringing kept me out of places like this for many years. It's only as I have grown older and more interested in jazz that I've begun to venture into such places. It is not a big deal to those who've frequented these places since college. I was determined not to miss out on a night of jazz in Paris.

I walked through the door as a jazz trio played the standard *You're Nobody Till Somebody Loves You*. I was happy to get out of the cold, pull off my coat, and sit down at the bar. A rather dapper looking bartender took my order (Gin Fizz) after which I found a table close to the piano.

There was only room for about a dozen tables. People were scattered around the few chairs and no one talked as we listened to the trio. They kept the set very smooth and low-key. I had found exactly what I was looking for. The chill of my night walk faded away as I sat with my eyes closed listening to the pianist pick his was through *Dancing Cheek to Cheek* and *All of Me*. A few times the piano player spoke rapid French between songs, and I did not catch a word of it, neither did I care to.

A very fussy waiter brought my drink. He was sort of a busybody, not afraid to move people who had taken a table without his instruction. He was polite, don't get me wrong, and he did joke with several patrons. I was intrigued at the

American couple who showed up not long after I took the first sips from my drink. He was a round, older man with white hair cut close to his scalp. His rosy cheeks fit in well with his enthusiasm for the jazz. He acted more like a teenager at a rock concert at times, cheering on the musicians, encouraging them with a vocal outburst now and then. He was overly chatty with the waiter, speaking over the music so that all of us could hear him order his drink. He was all smiles, all noise, and all American. She was less of the same. No smiles, no noise, and just a small glass of white wine. I wondered how many nights he'd dragged her to jazz performances like this. Maybe she was having the time of her life and I just couldn't tell.

The trio took a break, and I waited for them to restart. By the time they did, it was getting late. Not in actuality, but I knew Jennifer would begin to worry about me, and without a cell phone to call and let her know I had not become hopelessly lost, I decided to call it a night. I nodded as I passed the pianist, telling him *merci* and *c'est bon*.

I passed by Birdland Café just to see if there was live music. None. I stopped and paid my respects to Saint-Sulpice, marveling at the lights of the fountain as well as those on the church's façade. Yet another reason it was my favorite place in the city. Reluctantly I pulled my collar up to shield my neck from the wind as it blew along Rue du Vieux Colombier and climbed the eighty stairs back to the apartment.

<u>Journal Entry: April 20, afternoon</u>

I don't know if pigeons can smell but I suspect they can. I have a hot quiche Lorraine in a bag, and as I sit at the Saint-Sulpice fountain, the pigeons are gathering around me.

The quiche is not for me. It is for Jennifer for her breakfast tomorrow morning. I ordered it in French, in a nice pâtisserie on Rue Guisarde. The young girl smiled, and I thought she asked 'for here or to go?' I said 'à emporter' (which is the French way of saying 'to go') or I thought I did. She nodded and put it in the microwave. I suppose it could have been worse.

I am sitting on a bench at Saint-Sulpice and I was in the sun, but three older ladies crowded beside me, with only room for three. I gladly moved to the bench behind us and they happily said "Merci, Monsieur." But now I am not in the sun. It is a little chilly in the shade. But I am enjoying their French conversation. I understand one word in fifteen.

I mostly hear the fountain, as if a moderately sized waterfall were near. The wind fills in the rest of the major sound. There is a low constant cooing from the birds. The sounds of occasional car or bus brakes. When the traffic lights turn green, the motorcycles and scooters roar ahead, racing to the next stop light. The buses roar as well, but move slowly, as if they are too full of wine and French pastries. Smart Cars, Fiats, Peugots and BMWs fill out the remainder of the traffic.

The ladies have moved on and I return to the sunny side of the bench. Having finished my pavé Suisse, I will pull out Hemingway.

Chapter Six: A Day of Rest and a Night of Jazz

I'd never been a fan of Ernest Hemingway's. I had tried reading him back in High School, and I just couldn't. I put him down, and never picked him back up. Over the years, I've heard all the complaints about him; how he was full of himself and had a deliberate and ridiculous style. How he was an inveterate drunk who loved the sound of his own voice. Etc, Etc...

As I mentioned before, Woody Allen's movie *Midnight in Paris* taught me enough about Hemingway to tempt me back to his table. Reading of Paris, I learned of Papa's Paris memoir, *A Moveable Feast*. It intrigued me. I might not have liked his fiction, but who's to say I wouldn't like his stories about his life in Paris?

So I bought an ebook version of *A Moveable Feast* just days before we flew to Paris. I read a little here and there, but not much. I was in the process of rereading Dickens' *A Tale of Two*

Cities that Spring, and so I did not dive right into Hemingway.

Once in Paris, I began to pick a little more at Papa's memoir in the mornings as I watched the sun rise over Montparnasse. I enjoyed reading bits and pieces about the areas of Paris I had already discovered. I began to feel like I could relate to the man who had largely become a buffoon to the television masses.

On that Friday morning after our opera walk, Jennifer had finally had enough and was not in the least interested in getting out of the apartment. She was happy to curl up with her journal, busy at her poetry. I read Hemingway, and was content to keep off my feet as well, they were beginning to hurt just a tad. I was used to walking over twenty miles a week at home, but that was with tennis shoes. In Paris we had agreed to attempt to blend in with the locals and the word in the guidebooks was that the French do not wear tennis shoes. Maybe to play tennis they did, but even that did not seem to be a steadfast rule. Fashion trumped everything.

After a morning of laughing at Hemingway's views on Paris stairways, Paris weather, and his friend Ford Madox Ford, I became restless. I wanted to get out again and see Paris, so off I went and I saw Paris.

I found a little figurine shop on Rue Guisarde; *Au Plat d'Etain.* (This seems to mean 'the flat tin', which I take to be an idiom that doesn't really translate.) This place was really cool. Aside from all the little tin or lead soldiers (lead is no longer considered safe, I suppose!) there were all kinds of French celebrities of old: Monet, Manet, Molière, Voltaire, and so on. I was quite excited to find Jules Verne and Victor Hugo.

A very sweet but quiet lady watched me as I made my way around the shop, taking care not to miss the myriad of offerings displayed on the shelves. I wondered if she thought I was just window shopping and hoped I would leave. She could not have been aware that I had five children and I was searching for something that might be unique for one of them.

Once I'd found Hugo, I knew I wanted to get it for one of my sons who loves to read. I had to try out my French, first asking the price, and then letting her know I wanted to buy it. I could have pulled out my French book and read off the words like a full-blown tourist, but I always felt that would be too awkward. So I tried something far more graceful and pointed with my eyebrows as high as I could get them to go. I stammered a little, she came closer and smiled while also allowing me to see the lack of comprehension on her face.

If many Parisians knew English, this wasn't one of them. We finally were able to communicate a little, at least she understood my question enough to grab a calculator and type out the price so I could see it.

She was happy to conclude the sale, taking my credit card without the slightest problem. I had finally learned what the big deal was concerning our credit card.

European credit cards, for the most part, have the magnetic strip in a position that allows them to run the card from one end in their machines. They can just stick a little of the card into the handheld machine and it reads the whole thing. Our credit cards have the longer strip that must be read by sliding the card through the side of the reader. These little handheld readers were everywhere, and they read our American cards just fine, but the clerk had to know the proper method. Those first few problems I'd had were problems with the clerks, not the machines. It was a relief to find that my cards worked as promised.

The kind, figurine saleslady carefully boxed up Mr. Hugo, wrapped him in paper with a ribbon, and I was soon on my way. I did manage to compliment her shop (point all around and exclaim *"c'est beau!"*) and then thank her profusely. (*Merci, merci beaucoup.*) I have no idea how often she made a sale in that little shop, but I felt sure she hadn't sold a Victor Hugo in a long time.

After a little more walking and shopping, I stopped in at a pâtisserie and bought quiche Lorraine for Jennifer's breakfast while I grabbed a pavé suisse for me to eat right then. I stuffed the quiche in my camera bag and picked out a bench at Saint-Sulpice to enjoy some sun as I read *A Moveable Feast.*

Once I'd returned and showed off my purchases for Jennifer, she was ready to go out for the evening. I'd convinced her she should come out to the Café Laurent. As usual, I pushed a little more and added a little walk around Notre Dame. She was more than willing to trust me, and so off we went yet again.

Sure enough, the weather was perfect in the late afternoon. We rode the métro to Cité, popping up in *Place Luis Lepine.* The soccer players were not there that night. We walked around the corner of the Hôtel Dieu and Jennifer experienced her first real moment with Notre Dame Cathedral.

I knew I'd been right to add this to our little evening. She lost all traces of weariness as she stood at the west end of the square and took in the breath-taking view of the towers and that amazing façade.

As I did my best to photograph the amazing details of the portals, Jennifer found a seat on a stone bench and pulled out her journal. As the crowds moved around her, she paid them no mind, her eyes clearly on the grand image above her.

I was always struck by the multiplicity of languages one encountered in Paris. There, amidst the crowds, one could hear Spanish, Russian, Chinese, English with Australian accents, Arabic, English with British accents, and of course French. This was everywhere. The world comes to Paris, and you can touch the world if you are there.

One can also hear plenty of birds on a Spring night like the one we were experiencing. And there is ever the sound of pigeons cooing away at your feet.

We left the island, taking the bridge just west of the towers, Pont au Double, we stopped to take a few photos of the Seine and the Petit Pont which was just downstream. Jennifer took the camera and as she set up the shot, an older man had to wait for us. Jennifer put the camera back down and told him to go ahead and pass.

"No, no. You go ahead," he insisted in his heavy French accent. Pointing first at me then at the Seine, he added "You may never have *him* with *that* behind him ever again. It is so very beautiful."

Jennifer agreed with him, and he waited as she took several pictures of *me* with *that* behind me.

I had the feeling the old man was a local who just liked to come out and watch the tourists enjoy his city. He was not only polite, he had surprised us as he reminded us just how special that moment really was.

And he's right about the pictures, too. As much as I enjoy taking pictures, I am often self-conscious. So many films and television shows have mocked the image of the camera-toting tourist that I found I was occasionally embarrassed to pull out my camera and snap a few shots. But I eventually decided I didn't care about the mockers. I was in Paris, and if I passed up the chance to capture a moment on film, I'd regret it for a very long time. The old man's comment helped solidify that determination in me.

I made sure, after taking pictures, to put down my camera and soak in the sights without that contraption around my neck. I wasn't about to miss the city because I was always behind the lens. And yet, even after taking over three thousand pictures over a two-week period, I still think of times when I did not pull out my camera and I regret it.

Jennifer was feeling good enough to walk back to the Café Laurent. To energize her, I first took her down the Rue de la

Huchette, past all the little Greek restaurants and souvenir shops. I finally tempted her into stopping at a crêperie, where we discovered how special French crêpes can be. I was satisfied with the Crêpe Sucre, which was simply a big crêpe with sugar. Jennifer was more adventurous as she ordered the Crêpe Grand Marnier.

The man making the crêpes was a very cool dude who looked as if he were a movie star who had decided to fry crêpes for his adoring public. To make crêpes, batter is poured out onto a circular griddle, and the toppings, whatever you order, are tossed into it, then it is rolled up and dropped into a cone shaped wrapper.

I was suddenly a fan of crêpes.

Warmed by the crêpes and coffee, we cut across Place Saint-Michel and Jennifer stopped in at her favorite souvenir shop to check out their scarves. To her delight, the same clerk she'd spoken with three nights before remembered her. He asked how the vacation was going. They talked again, at great length, and when she chose a scarf to buy, he insisted she grab another one at no extra cost.

As we prepared to leave, I asked him his name.

"David," he proudly announced. I convinced him to pose for a picture with Jennifer, which he seemed embarrassed to do. But the sincere smile on his face says it all. He loved the attention.

We made our way down Rue Saint-André des Arts, cutting across Rue André Mazet to reach Rue Dauphine. In no time, we were sitting down in the Café Laurent. The jazz trio was now a quartet; an electric guitarist had been added for the evening. Instead of old standards, the group was playing a more upbeat mix of what I would call fusion jazz.

The same white-haired gentleman and his wife returned for the evening, and the fussy waiter took care of us. He was far more personable with me than the night before, and I would guess he was more relaxed with Jennifer there, translating.

Right away, she noticed something I should have but did not the night before: the waiter's accent was definitely German. The café was a little more crowded that night, and the more lively set from the musicians kept everyone's toes tapping. We were able to sit back and enjoy the music as they worked through their set.

Finally, tired from what had only been a short day, we headed home. But not before I took us down a side street that we had not previously used. On this street, Rue Christine, I discovered an old movie theater advertising classic movies. To my surprise and joy I found that they were showing Orson Welles' *The Lady from Shanghai* the next night. I wasn't about to miss it.

We made it home, the memories of smooth jazz still in our heads as we drifted off to sleep. It had been a magnificent week. Already we'd spent six days of wonder in Paris. It did not seem as if it could get any better.

Chapter Seven: The Eiffel Tower and the Little Girl on Swan Alley

It was Saturday. The last day of our first week. When we had arrived in Paris it had seemed like we had all the time in the world. Suddenly, I was beginning to wonder how we would be able to see anything before we would be forced to board that great big AirFrance plane and head out over the Atlantic. How could we make sure we made the most of our time?

Another night of rest and we felt ready to tackle a big day. And really, it was high time we looked around in our own back yard. And without much effort we could take that look around and find the Eiffel Tower. It wasn't all that far away, just under two miles on foot.

The funny thing about our trip to Paris was the fact that neither one of us had any interest in the Eiffel Tower. Jennifer had always said she thought it was ugly. I just thought it suffered from too much exposure; *everything* connected to Paris—be it movies, books, commercials, or sporting events—used the Eiffel Tower in some way. And I tend to shun whatever is popular. So for us, the Eiffel Tower was far down on our list of places to see.

There were, however, two places I did want to see. The first one was Rodin's museum. The second, as you might guess, was a movie location.

Auguste Rodin worked in Paris out of the Hôtel Biron for most of his career. This stately home was built in the early 1700s. Once its owner had been guillotined in 1793, it served in many different capacities, including the Russian Embassy and a young girl's Catholic school. But it was Rodin's use of the property that ensured its survival. Near the end of his career, he campaigned to turn the Hôtel Biron into a museum dedicated to his work. The French Government agreed, since Rodin willed all of his work to them on the condition that they do what he said. It has paid off for them, since the *Musée Rodin* receives over 700,000 visitors a year.

I'm intrigued by sculpture, though I cannot say I am a great fan. I tend to like paintings more. But I think I am dubious of sculpture because so much of it is not very well done. I am, however, always impressed with Rodin. His figures are not just real to life. They come to life. And that's the kind of compliment I rarely give out. Van Gogh's paintings come to life. Not many others do. So Rodin's museum was definitely on my list.

Now as to the movie location, this one was about tops on my list for Paris movie sites. The 1988 noir thriller *Frantic* is the best Parisian movie I've ever seen. If you've never seen it, and get the opportunity, make sure you take advantage of it. It's a very taut thriller that pulls you deeper and deeper into a man's frantic search for his missing wife. The location shots are of a darker Paris, despite the fact that this couple is visiting Paris on a business/vacation. The usual tourist scenes are omitted, or they appear in the background and go unnoticed. The climax is filmed at the base of the replica Statue of Liberty which stands on a small island in the Seine. So as not to spoil the movie, I'll just say that one of the prominent characters has a very dramatic death scene in the closing moments of the film. All of this takes place on the island, and since I first saw the film, I wanted to know more about this very evocative location.

It took some digging around the Internet before I'd finally found the location. The Liberty Statue stands on the south end of the Île aux Cygnes, the Island of the Swans. This is a manmade island in the middle of the Seine, just south of the Eiffel Tower. It was built to help protect the port of Grenelle in the early 1800s. The island is only 36 feet wide at its widest, and is not quite one thousand yards long.

The final scene of the movie, where Harrison Ford grapples with his wife's kidnappers, features the Liberty Statue and the Pont de Grenelle which straddles that end of the island. This I had to see.

So if we wanted to check out these locations, we decided to add the Eiffel Tower into the trip, since it was right in the middle of them. Actually, I just figured we could not avoid it as we walked from one to the other. Jennifer, however, had begun to think that we really should take time to see the tower. After all, Paris and Eiffel's tower are interminably entwined. If you love one, you really should love the other. If only for their relation to each other.

Our hesitancy about the Tower was nothing novel. Many Parisians hated it when it was erected, a great deal of them were actually horrified. Campaigns were run to have it torn down. The artistic community, in particular, declared it to be blasphemous. Guy de Maupassant probably said it best when he famously quipped that he ate lunch daily in the Tower's restaurant since it was the only place in the city where he could not see the darned thing.

But as they say, when in Rome…so off we rode on the 87 Bus, down Rue de Babylone to the little François Xavier bus stop. We were just steps away from the Boulevard des Invalides. This wide thoroughfare was full of traffic and holiday-like energy on what was shaping up to be a gorgeous Saturday—the sun was shining through banks of fluffy clouds, the temperature was warmer than it had been since we arrived, and the sunlight sparkled off the gilded dome of des Invalides. This would prove to be providential, since many of our photographs taken in the Rodin garden would have this bright icon as a backdrop.

The museum was everything the Orsay was not—spacious, inviting, peaceful. Though there are substantial indoor galleries, we were simply happy to stay outside in the sculpture garden, enjoying the weather and Rodin's unrivaled masterpieces. The crowds were thin, to the point that we had time alone to admire and photograph the ponderous Thinker.

There is a reason that Rodin's name is just about the only modern sculptor that most people think of when the subject is discussed. I am not one to put too much faith in the magic of famous artists—I tend to believe that many lesser known artists are just as good as the famous ones—but Rodin is an exception to this rule. His pieces grab your attention like no other. They pulse with life; the hands, the muscles, even the toes on the Thinker look strong and fleshy, as if they are about to dig into the base to propel the man from his sitting position to a sudden explosion of action. As if all that thought is about to be transformed into turbulent motion.

The Thinker sits upon a pedestal that is nearly eight feet off the ground. It seems he is sitting on the edge of a precipice, contemplating a jump. From below, you look up at him in awe, mesmerized by Rodin's skill and sheer profundity.

Just down the path you'll find Rodin's *Monument to Balzac*, which has a story that I just love. At the height of his fame, Rodin was commissioned to create a monument to the much-loved writer Honore de Balzac by the *Société des Gens des Lettres*. This writer's group was angered when Rodin displayed the statue. Balzac, who was a large, round man, was a challenge for Rodin. He spent many years working on the concept and model. Eventually, he chose to portray the novelist wrapped in a robe, his head tossed back, his features deeply scarred. The *Société* rejected the work, Rodin paid back their commission and kept his Balzac. It is now considered to be one of his masterpieces.

As a writer, I love that story. First of all for the fact that a man as renowned as Rodin can be collectively criticized for his ideas, and that he can stand by his art enough to give back the money and hold onto his creation. A true inspiration to writers and artists the world over who believe that no one likes our work and since you don't we'll just keep it to ourselves. *La Vie des Artistes*.

The sculpture garden and pool make for one of the most peaceful locations in the city. Walled in from the surrounding neighborhood, this hideaway would be my place of choice for a weekly meditation if I lived in the city. If you visit the museum, be sure to sit on one of the benches at the far end of the garden and look back at the chateaux. Then just be still. Well, go ahead and take a few pictures, because it is as beautiful as Versailles and the Luxembourg gardens; just a smaller scale. But once you've captured it on film (or disk, or drive, or your phone) then put down the camera, turn off your iPod, pull off your backpack, stop thinking about where you are going to eat lunch, forget about all the money you've spent on your trip, and just be still. Don't take it all in, soak up the atmosphere, ponder the works of art you see, or even smell the trees and the flowers blooming—just be *still*.

Time stops here. And for all the busyness of your Paris vacation, make sure you do too. Let out a breath.

After a while, you'll have to move on. And you should. There is so much more to see. But don't forget your backpack on that bench.

Not being well versed in Rodin's work, both Jennifer and I were able to discover one of the sculptor's most famous works in person. Not ever having seen it before, we were in awe as we approached Rodin's *The Gates of Hell*. This massive entrance was once intended to be the entrance for a museum that never came to fruition. Rodin spent 37 years working on this epic work of art, and died before he could finish it. With over 180 figures on it, many of which he eventually did as independent works (including *The Thinker, The Kiss,* and *The Three Shades*) this unbelievable vision represents Rodin's view of Dante's *Inferno*. It is terrible to behold.

Just beyond this spectacular vision you can find *The Burghers of Calais*. Yet another piece for which Rodin was vilified, Rodin depicted Calais' sacrificial heroes as weak and pitiful. They were, after all, walking to their doom, to save the town from the English sword. The people of Calais just wanted to remember them in a more heroic light.

Filled with the wonder of Rodin's world, we left it behind, though we would certainly always remember it with awe.

When we were processing through airport security in Houston, the man who checked our passports and asked about our travel intentions insisted that when we were in Paris we should visit Napoleon's tomb. As much as I love history, I was not interested in Napoleon on this trip. He was, when all is said and done, just a little man who caused far too much destruction for the European people. I had no intention of paying respects at his grave.

Les Invalides, the site of Napoleon's exhalted tomb, is a

complex of buildings erected as a memorial to the military history of France as well as a retirement home for veterans. It was nowhere on our list of things to do and we only entered its grounds to pass through them to the other side.

We did take advantage of a nice cafeteria-style coffee shop that we found. After this energy-booster, we left, with every intention of moving on to the Eiffel Tower.

This was more difficult than it should have been. We passed through a flower garden, and came to an impassable concrete ditch. Following it along the perimeter, I finally dug through my historical memory banks until I realized that our obstacle had to be a moat, or something close to that. Though it was empty of water, and had a nice lawn in the bottom, this moat forced us to swing all the way back to a different part of the grounds where we were eventually able to escape across an access point that was not a drawbridge. (Sort of disappointing, you know?)

A short walk along Avenue de Tourville brought us to the Place de l'École Militaire, which connected us to the Champ de Mars. And that, readers, is possibly the best family park in the city.

The site of the amazing 1889 *Exposition Universelle* which featured the brand new Eiffel Tower, this field has been the central point of many French festivals and historic celebrations. It is also the point from which the world's first hydrogen-filled balloon was launched in 1783.

After a flurry of picture taking, we walked out onto the mall. The park, with the Tower at the far end, was full of families who had come out to enjoy the warm, spring day. Forget the fact that the Eiffel Tower is an overused iconic image for this tourist destination. All I could see were Parisians out enjoying their local city park. Couples were sitting in the grass, reading or just snuggling with each other. Kids ran after soccer balls. Little girls were climbing all over a playground set—a cheesy plastic and aluminum castle—off to one side. Behind them boys played a pick-up game of basketball. A white-haired grandfather let his grandson win on the outdoor ping-pong tables while a young girl in a sandbox, wearing a long black coat, fed the pigeons flocking around her.

I suddenly wished I were not a tourist. I wanted to be a Parisian. I wanted this to be my park too. I didn't want to be an outsider, disturbing their family time. And yet it was an inescapable reality. I still did not know the language enough to feel like I fit in. Surrounded by these families, I could hear them chatting away, could hear the kids squeal with laughter, could hear the parents warn them not to run too far, all of it in a language I did not understand. This single barrier kept me apart. It kept me in an observation mode much like a time-traveler who can visit a point in the past but cannot interact with what he sees.

Jennifer fell right into her poet's mode, dropping onto a bench under the box-topped London plane trees. (Of course, in France, they do not call them *London* plane trees. They call them *platane a feuille d'erable*: plane tree with maple leaf.) As per our unspoken agreement, I wandered off with the camera, leaving her to her thoughts, ink, and paper.

And as I walked the Field of Mars, snapping shot after shot of children, old men, couples, and the massive tower, I eventually began to get *it*. The Tower. Eiffel's Folly. That great big monstrosity of steel that drove Maupassant crazy. That simple pointy shape that is slapped on, printed on, engraved on and painted on every chintzy trinket sold in Paris *clicked* in my head. I can't really say why. It just did. And as I walked ever closer to it, and bent my head back to look up at it, it won me over again each step of the way.

I've stood at the base of the Sears Tower. I've lain in the grass beneath the St. Louis Arch and gaped at that delicate miracle. I've been knocked out by the art deco design of

Rockefeller Center. But nothing like the Eiffel Tower has ever hit me in this manner. This massive, dark, raw and powerful colossus stands planted in the earth like some alien creature from a Jules Verne science fiction novel. Yet at the same time, its intricate and graceful design adds intelligence and beauty to offset that initial brash impression.

Does everyone get that? I don't know. Most tourists just posed for silly pictures from afar, with the man or woman in the frame holding up the tower in the palm of their hand or maybe pretending to push it over. And that's fine. That's part of its magic. In addition to being powerful and beautiful it is also whimsical. It seems to be everything to everyone; a universal appeal.

Toward the middle of the park, on the west side under the trees, I found a little carousel, a *chevaux de Bois*, which looks like it had been there since before the Eiffel Tower. That's not to say it was old and run-down. This wooden gem is in great working order. When I found it, it was full of children, ready to begin its spinning adventure. The operator, an older gentleman with dark bushy eyebrows and matching mustache, was just making sure the kids were settled properly in their seats. Once the kids were ready, he grabbed one of the horse's poles and began to push. After achieving the desired speed, he slipped inside the circle of horses, and I saw that the machine was operated by hand-crank. He began to crank away, his initial push making it much easier for the horses to reach a comfortable trot which then required little effort for the hand crank to maintain.

Jennifer finally put down her pen and we strolled up to the Tower, our heads tilted in order to view the top of that one-thousand-foot structure, which was the tallest man-made structure in the world from 1889 to 1930. It's pretty cool to realize this, since as a native Illinois kid, I was always entranced by the Sears Tower, which held its own world height record from 1973 to 1998.

And as we stood there near the base of this modern Wonder of the World, I couldn't help but shake my head at the thought that this was really happening. Here I was, just a kid from the fields of Illinois, standing in one of the grandest locations the world has ever known, where people come from every corner of the globe to stand and stare and become a part of something greater than the little worlds we inhabit during our daily isolation from the planet at large.

I don't care if you aren't interested in Paris, or France, or even Europe. Sacrifice enough in life to save up some money and travel to a place that will mean as much to you. Go stand on Golgotha, or look out over the Great Wall of China, or plant your feet in the middle of Red Square and marvel at St. Basil's Cathedral.

Near the base of the Tower, just after crossing Gustave Eiffel Avenue, I spotted a tall man with a ponytail that hung down to his belt. He was taking pictures of a woman, and it was obvious, from his manner and large camera, that he knew what he was doing. I offered to take their picture together, and he agreed. He was rather demanding about how I orient his camera and take the picture, which I didn't mind.

When I asked him to take our picture, he nodded, though he rolled his eyes at the same time, as if to say "yeah, I saw that coming," which I didn't mind either. You have to be bold to get some help. Now, as he took my camera, which is not top of the line, but better than average, he looked annoyed to see it was on the easy button. I generally let the camera do the thinking, setting it on the green icon which is essentially the dummy setting. Our *professional* began fiddling with the knobs and buttons, resetting it to his own preferences. I didn't mind this either. Though I sort of resented the condescending look he shot my way. But if it meant he was going to take a great picture, what did I care what he thought of me?

So we smiled, arms around each other, and waited as he took three pictures, changing the settings a few times in between. He very politely returned the settings to the idiot position and handed back the camera as all four of us nodded repeatedly saying *merci, merci boucoup.*

I'd just like to add here that when I downloaded the pictures, only one of his pictures turned out well. The others were too dark. So much for his skill. I'll stick with the dummy shots. I may not be the most highly trained photographer, but I know when a computer is smarter than I am and I'm not afraid to take advantage of it.

One more note on taking pictures for other couples. While Jennifer sat in the shadow of the Tower to jot down a few more notes, I ran off toward a little concession stand tucked in behind some trees on the west side of the park. As I headed down a sidewalk, I saw a couple taking pictures. Of course, the man was taking the woman's picture with the Tower behind her. After pausing to allow them to get the shot, as I passed, I offered to take their picture for them. This time, without any *quid pro quo.* I was alone.

Without skipping a beat, the man, in a strong German accent, narrowed his brows, frowned at me and said "No!" as if I'd just asked the man if I could throw myself upon his wife. (Which, in Paris, may not be so very preposterous...) So I just smiled, said "okay" in my happy-go-lucky American accent, and kept moving, slightly concerned that the offended German would come after me with a dueling sword.

A cup of *café au lait* and a beignet erased the German from my mind (temporarily) and Jennifer and I strolled under the Tower and out onto Quai Branly as we munched away at our New Orleans style snack.

We did not go up into the tower. Jennifer does not handle heights well and I had *Frantic* on my mind. Clouds had been turning gray and heavy throughout the afternoon and I began to worry that we would get washed out. I began to push us along a little faster.

The riverside view along this stretch of the Seine was a little more modern. You could see cars zooming along the expressway on the right bank. We were completely enthralled by the boats tied up alongside the quay, and it was hard to keep moving with so many great views to shoot.

Along this route is a raised walk called the Promenade d'Australie, and I recommend it to anyone who wants a pleasant place to view the river. You get a magnificent view of the Pont de Bir-Hakeim, which is best known for its role in the movie *Inception* though I prefer to remember it for its cameo appearance in Jules Dassin's French Film Noir classic *Rififi*.

The bridge supports have gorgeous cast-iron figures that appear to be laboring to affix ornamental plates to the supports. The bridge surface has two decks, the first for car and truck traffic, the second, raised deck accommodates train traffic for the RER and métro.

This was the bridge I was looking for, since it was the access point for the east end of the Île aux Cygnes. We were almost to my film destination. I could feel it. I could almost touch it. I could also feel the rain begin to fall.

And just like that, a good downpour hit us. I tucked the camera into my bag, we huddled under our umbrellas, and I wasn't sure what we should do next. It looked like it was going to rain for a while. So I shifted gears and looked along the shops on the Quai de Grenelle.

We were in luck. Directly across the street from us was a pizzeria. *Jolanda's* red awning said it all: *ristorante Italiano— pizzeria*. I didn't have to sell Jennifer on the idea. She was getting tired, and the sudden rain brought a cold wind with it. It was now mid-afternoon, about three o'clock, and our usual late lunch/early dinner was a welcome plan. Ducking under the awning, we stepped inside and a waiter was more than happy to lead us to a corner table.

Our waiter, a tall, smiling young man with a slightly haughty look in his eye handed us menus and stood by as we looked over the drink options. Jennifer surprised me with something very close to a shout:

"Oh my God! Iced Tea!"

The waiter grinned and folded his hands together as if to say "how cute."

Jennifer drinks iced tea at home more than she drinks coffee. She explained to the waiter that she had not seen iced tea since arriving in France.

"Madame will have iced tea?" he asked. Jennifer nodded and said she would. He turned to me. In substandard French I said I would take Sprite. My French didn't sound too bad, but when I ended the sentence with *Sprite*, he raised an eyebrow that clearly said "of course you will."

A big screen TV displayed sports news, sort of a French ESPN, and we were able to relax and enjoy some time off our feet.

Though I had thought the waiter to be terribly pompous, I could not have been more wrong. When he brought our drinks, he set Jennifer's tea down and exclaimed "Oh my God! Iced Tea!" His impersonation of her carried just the right amount of humor without a shred of cruel mockery. He had us all laughing.

Several times during our meal he passed by to see if we needed refills. Of course, he was quick to say *iced tea!* with flair each time. The food was great, and we watched the sky dump rain until it ran out. The sun battled its way through the clouds just before we were ready to leave the restaurant.

As we threaded our way through the now crowded dining room, our waiter spotted us one last time and as we thanked him, he pointed at Jennifer and called out "*Madame* Iced Tea!"

We quickly made our way across the street and out onto

the Pont de Bir-Hakeim. Passing under the great ironwork of the viaduct, we found a broad staircase leading down to the narrow Island of Swans. We could not have been more charmed.

Since returning home, I've done many Internet searches for background information on the Île aux Cygnes. Nearly every review or blog says the same thing: everyone is surprised and overcome by the island's charm. And that's truly the best way to say it. It knocks you down with its simplicity and graceful lines.

The island is wide enough to contain a paving stone walkway about ten or twelve feet wide, with just a hint of grass growing beside the walk, a line of trees on both sides, all of which is capped off with an iron fence on each bank. There are street lamps spaced along the walk, and outward-facing benches scattered among the trees.

We walked along the Seine, snapping pictures of boats moored along the quays as well as boats moving upstream and downstream. We laughed at the boat which had been christened with the name *Mississippi*, which must sound foreign and exotic to them. (As if we had named a boat *Dordogne*.) A large luxury cruiser hosted a party with loud 1950's American Rock and Roll playing from its sound system.

Nearing the Grenelle bridge, I was excited to see the *Frantic* filming site. But as we walked under the bridge, most of it did not look right. I walked to the far edge of the island, turned to look back at the base of the statue and the bridge supports, and I just could not fit the image in with the scene in the movie. I took a picture of it, but wondered aloud why it did not look right.

Jennifer wasn't listening. She was reading the inscription at the base of the quarter sized replica of Lady Liberty. She drew my attention to it. In French, it tells of how the Parisian community in the United States gave the statue to the city of

Paris.

As we backed up to look at Dame Liberty, a dozen boisterous young people crowded around the statue. They were mostly teenagers, or maybe in their twenties. All quite excited. After viewing this little Statue of Liberty, one of the boys, in a German accent, shouted "Freakin' USA! Yeah!" A little cheer went up from the group.

That's when one of them turned around and asked if I could take their picture. He asked in English. I suppose I was caught up in their merriment. Or I just felt like yanking their chains.

"Sorry, no English" I said in my worst French accented English.

The young man looked disappointed for a moment. I came to his rescue by switching to the most American sounding accent I could muster.

"No, I'm jus' kiddin'. I speak English. Sure I'll take yer picture!"

The whole group got a pretty good laugh out of that. I suppose it had more to do with their admiration for the United States than for my poor attempt at humor. They lit up like Tannenbaums and I goofed around with them, telling them all to smash in closely for the picture, then I backed up to the edge of the island while they played along and told me to keep backing up.

They all clowned around for the picture and as they hurried off when we were done I went back to worrying over the changes on the island that made me wonder if I had the right spot.

Of course, it had to be the right spot. The movie had been filmed at the base of the statue. But later, back home, when I played the DVD and compared it to the photo I'd taken, I could see where the fencing had been changed, a protective seawall at the edge of the island had been removed, and one small tree had been taken out while another small one had grown considerably in the last 25 years.

Somewhat disappointed that my movie site had left me more puzzled than excited, we began to retrace our steps across the island. I had not felt the trip was wasted time, but I had certainly begun to feel like I had missed out on something.

I couldn't have been more wrong.

As we strolled along the *Allée des Cygnes*, Jennifer pointed at a little girl walking in front of us. She was splashing through the puddles along the path. She was, to put it mildly, one of the cutest little characters we'd ever seen.

Let me give you some details:

First of all, this little girl, maybe three or four years old, wore a dark blue and violet winter coat that hung down to the tops of her pink Winnie-the-Pooh galoshes. On her head was a pink and gray stocking cap shaped like a bear's head with round ears, coal black eyes, a pink nose, and a little girl's face sticking out of its wide open mouth. In one hand she carried a stuffed monkey by its tail, while in the other hand, she held a red bucket with a panda bear smiley face on its side, plastic sand tools stuck out of the bucket's mouth. Trailing behind her were two pug-nosed dogs that were feeling quite frisky towards each other. The girl's mother, in a jet-black coat and periwinkle tennis shoes, walked beside her while pushing a stroller that presumably held a baby under many layers of blankets.

I had already put my camera away. But I knew I had to get a picture of this French fashion icon. So I dug the camera out of my bag as quickly as I could and snapped a few pictures. She heard the camera, and immediately knew what I was doing. And she liked it. She spun around, arms held out to display the wonderful items in her hands, and waited for me to take another picture.

As I did, Jennifer called out to her, telling her in the

French language she was pretty and thanking her for letting us take her picture. She waited, in case I was going to take more pictures. When she saw I was done, she turned around and continued her journey.

I pulled the camera up to my eye and snapped a few more. She heard me again and turned right back around. Her smile could have been visible from a satellite. But I could see her mother, who had patiently stopped with her, would never get anywhere if this continued. So I kept my camera at my hip and with Jennifer's prompting told her *"C'est tout!"* "That's all!" The girl waited, not sure if she believed me. She eventually turned and walked on. We sang out a few *bonjours* and then slowed to allow space to grow between us.

What a perfect afternoon it turned out to be. We walked back to the Eiffel Tower, enjoying the stroll along the quay, and that would have been the end of the day if we had taken the Batobus back along the river toward home. However, we decided to look for the street bus so we ascended the stairs back up to street level.

To cross Quai Branly at the base of the Tower, we joined a group of tourists who began to cross when the little green stick figure told us we could cross. But at the halfway point in the four lane crossing, a tall gendarme, in heavy riot gear (minus the shield and helmet) stepped out from behind a large blue van and put his arms out from his sides and told us all to stop right where we were.

The traffic lights changed, we were in the middle of the road, and the gendarme stared straight ahead. I was only about eight inches from him. We were nearly face to face.

Out of the corner of my eye, I realized there must have been about seven or eight large blue vans with *Gendarmerie* plastered across their doors. Scores of French Police milled about. Our gendarme held us back while the driver of the van directly behind him repositioned it.

This gendarme, trying to maintain a neutral expression as we stood nose to nose, could obviously see how silly all of this looked. Cracking just a hint of a smile, he spoke:

"*Bienvenue à Paris!*" (Welcome to Paris!) He broke into a full-blown smile as all of us facing him laughed at his little joke.

Once allowed to pass, we stepped beyond the vans and Jennifer suggested I take a picture for the kids. When I pulled up my camera and took the shot, I forgot that the flash was on. A dozen *gendarmerie* spun at the sound of my camera and the flash of the bulb. They weren't smiling as the little girl with the Pooh-Bear boots had smiled. I put the camera down quickly and led Jennifer away. It was then I began to notice they were pulling out those see-through bullet-proof shields that we only see on the nightly news when something has gotten out of hand in Europe.

Then I remembered two things. *We* were in Europe, and the French Presidential election was the next day.

"Oh, Lord," I said to Jennifer. "Someone's about to protest something and we're in the wrong place. We'd better get out of here."

And we did. I never learned what was really going on and I didn't need to. We walked to the south end of the Champ-de-Mars and caught the 87 bus back down at the Place de l'École Militaire, and were happy to ride it back to our doorstep at Michel Debré.

What had been a not-so-exciting plan had turned out to be one of our best days yet. It had not been a day of monuments as grand as the Pantheon and the Catacombs, but it had given us a closer feel for the people of Paris in their natural habitat. The day left us with much to think about and images we would remember for the rest of our lives.

I returned to Rue Christine that night alone. There was a line outside the old theater. Once the usher took our tickets and led us downstairs to the theater, I had to remove my coat and sweater. It was hot. The place had been recently renovated. The seats were new, the screen new. It was quite small, about a third of the size of a movie theater in our multiplexes.

I settled into the first row, which was not as close to the screen as most first rows usually are. And the screen was not so big that I could not see well from that close distance. As the lights went down and the old Columbia Pictures logo appeared on screen—you know the one, that grand lady with the over-active torch that never runs out of fuel—I couldn't believe my luck; an Orson Welles picture show in an old French movie house. As the commercial says—priceless.

The only disappointing part of the night was discovering *The Lady from Shanghai* was not dubbed into French. I'd been wondering just how much of the dialogue I'd be able to understand with my recently acquired knowledge of the language. (A meager amount of knowledge, to be sure!) I hoped that since I knew the movie, I'd be able to pick up more of the language through context. But the movie used the original English dialogue, the only French modification being the subtitles across the bottom of the screen.

So I did my best to read along, which was a great education in itself. And this also meant I was not deprived of hearing Orson Welles' horrible Irish brogue.

You have to love Paris. Later, around the corner from the theater, I found a bookstore that was still open (it was past 10 PM). Even better, the bookstore was run by Taschen, a German company that publishes the greatest retro collection books in the world. I nearly cried at the low prices (cheaper in Europe than in the States, which I suppose has to do with tariffs or what-not) and the fact that we were limited on the weight of our luggage on the flight home.

Walking home that Saturday night, I ran into a Dixieland

band on Rue de Buci. The old trumpet player leading the group sang *What a Wonderful World* and *The White Cliffs of Dover*. His accent was pure Jersey. But after their performance he said he was from California. I thought it was funny that I'd traveled over five thousand miles from Louisiana to stand on a street in Paris and listen to Dixieland Jazz played by a Jersey boy from California.

What a wonderful world.

Chapter Eight: A Solo Walk through the Heart of Paris

I turned onto Rue Charlemagne. The streets were deserted. I glanced down an alley on the left. Nothing. To my right, another street branched off; curling back to the left, an ancient turreted castle loomed just beyond the bend.

Jennifer was nowhere to be seen.

I would soon see devils leering down at me; mouths dripping, eyes as black as night.

As fun as the above teaser sounds, it wasn't as dramatic as all that. But every line of it is true.

Even God rested after six days of work. And Jennifer made sure to follow his lead. Sunday was a total day of rest for her. She'd earned it. We'd pushed hard for a week and there was much for her to take in. She stayed bundled up in the apartment with her pens, her paper and her thoughts.

Of course, to start Sunday off right, we'd made sure to

stock up on food from the local Franprix when we'd returned from our Eiffel Tower trip. We'd already seen how deserted the neighborhood could look on Sunday. Fool me once…as the saying goes.

After my own day of rest, which consisted of reading Hemingway, blogging, and eating croissants and Madeleines, I determined to head back out for a walk around the historic Marais district on the Right Bank. There were several sites I wanted to see that I knew would not be high on Jennifer's list, and since she was taking the day off, it was a great chance for me to get out and wander.

That Sunday on the Seine, as I've come to think of it, was a four and a half hour tour I'll never forget. And not just because of the nearly four hundred pictures I shot. (Thank God for digital cameras. My film costs alone would have made the trip impossible, let alone the processing costs.) Photos can help recreate a tour like that, but the impression Paris left on my mind after that day will never fade away. It was the day I ceased feeling like that time-traveler with an eyes-only view of the past. It was the day I began to feel as if I were a part of the city.

I still suffered from the language barrier. My biggest regret on the trip was that I had not learned more of the language before we left. I had almost two years to do so. I could have become quite proficient, considering the convenience of online language programs and the fact that my wife has extensive knowledge of French. My only excuse is that I believed the reports that nearly everyone in France speaks English. If they do, they didn't always let me know.

And even if they did, I wish I had been able to show them the respect and courtesy of learning and speaking their language in their homeland.

Make no mistake; you do *not* have to know French to make this trip. You can still enjoy it beyond imagining. But if you want to do more than scratch the surface of this city, you'll want to be able to talk with the locals. I have already determined to learn the language if I ever go back.

After an extensive and slow walk through the Latin Quarter, taking my time to capture many of the great bits of history and architecture, I found my way to the Hôtel de Cluny, a museum dedicated to the Middle Ages. This awesome structure, which is more like a castle than a chateau, was built around 1500, though the original building was constructed nearly two hundred years before that.

I see more reviews of this museum popping up all the time as it gains popularity through the Internet. I had every intention of taking the tour, especially to see the fifteenth century tapestry series *The Lady and the Unicorn*. I did not take it that Sunday, since Jennifer and I had planned to do so later in the week. We never made it, it was dropped from the list as we adapted our plans according to our experiences and state of health. As the week wore on, we wanted to focus more on seeing the city and less on museums. But I could not know this at the time and so after a walk around the courtyard, I left Hôtel de Cluny behind.

From there I headed north, intent on crossing the Seine via the Île de la Cité and Île Saint-Louis.

And that's when it started to rain harder than I had seen it rain since we'd arrived. I was stuck in the smaller streets east of Saint-Julien-le-Pauvre. I still am not sure where I ended up hiding from the downpour—it was the entrance to an underground parking lot tucked in a tiny little street that I have never been able to find again with Google Earth's street view. It eventually stopped raining enough to draw me out. I emerged on the Seine across from Notre Dame and was pleasantly surprised to see that many of the *bouquinistes* were still open.

These historic booksellers have operated on the banks of

the Seine as far back at the 16th century. They have had a regular licensed concession since 1859. Their wares stored in government approved green boxes (about nine hundred of them), the booksellers open their boxes for business whenever the heck they feel like it. There is a minimum of days per week they must be opened, but beyond that, their hours are flexible.

I'd been looking to browse their world-famous stock since we'd arrived, but I had never seen them opened. I began to worry that they did not open so early in the season. Or that the rain was keeping them shut tight. Thus my joy at finding them opened on that drizzling afternoon.

And the drizzle started to return to a heavy rain. To my surprise, the *bouquinistes* showed no concern. The raised covers on the boxes act as awnings. All of the books, with a few exceptions, are individually wrapped in plastic. The booksellers know not to trust the European weather.

I ducked under the nearest box cover to keep my camera bag dry. The bookseller for that box was standing in the rain, wearing an old down-filled parka with its hood tied firmly around his head. Taking care not to drip on his books, I began to sift through his shelves.

What a delight to pick through the titles. His box was full of old science fiction, mystery books, and even poetry. All of it, of course, in French. I was able to pick up a few gifts, including an old sci-fi novel entitled *La Guerre Des Robots* by B.R. Bruss. I even found some new X-Men and Star Wars comics for my kids. I figured the French versions would be fun to show in French class. I snagged a French volume of Baudelaire's *Fleurs du Mal* for Jennifer.

By the time I'd finished making my careful selections (space and weight still a concern for that flight home), the rain had stopped and the sun broke free of the clouds.

With the sun came the tourists and the bridges around Notre Dame filled quickly, as couples and tour groups milled about, enjoying the sudden light. Along the rails of the Pont de l'Archevêché, the bridge on the southeast corner of the Cathedral, lovers the world over come and clamp a lock on the bridge railing, with their names written on the lock. Tradition then dictates that they throw the key into the river. As my father pointed out, this means their love is in-Seine.

Street performers were out in full force; an accordion player (an iconic French image that I only saw once), a guitar player, and even a piano player who brought a small piano on big fat wheels. None of these musicians were playing together, though they were within hearing distance of each other on the Pont Saint-Louis. I dropped a Euro in the basket for the first guy, but I wasn't going to bankroll the whole orchestra.

Crossing onto the Île Saint-Louis, I did not stop to explore it. The Pont Louis Philippe guided me to the Right Bank where I made my way to Rue Charlemagne.

This little area of the Marais is very old. As I mentioned in my dramatic opening teaser, the streets were deserted. That little alley to the left is the Rue du Prévôt , one of the more picturesque alleys in Paris. A photographer's delight. Heading in the other direction, down that curved lane called Rue du Figuier, I found the primary goal of my Sunday tour: the Hôtel de Sens.

The Hôtel de Sens is not well known by Parisian tourists. It is out of the way, just off the main Rue de Rivoli. It has a fairytale appearance, like something you might see in *Beauty and the Beast*. It was built around the same time as Hôtel de Cluny, from 1498 to 1519. At one time, like many historical sites in Paris, it had become extremely rundown, but it has since been restored.

As I circled this treasure—taking photographs, as you might guess—a man about my age approached and asked if I would mind taking his picture in front of the hotel. I was happy to, of course. Though I found his conditions sort of odd.

"Would you please take it with all these bushes showing in front of me?" he asked, indicating a row of shrubbery on the street opposite the Hotel. His accent was British, and he was in fact driving a Land Rover which he must have brought over on the Chunnel Train.

"No problem," I answered, promptly lining up the shot and snapping the picture. He quickly scanned the results.

"Uh, if you don't mind, I just need…" he turned and bent his knees, to show me the angle he wanted. With the camera in hand, he framed the shot and pointed where he wanted to be in it. Half of the shot included the shrubbery. I couldn't help but think about the Knights of Ni! who demanded shrubbery from King Arthur in that old Monty Python movie. I kept a straight face and did as he asked.

He was happier than a fifteen-year-old boy at the Moulin Rouge. Maybe he was a landscape artist who was writing a book. I dunno. But I was glad to help the guy out. It seemed unlikely that two men from separate worlds would meet on the same day as they visited an out-of-the-way old house in the middle of Paris.

We chatted a little, expressing our admiration for the wonderful old palace, then went back to our separate worlds.

Somewhere in London or Surrey there is a photograph on a wall of a man in front of the Hôtel de Sens with a great shot of shrubbery in the foreground. I know, I made sure the shrubbery looked good. It obviously meant a lot to him.

If you should take the time to look up this wonderful jewel, be sure to notice the cannonball stuck in the wall just off to the side of the left turret (it's left if you're facing the main gate). Some idiot during the July Revolution of 1830 not only pointed a loaded cannon at this irreplaceable landmark, but he actually fired the stupid thing. Thankfully, the walls were stronger than his intellect.

The day I made this tour was Sunday, April the 22nd, a Presidential Election day for France. What intrigued me most was that you would not have known it unless you were paying attention. Just across the street from the Hôtel de Sens was an old school building bearing the words *École Primaire Communale des Filles*, which means it was a girl's elementary school many years ago. It is still a school today; a paper sign tacked to a bulletin board at the entrance reads *École Élémentaire Ave Maria*. Interestingly enough, the original stone inscription shows heavy damage, as if someone had chiseled or hammered away at it, which is likely, considering the passionate uprisings that have occurred over the years. The French like to make all of these signs and symbols in permanent stone, then go to great lengths to erase them when they become enraged.

But this election was quite peaceful, and I watched old people and young men and tired ladies stand in line at the school for the chance to cast their ballot. It looked much like our own elections at home, where little old ladies run the election process to choose the leaders of a superpower. I've always been fascinated by that fact. I could not see who was running the show in the school but I would not have been surprised to find a few tough old birds like our League of Women Voters.

There is one last little irony about this voting location. The school was built against a portion of what was once King Phillipe-Auguste's Wall (1190 to 1210 AD), which he ordered to be built for the city's defense against the Plantagenets of Norman England while he was away on the Third Crusade. The wall was covered for many years, and it wasn't until a row of houses was torn down that it was discovered. So King Philip's wall now shelters a voting booth for the French democratic government.

As rain began to fall again, I slipped down the aforementioned Rue de Privot and came out at the café l'Éléphant du Nil, a café which I'd been anticipating for many months. I'd learned of it while researching Paris and it looked too good to pass up. I took a small table, ordered a cappuccino and a crème brûlée and wrote in my journal as Depeche Mode played over the café's speakers.

I was getting better at interacting with the waitresses and I could have stayed there for hours. But I knew that Jennifer would begin to worry about me, so I called for the check (*l'addition, s'il vous plaît*) and headed back out to the streets.

After watching kids ride a tacky, 1990's sort of carnival carousel, complete with characters like *The Simpsons* and *The Incredibles* painted onto buses and motorbikes and spaceships, I turned west and strolled down Rue François Miron.

This quiet street, running parallel to the busier Rue de Rivoli, is perfect for an afternoon walk. The sun finds its way into the street and you can wander along, taking note of the many faces carved into the stone above the doors and windows of the buildings. There are historical stories everywhere you turn, if you only know where to look.

I learned much of the history of this area from Leonard Pitt's book *Walks Through Lost Paris* which I'd read just months before our visit. His book tries to reconstruct much of what was lost when Baron Hausmann destroyed so much of Paris to complete his vision.

It was his story on the Hôtel de Beauvais, where the Queen Mother had stood on her balcony to watch King Louis the XIV and his bride enter the city after his coronation, that led me to find it and photograph it, even though I'd left the book in the apartment and forgotten most of the details. It was only later that I found I'd not only photographed the right balcony, but I'd also taken shots of two other historical entrances that I had seemingly forgotten about. I guess his book had more influence on me than I'd suspected.

If you ever get the chance to visit France and you decide you want to follow along on this tour, you'll be able to stop by the Église Saint-Gervais-et-Saint-Protais, where a German shell fired 75 miles outside of Paris by the infamous "Paris Gun" struck the church during a Good Friday service in 1918, killing 88 people. Paris never runs out of ghosts.

Continuing in this direction will lead you to the highly decorative spectacle that is the Hôtel de Ville, home of the city's administrative government. This municipal seat has been in the same location since 1357. Built during the 1500s and finished in 1628, its distinctive French Renaissance design stands out as the embodiment of French glamour and design. This too was burned to a shell by the Communards in the early 1870s. (Stop doing that!) Its restoration included over 300 statues of famous Frenchmen, along with lions and griffins and medieval soldiers in suits of armor. It is so charming it is almost too much, as if Disney was asked to design the most outlandish French building its Imagineers could create.

While admiring the far-out décor (and really, I did like it, despite what many writers say about the nearly make-believe effect of the restoration) a big guy saw me pulling out my pack of Stride gum, something I always have with me, and he fearlessly approached and caught my attention.

"Gum? May I?" He asked, his French accent an odd

match with his large and rough appearance. "Can I have a piece?"

"Oui, oui," I nodded and handed him one. He unwrapped it quickly, as if he were afraid I would change my mind, and gave me a huge smile as he popped it in his mouth. As he ambled away, he looked back and pointed at his gum with a big nod and bigger smile.

Now I can be a bit suspicious of people who approach me like that. At home, and certainly when I'm abroad. So I was a bit on my guard, in case he was a pickpocket or he had a friend with sticky fingers while he held my attention. I didn't mind giving him the gum, but I increased my level of vigilance since the square in front of the Hôtel de Ville was crowded. But nothing sinister came of it and I finally concluded that the man just wanted to get some American gum. If that's all it was, I wish I had thought to hand him the rest of the pack. If one piece made him happy, the pack might have turned his entire week into a holiday.

Some more light, rain showers hit as I sought out my next destination. And this time, the rain was fortuitous. I'd never heard of the *Tour Saint-Jacques* until I began to study Paris. This magnificent tower was once a bell-tower for the 16th century church of Saint-Jacques-de-la-Boucherie. The church was razed during the French Revolution. (Seriously, guys; stop,

stop, stop!)

Now as I mentioned, the rain returned for a short time. The tower, full of gothic design and imagery, had many bizarre and surreal gargoyles and grotesques. As I neared the base of the tower, in the little flower garden that surrounds it, I looked up and saw that the gargoyles, in particular one devilish character, had rain dripping slowly from its mouth. It looked quite ominous.

Though many scholars argue over the purpose of the faces designed for gargoyles, there is general agreement that they were meant to remind the laypeople—peasants—that the devil was real and to be feared. This encouraged them to come to the church for salvation and protection. Now, if I were an uneducated peasant (well, at least I'm somewhat educated—one out of two ain't bad), I would have no problem imagining the devil after seeing those stone devils *drool*. It's a great effect. It had to be terribly useful for the church officials.

Just a few steps away from the tower you'll find Place du Châtelet with its water-spouting sphinxes. A golden statue of Nike (as in Victory, not the shoe, kids) stands atop a column dedicated in the early 1800s to French military victories, one of which was the Battle of the Pyramids, which explains the whole Egyptian motif.

Back on the banks of the Seine, I hurried down the Right Bank to Pont Neuf, site of yet another movie scene, this time from *The Bourne Identity*. I did not linger long—in case government agents were staking out the bridge—and headed further west. I found a walkway down onto the riverbank, and sat on a bench to watch the water flow. By now the sun was getting lower and golden light

Saint James of the Butchery was the church of choice for many of those who made their living in the nearby food stalls of Les Halles, the Parisian food markets that kept food on the table for most of Paris for over 800 years.

glittered everywhere. Lovers strolled along the Pont de Arts and I found another place to be still.

It didn't hurt to get off my feet for a little while too. I wasn't far from home, but I wanted to check out one last location. A little place called the Louvre.

We were finally planning to visit the Louvre in the morning. Jennifer was ready to see some of the world's greatest art, and I knew that the forecast called for rain all day. We were expecting to spend most of the day inside.

I had decided to go ahead and scout it out. I don't like surprises as much as I used to. So once I'd had my fill of the Seine flowing by, I climbed back up the ramp and looked for a way inside the Louvre.

At the point where Pont des Arts reaches the Right Bank, you can enter the Louvre through an arch that leads into the *Cour Carrée*. This courtyard, the "Square Courtyard," was built by Napoleon I, and is surrounded by what is known as the "old Louvre." Three sides of it make up the Pavillon de l'Horloge, the west side is the Pavillon Sully. If you want to find a place in the center of Paris that is quiet, sublime, and completely isolates you from everything else, find this courtyard.

You're completely surrounded by stone. The only things not made of stone are windows that glitter with sunlight in the late afternoon. A modest, circular fountain sits in the center of the courtyard, and its water would be the only other element you would see besides stone and glass. You see nothing beyond the roofline. No Eiffel Tower, no cathedral or monument. No antenna or lamppost, save for one flagpole waving the French Tri-Color over the Sully Pavilion.

Even the roar of traffic on Quai François Mitterrand, which ricochets inside the arched stone entry, cannot be heard once you step fully into the courtyard. This immaculate, inner sanctum is the perfect place to pull back and allow one's self time to think. To wonder at all that has been seen. To sort out emotions. Or, as one man chose to do while I was there, to sit on a bench and woo his lover with his guitar.

From this point, I stepped through the arch of the Sully Pavilion and was treated to the sun-filled *Cour Napoleon*, which is twice the size of the *Cour Carrée*. This courtyard, built by Napolean III, is dominated by the Richelieu and Denon Pavilions on the north and south sides, both of which face the modern glass pyramid that is forever linked to that Dan Brown literary marvel (that is, we marvel that so many people read the silly thing) *The Da Vinci Code*.

I will admit that I've never liked that odd-looking trinket I.M. Pei rammed into the center of the Louvre. I still cannot bring myself to admire it. However, I can see what he was trying to do. There is a certain artistic flare to the whole affair, I suppose. But in the end, when you look at all that stone surrounding it, the pyramid just looks temporary, as if a child built a cute snowman in his parent's front yard and everyone knows it will only last until spring melts it into nonexistence.

But the sun did not melt Pei's Pyramid, though it did add a golden patina to the courtyard that was perfect for my camera. I felt a little guilty that I had peeked inside without Jennifer, but it turned out to be quite fortunate, since the forecast turned out to be correct; it rained the next day, and the courtyard looked nothing like it had that Sunday evening.

And here's the kind of information I want to pass on to anyone considering a trip to Paris. Though you'll be told the Louvre is outrageously crowded (which it was when we took the tour), you should know that there are times you can find it as I did, nearly empty, with only a sprinkling of tourists scattered around. That Sunday evening, the entire Louvre complex, including the open gardens leading out to the Tuileries, was calm, hushed and completely relaxing. It costs nothing to wander the courtyards, which are full of impressive statues and reliefs along the walls and roofs of the pavilions.

Not all of Paris is buzzing with iconic *joie de vive*.

Cloudbanks to the west were rolling in. I had the feeling I was about to be hit with another downpour. So I reluctantly crossed the Seine, made my way through the Saint-Germain neighborhood, stopping only to help out two Scandinavian ladies who were looking for Saint-Séverin. (That was one I knew. They were way off the mark but I sent them in the right direction.)

I climbed our charming staircase, and settled into the apartment to sort through the pictures I'd snapped. The tour I'd taken was extraordinary. Unfortunately I would pay the price the next day for all that walking. But it's a price I'd gladly pay again.

Chapter Nine: The Wonders of the Ancient World

We had been in Paris for a week. As much as we had longed to see the wonders of the Louvre, we had held off for a time, determined to have our feet on the ground before we viewed the greatest pieces of art the world has ever known. Going sooner would have been like opening the biggest present on Christmas morning first. Or eating the main course first. It just felt wrong.

So after a week of discovering Paris, its cemeteries and memorials and streets and cathedrals, we awoke Monday morning ready to open our big present.

Taking a bus from Michel Debré Station, we promptly headed in the wrong direction. Instead of meandering down Raspail Boulevard, the bus rattled down Rue de Sévres. I was savvy enough with the buses now to read the web-like routes on the buses' overhead panels, and so I knew right away a mistake had been made. Honestly, to this day, I suspect the bus driver made the mistake, but I'll cut him some slack. It might have been his first day on the job. Since this was probably my second or third time on a Parisian bus, I will have the good graces to acknowledge that he might not have been as experienced in these things.

After giving the poor, misguided driver a chance to correct his mistake, which he never did, we jumped off at the little Bac-Saint-Placide bus stop and caught the next bus going in the other direction to jump off again at Sévres-Babylone where we dropped into the Number 12 métro line.

One little benefit of this mistake was that we were finally able to solve a small puzzle we'd had since our first day in Paris. A French flag was visible above the rooftops from our apartment windows. It was a perfect prop for the view, constantly reminding us that we were in France. Sure, the rooftops looked like Paris, but this little validation was a nice touch. I had joked that it was put up there for the tourists. Coming back down Rue de Sévres, we could see that the flag was in fact on top of the Lutetia Hotel.

I've only recently discovered that the Lutetia was the hangout for German officers of the *Abwehr*, the German Army's Intelligence Service. From there they worked at rounding up French *Resistance* Fighters. How heartbroken it must have made the residents of the 6th *arrondissement*. Yet how meaningful must it be now to some of the elder neighbors to see *le drapeau tricolore* proudly flying above that venerable edifice each and every day.

With this mystery solved, I had to crack the mystery of my transit error. I'd written down Bus 39, which was the bus we'd taken, and according to the bus map in the métro station, Bus 39 had done what it was supposed to do. So the bus driver was off the hook. Why I'd written down the wrong number was anybody's guess, but I conveniently blamed it on Bing

Maps, since that's the online planner I'd used.

So we hopped aboard the Number 12 train, with every intention of riding to Concorde Station where we would then connect with the Number 1 line which would get us to the Louvre.

But I knew better. As we rode along on the 12, I saw a sign that said the next station could be used to reach the Musée d'Orsay. This had to be the métro entrance I'd seen directly in front of the museum, and I knew it was right across the Seine from the Louvre. Simple. So I assured Jennifer I was going to make the trip easier and we slipped out of the train, up the stairs.

We were on Boulevard Saint-Germain, several blocks shy of the Orsay, at Solferino station. It turns out the station I'd seen at the Orsay was an RER station, which services the bigger trains that do not always connect with métro stations.

At this point I gave up on transit routes and we walked the rest of the way to the Louvre, which we could have done from the start. Soon enough, we walked across the Pont Royal and I introduced Jennifer to the *Cour Napoleon*.

Running a little late, a line had already formed by the time we arrived and we had to wait beside the pyramid before we could get inside. Fortunately, the rain held off long enough for us to clear through security.

Again, the question of the museum pass comes into play. One of the obstacles that the museum pass is supposed to clear out is the long wait. However, we did not wait more than thirty minutes to get inside. Once there, we bought tickets at ticket-machines with only about a two or three minute delay. This was a Monday in April, and though certainly crowded, it was not unbearable. The longest wait we endured was at the Paul counter. (But coffee and *pain de chocolat* is so worth any wait.)

Fortified with caffeine, we set off for the Denon wing,

where we went straight for the jugular, to put it delicately.

The Louvre is best known for two works of art; *La Joconde* and *Aphrodite tes Melou*. (That's the *Mona Lisa*, and the *Venus De Milo* to you and me.) Both of these can be seen by heading into the Denon wing. The Venus de Milo is actually in the Sully Pavilion, but it is only a few steps from the end of the Denon Pavilion.

I had one other *biggie* that I was looking for: *Nike of Samothrace*. This is also in the same area, so we wasted no time getting there.

Take an immediate left and pass through a large gallery of statues and sunlight and you will see Nike of Samothrace at the top of the grand Daru staircase. This ancient, broken, gorgeous image represents the winged goddess of Victory. It is one of the best surviving works of art from ancient times. Missing its head and arms, it appears enticing and mystical.

Nike has been on display since 1884 in this location. Only once was she removed; in 1939, in preparation for the coming war with Germany, she was lowered down the staircase on a wooden ramp and hidden outside Paris. In fact, nearly every painting was removed from the Louvre at that time, and most of the statues. Various stories, some of them contradictory, say the most valuable pieces were walled up in basements or simply housed in chateaux around the country. It is a sign of the importance of these works that such care was taken. Many great works of art were plundered or destroyed during the war. Oddly enough, according to officials at the Louvre, the Germans were aware of the location of most of these pieces but left them alone.

These are no ordinary museum pieces.

I won't provide a detailed tour of the Louvre. There are other books far more suited to that purpose. However, I can tell you the impression it left on us.

It is shocking to walk into a small room and look upon a

plaster fresco and realize you are looking at a 530-year-old Botticelli. An ancient statue is one thing. A painting that has survived for centuries is something else entirely.

The Mona Lisa takes center stage in the *Salle des Etats*, a rather modern looking room that drives me sort of crazy. Let me set the stage:

This square gallery has a free-standing wall that essentially divides the gallery into one large area and a smaller area behind it. On the wall, facing the large open gallery, is the Mona Lisa. She is a small painting, measuring only 30 inches by 21 inches. She is in a wooden frame, covered by super special bulletproof glass. This is reasonable considering a vandal threw acid on it in 1956 and later that same year someone hit it with a rock. Both attacks damaged the painting. So I am cool with protecting her.

What I don't understand is the mad crush of people trying to get near her to take her picture. First of all, you can download the image for free from about anywhere on the web. It's in the public domain and there are many good digital copies available. Secondly, your picture of the Mona Lisa will look *horrible*. You are not allowed to get closer than about 12 feet from her. No matter how good the lighting is in the gallery, all of it reflects off the glass. So do all the colored laser eyes on everyone's cameras as they line up their digital cameras.

I watched one lady push to the front of the crowd. She stood there shooting about seven or eight pictures of the Mona Lisa with her phone. After that, she continued to stand in the front, blocking many people's view, while she made a phone call and had a conversation in a room where it is nearly impossible to hear someone talking next to you. ("I'm here at the Mona Lisa! What? What? I can't hear you! What? No, I'm at the Mona Lisa! I posted it to Facebook! Huh? No, the Mona Lisa!")

My last bit of whining about this scene has more to do with the other paintings in the room. I was aghast to see that the majority of the tourists were completely ignoring the other works of art, of which, frankly, I felt many were far superior to the Mona Lisa.

The best thing to do with that throng of Mona Lisa nuts is put them behind you. Face the opposite direction and you'll see Veronese's *The Wedding Feast at Cana*. This gigantic painting (about 21 feet by 30 feet) takes the biblical story of the Canaan Wedding feast and sets it in Venice in modern times. Well, modern times for 1553. The detail on such an epic scale must have taken years to fill in. Veronese takes no shortcuts. His mastery of the total image is evident no matter where you look on the ridiculously huge canvas.

Even more amazing is the realization that Napoleon's troops cut it in half for shipment to France. Some people do things I would never conceive of doing. That is one of them.

Da Vincis, Raphaels, Titians, and Caravaggios fill the Italian gallery with a mind-numbing display of genius. We spent most of our pre-lunch tour here. If the art in these rooms does not move you, you should probably be checked by a doctor.

There is a great little café at the west end of the Denon Pavilion overlooking the Mollien staircase. Le Café Mollien has an excellent light lunch menu, and you can dine with one of the best views in Paris. From where I sat, I could look into a gallery of oversized French paintings from the 19th century. Jennifer could look out the windows of the palace and see the gardens in the *Cour du Carrousel*. It is an amazing spot to have lunch.

We spent the next few hours walking in awe through the galleries. So many of the paintings were ten and fifteen feet across, I couldn't help thinking how difficult it must have been to move and hang them. It is just too intimidating to consider.

Room With No View *Excerpt, April 25, 2012*

For a generation that is being raised to watch movies on the iPhone, it is important to remember how much is lost when viewing great works of art online instead of personally standing in front of them. I do not mean to suggest that great works of art cannot be viewed online. To the contrary, it is one of the great benefits to people the world over that so many paintings and sculptures can be seen by people who will never get the chance to see them in person. Yes, something is lost seeing great canvases on a small digital screen, the same as three-dimensional sculpture on a two-dimensional plane. Yet great works of art can lose a little something and still be great. They are, after all, great...

The first thing that caught my attention at the Louvre was the sheer scale of the galleries. The long halls in the Denon Wing, where so many Italian and French Paintings are hung, are immense...I was in awe of Veronese's The Wedding Feast at Cana which is a staggering 21 feet and 10 inches by 32 feet and six inches. (A painting looted from Venice by Napoleon, who had his troops cut it in half to ship it back to France.) Frankly, I don't even have a wall that is 32 feet long in my house, let alone 21 feet high. And that's always the problem with buying art prints and posters. I just don't have much wall space left.

To give an example of what is lost when viewing smaller copies of these epic masterpieces, let's take a closer look at a painting by Salvator Rosa. *Heroic Battle*, from 1652, is a grand depiction of a battle that only measures seven feet by eleven and a half feet. Modest, compared to Jacques-Louis David's thirteen foot by seventeen foot Leonidas at Thermopylae (which, by the way, was the original 300 big screen feature, nearly 200 years before Zack Snyder's version.) It is a busy painting, depicting the chaos and glory of a sixteenth or seventeenth century melee. As a whole, the eye takes in the ruins of a temple, and the struggles of the mounted soldiers as they are deep in the thick of the fight. But that is not what I noticed as soon

as I stepped in front. What drew me was the fear in the eyes of the foot soldier about to be trampled by one of those warhorses. There is nothing glorious in his terror. Yes, he is wearing a totally awesome arm shield, which has its own face designed to bring terror to his opponent, but he cannot manage to look as menacing. It is easy to forget about scaring the other guy when you see a 1500 pound horse about to land on you. And Rosa does a great job of depicting this. That stab of white paint on the eye jumps out at you.

Off to the left, you can see another foot soldier. His face is eerily similar to the first one, though his color is much more death-like. Where the man with the arm shield is full of terror and color, this man has the pallor of a corpse. That same look of terror is there, but you can see that

his arm has been severed, he has bled out, and his face looks as dead as the hand that lies next to him. If only he had been fortunate enough to get one of those arm shields, he might have lived long enough to be trampled by a horse. This seems too much of a coincidence to believe Rosa did not depict this on purpose. The faces are too alike, the protected arm and the severed arm are on the same side. These are the kinds of details the viewer is supposed to pick up on such a large piece. It is what can be missed when you can only see this on a 1/10 scale display.

I'm intrigued by these giant paintings. Caring for them must be a headache. The larger ones are not covered in glass, as many of the smaller ones are. So that must mean dust is a problem. In fact,

Veronese's The Wedding at Cana was actually dropped in 1992 when an attempt was made to raise it higher on the wall. The 1.5 ton painting fell over when a support gave way. The canvas was torn in four places. Sadly, this happened just two days after water had dripped on it from a leaking air vent. All of this after it successfully survived WWII by being rolled up and moved around in a truck as it was hidden from the Nazis. One more impressive feature of these massive paintings is the fact that they have been copied from time to time. David's The Coronation of Napoleon, a 20 by 32 foot painting… once hung at Versailles, but was moved to the Louvre, then a full-sized replica painted by David himself was rehung at Versailles. This kind of dedication to art is difficult to understand. The first painting took him almost two years to complete. Imagine if Peter Jackson, once completing the Lord of the Rings movies, shot them over again. Sure, it can be done, but couldn't David have simply made a copy of his painting that only measured five by eight feet? That would still have been impressive.

The spacious galleries of the Italian and French painters were sorely missed once we entered the Sully Pavilion's collection of Greek antiquities. It was here we began to feel the pinch of the crowd. We wove our way through this throng of statue gawkers, pausing long enough to see the Venus di Milo and, at the other end of the gallery, the even more impressive *Pallas of Velletri*, a first century marble reproduction of a (now lost) bronze effigy of Athena from 430 BC as described by Pliny the Elder. Her cloak is secured by an aegis which depicts the head of Medusa, complete with her serpent hairstyle.

An historical note on Athena for history buffs: Athena was sold to France by the art restorer Pacetti in the late 1700s. The French were moving it when the Neapolitan Government confiscated it. This was during the War of the Second Coalition, an attempt by the European Royals to punish the French for so rudely murdering the French Royal family. The statue would actually be named in the ensuing Treaty of Florence, turning it over to France. The treaty also included the transfer of the Principality of Piombino and the State of Presidi to France, who then traded these territories to Spain for Louisiana, which eventually enabled Napoleon to sell Louisiana to Thomas Jefferson so that I could find a home on the Gulf Coast.

Not long after we began to delve into the mysteries of the Egyptian antiquities, the crowds became too much. We were worn down and ready to get out. I was beginning to feel the effects of that extensive walking tour I'd taken the day before and we decided to call it a day. After perusing the Louvre's bookstore for family gifts, we stepped out of the glass pyramid into the Napoleon Courtyard and caught the 39 bus which dropped us off right at our local Franprix grocery store.

We'd come to love our little grocery store. It was small, older, and included a second level accessible by two different stairs, one of which was a creaky old spiral staircase tucked into the corner behind the lunchmeat cooler.

We were quickly becoming accustomed to city shopping. The small apartment, with its small cabinets and refrigerator, forced us to buy only a few groceries at a time. Back home, with five children in our large house, Jennifer loads up the car on a weekly shopping trip. In Paris, we would stop off at the Franprix nearly every afternoon to pick up a few fresh fruits, milk, orange juice, or fresh bread.

This was one of the benefits of choosing an apartment

over a hotel. We were able to cook for ourselves, and sample the goods available to Parisians in their daily lives. We tried out their frozen dinners, chips, factory packaged croissants and pain de chocolat, and many other local products. I was, of course, impressed with their prices on French wine (which is just local wine, you know, without all the levies or tariffs or whatever it is that makes it so expensive in the States). I enjoyed their ice cream, though I was puzzled that I could not find a French Vanilla flavor. (That's a joke, guys. You see, they had vanilla, but…oh, never mind.)

We loaded up on goodies (be sure to buy some Madeleine snack cakes while you're there) and were safely tucked into the apartment in time to cook dinner.

One special aspect of our trip was our ability to share photographs and stories with all of our friends and family back home. We were greatly encouraged by all the comments and advice from friends around the world. It motivated me to raise my photographic standards for my blog.

As I mentioned before, we are not the most active couple in the evenings. We don't dance the night away at clubs or reserve tables at four-star restaurants for full-blown dinners late in the evening. We eat early, and enjoy watching a movie or reading a book. But we just don't get out at night very much. This was our time to relax and rest after our day of sightseeing.

But since we'd closed up shop early that day, I decided to take another trip out into my favorite neighborhood again, only this time I waited for the sun to go down. I had seen a bit of the Latin Quarter the night I'd gone to the Christine Theater to watch Rita Hayworth and Orson Welles. This time, I was going to take a look at the City of Light through my camera lens.

I'd become more comfortable with trekking through the

Parisian streets at night. If there were parts of the city that were dangerous at night I had not stumbled upon them yet. One night, I had even noticed an elderly woman with her hands full of groceries walking down a darkened street seemingly without reservation and it occurred to me that I was not imagining things. There was nothing on the streets that might cause me alarm. I can only speak for the few nights I was out and about during that fortnight in April. And I can only say what it was like in the Latin Quarter, since I did not venture beyond it in the dark.

Right off the bat I discovered the voyeuristic pull of the brightly lit café windows. The glamorous scenes displayed in those windows were perfect subjects for the camera. While I love looking at Robert Doineau's famed black and white photographs of Paris, which include many wonderful night scenes, his black and white images cannot convey the artistic brilliance of cafés at night; their neon signs glowing above shadow-riddled red or green canopies, the brightly lit sidewalk tables with their yellow cane chairs, the blues and reds of the inner dining rooms, the soft glow of beer logos behind dark, glossy bars. I felt like a modern day Edward Hopper.

These little scenes were life-sized HDTV sets with the widest screens possible. All of them peopled with a myriad of characters that could become anything. And the best part of it was that in Paris, there is at least one café at every corner, and plenty in between.

Turning away from the café scenes, I was even more won over by the Seine as it ran alongside Notre Dame. The cobblestone quays, lit with street lamps (quay lamps?), fuse with the bridges, perfectly framing the sparkling waters that flow beneath the city lights. From Saint-Michel fountain to Notre Dame, the river is alive with lights the color of gold and pearls and silver medallions. The tourist-filled batobuses, far from an annoyance, add color and wonder to the scene as they glide by, shining their spotlights up at Notre Dame's flying buttresses and the statue of Henry the Great.

Notre Dame stands out, of course, lit for all the world to see. And all the world does as those boats glide by. In the square below her towers, I found only street lamps, puddles left over from the day's rain, and a few pairs of lovers. I could not believe I was free to photograph it alone. It seemed unlikely that something this magnificent should be empty so early in the evening. It was only about eleven o'clock at night. That's early for Paris. And it was not as cold as I had expected it to be. But the square was vacant nonetheless.

Well, it wasn't completely empty. I was, in fact, not alone.

As I crossed the Petit Pont and stepped out into the lamp-lit gravel, I heard rustling in the bushes beside the quay wall. I assumed it was birds settling in for the night. My knowledge of wildlife is not very broad but I should have been able to guess what was making all that racket.

Up near the statue of Charlemagne, as I lined up shots of the brightly lit cathedral façade, I saw movement not ten or fifteen feet in front of me. With my camera I tracked it and focused on it to identify my new companion.

I should have been disgusted. I should at least have been annoyed. But thanks to Pixar, I was actually delighted to see a rat in Paris. This little guy was the spitting image of Paul Lynde's Templeton in *Charlotte's Web*. He was much too long and thin to resemble *Ratatouille's* Remy. I watched him cross the open ground and approach the green trash bag hanging from the Parisian's idea of a safe trash can.

In the wake of terrorist bombings in the mid-nineties, the last of which killed eight people at the Saint-Michel métro station in 1996, the government had replaced all of their trash cans with metal frames that hold semi-opaque green trash bags with *vigilance* printed on them. I'd been seeing them everywhere and thought that they were an ugly choice for such a beautifully managed city. It turns out I was right. It is an ugly choice, for an ugly world, but probably the right choice.

The rat ducked under the hanging trash bag and began to look around for any food dropped by the tourists. He nibbled on a few things then skipped back across the open ground and ducked into the bushes.

Intrigued, I followed him. At the edge of the grass, I began to notice a few of his friends. As they foraged for something to eat, and as I focused my camera on them and lit them up with my flash, I realized that there were more of them than I had first thought. I wondered just how aggressive they could become. I'd never heard of a tourist being eaten by rats, but I did not want to be the first one to make the evening news so I decided to leave them alone.

At least they weren't wolves.

On the very spot I was standing, on what is called the parvis of the cathedral, in the winter of 1450, the people of Paris finally trapped and killed a pack of wolves that had terrorized the city, killing forty people. Yet another layer of history that covers this amazing city; yet more ghosts lingering in the shadows among the rats.

I slowly worked my way back through the Latin Quarter— Rue Galande, Saint-Julien-le-Pauvre, Saint-Séverin, Rue de la Harpe. The night was getting colder, but there were still people sitting at the sidewalk tables, wrapped in coats and scarves as they shared bottles of wine and baskets of bread.

I was surprised to see many of the brasseries and cafés closing their doors before midnight. I had been under the impression that the world of Paris stayed open all night. But even Parisian waiters and bartenders must sleep sometime and I watched many of them stack their chairs or tally their receipts as they prepared to put their establishments to bed.

There is a French word that describes someone who walks around in the dark; *noctambule*. A night owl. This nocturnal observer has historical and literary roots in the writings of Nicolas-Edme Restif de la Bretonne. His eight volume *Les Nuits de Paris ou le Spectateur Nocturne*, published between 1788 and 1794, details one thousand and one nights during which he prowls the city, watching and cataloging the lives of Parisians as night. I had never heard of it until after I left France. I was delighted to read of this, it made all the sense in the world to me. Paris is an ideal place to practise *noctambulisme*. This city is turned inside out. Where else can you find so many tables and chairs outside on the streets? Certainly no place this cold. Yet the people of Paris are determined to continue this practice, using space heaters and plastic enclosures to allow them a few more weeks out on the sidewalks; a few more weeks to sit in the glow of neon late into the night, talking and drinking with friends.

I walked the last few blocks to Saint-Sulpice, sharing the sidewalks and the night with a few couples who walked hand-in-hand. I stopped at the cathedral. The lights in the nave illuminated its great stained-glass windows. Its towers were lit with golden spotlights while its fountain was lit with pale light from within the waters.

I was alone at the fountain. After all, this was no Hollywood fantasy. Ernest Hemingway did not come walking into the square from Rue Bonaparte, a route he says he walked on his way from the cafés back to the rooms his family rented on Rue de Vaugirard. It's said he often stopped at the Saint-Sulpice fountain but he did not do so that night while I was there.

And I, too, had to complete what was becoming my usual route back to the rooms we were renting on Rue du Vieux Colombier. The next day we would revisit Montmartre cemetery.

Chapter Ten: A Walk Amongst the Montmartre Dead

There is no way to tell, when walking amongst the black and green-stained crypts of the cemeteries of Paris, whether or not the figures walking toward you are living people or the spirits of those who have been buried beneath your feet. Just as you cannot tell if you are passing an unseen spirit, since by its nature it is unseen, and since no one can argue that you did or did not pass by it, neither can you argue that the woman who passes by with a bouquet of flowers in her hand, her head covered with a black and tan scarf, her steps unsteady and weak, is one of the living or the dead. One could argue that the woman could be stopped, grabbed hold of, and a pulse could be taken. One could pull her close and determine if the warmth of life flows from her lips. But that is something no one would ever do. It is not allowed. It is not how rational beings act. And so the fact remains: there is no way to tell if the figures you pass in Montmartre Cemetery, or Montparnasse

Cemetery, or Père Lachaise Cemetery, are tourists, Parisians, ghosts, or angels.

As we made our way down the Avenue de la Croix, which is indeed *down* in this sunken burial ground, we stepped carefully over the cracked and pot-holed macadam surface as it crossed the Avenue de Montmorency. I had attempted to find Stendhal's grave, which, according to the English version of the map we were given, should have been to our left before the intersection. I did my best not to slip on the wet cobblestones and uneven borders of the tightly packed monument bases, while at the same time, holding my umbrella at an angle to best protect the nylon backpack holding my camera equipment. I did not see Stendhal anywhere. And if the deceased author saw me he did not attempt to get my attention. That was fine with me, since *The Red and the Black* had not really captured my attention nearly twenty years before. I was more interested in finding Edgar Degas' resting place. He could always capture my attention. Not just with bathing nudes, though that wasn't a bad way to draw my attention, but I learned to appreciate his art after visiting his temporary home in New Orleans ten years before on my first vacation in the Big Easy. His depiction of the Cotton Exchange is high on my list of favorite scenes. So giving up on Stendhal physically, as I had literarily, we crossed Montmorency and continued down into the northwestern portion of the cemetery.

On our left, we passed an old woman who was busy cleaning around what I presumed to be her family crypt. Rain was still falling in a steady drizzle but this did not hinder her. She had a broom in her hands, and was short-brushing the edge of the crypt's stone base. Her headscarf was tied neatly under her chin, her heavy black shoes gently scuffing the stone as she backed up, then advanced again on the debris that littered it. The wet detritus of tree buds, old leaves, and bits of trash clung stubbornly enough that her strokes required real effort to clear the base. I nodded toward her, to make Jennifer aware of her. It was something we were used to seeing in New Orleans. There too, the living take greater care of the dead, or at least of their memories, than most Americans do. At best, Americans attempt to buy this sort of devotion with perpetual care, which is nothing like the tender efforts of a seventy or eighty-year-old woman scrubbing concrete and stone in fifty-degree rain.

I was worried about my cameras getting wet. Jennifer was worried about finding the crypt we sought. This woman was worried about clearing away debris that the next wind and rain would wash back up upon her family's tomb. She would have to do it all over again very soon. Or give up in the end. Judging by the neatness of that crypt, she hadn't given up for many, many years. I had a feeling she wouldn't give up as long as she could still clutch a broom in her gnarled hands.

If I had known the language, I would have been tempted to stop and speak with her; ask about her family, ask why she was putting forth such an effort. But I didn't, and so we left her to her work. I suppose that, though I did not know the details, I could guess easily enough why she did it. Duty or love, or both. Maybe she would not know which. Some of us can tell the difference. For some of us, a difference between the two does not exist.

We descended further toward the northwest corner of the cemetery.

Once a gypsum quarry, this sunken graveyard is one of the most beautiful cemeteries I have visited. Originally a site for mass graves after the French Revolution, it became, in time, a revered resting place for the upper-class citizens of the Right Bank. With only two entrances, this man-made canyon landscape is the size of 11 hectares, which some quick and broad calculations tells me is comparable to 25 football fields clumped together. With over 700 trees and 20,000 residents (most of whom are not in single graves, again something we are accustomed to seeing in New Orleans but not the rest of the United States), it has multiple levels accessed by sloping avenues and stone staircases.

It is a photographer's paradise.

It is not a researcher's paradise.

We had decided to come back to Montmartre Cemetery when it was open, to seek out a borrowed grave. Jennifer had been researching the life of Madame LaLaurie, the wicked New Orleans socialite infamous for her horrific treatment of her slaves. Jennifer was in the process of writing an epic verse retelling of the story, and had already seen several cantos of it published before our trip. She knew that Madame LaLaurie had fled from New Orleans to Paris after the public discovery of her atrocities.

Marie Delphine LaLaurie had brazenly moved into Parisian society, taking up residence in the Madeleine district, and leading a well-to-do life until her death in 1842. For a time, her body was interred at Montmartre Cemetery, where Jennifer hoped to find the crypt.

It would have been difficult even if she had remembered to bring the research book containing the grave's description. The book contained a photograph of the crypt but we had forgotten it back in our apartment. We both thought, however, that we would recognize the grave. One of us remarked that the name on the stele, which neither could quite remember, started with a *P*. And it was in open sunshine, which should have made it easier, since so much of the cemetery lay covered in shade from the hundreds of maples that crowd the monuments. Armed with these images from our memories, we arrived at that gypsum-mine-necropolis prepared to seek out the borrowed, temporary grave of a New Orleans fiend.

Some memories hold on tightly, and we can simply call

them up when they are needed. Other memories die as easily as a fragile man and can only be recalled as a ghost of what we actually remember. These are memories never to be trusted-- they are always distorted, deceiving, and often completely false. Such was the case with our collective memory of the crypt for which we were searching. We never found it. And when we returned home and dug out the original photo we found our memory of it had been completely wrong.

The entrance to this lower realm is down a flight of steps that connects the southwest end of the Rue Coulaincourt viaduct and the northeast end of the very short Avenue Rachel. One would hardly know it was there. A few days before, we had attempted to enter through the Joseph-de-Maistre Gate, at the other end of the viaduct, when we had approached the cemetery from the top of Montmartre and Sacré-Cœur Basilica. The gate had been locked. We had arrived too late. A Frenchman, eager to help, had told us of the other gate, pointing out we would need to cross the bridge and take the steps on the immediate left. That gate had also been locked, and so we had been forced to come this second day.

Entering the cemetery leaves one unbalanced. The sight of the blue, iron bridge, more like New York than Paris, astride the cemetery at its odd angle to the entrance left me doubtful that we had indeed found the famous graveyard. There was no denying that the crypts that could be seen, including those *under* the bridge, were quite impressive, and certainly what we had expected to find. But it looked as if the city planners had plunked this cold, dreary bridge on this lovely and sacred sight, in a drunken mistake. That might make sense in an American city. It was not something we had come to expect in Paris.

But as rain began to fall more heavily than we had previously seen in Paris, moments after we stepped into the information office and requested a map in English, the bridge proved to be providential as cover from the shower. We sat on a bench, taking a break from our walk up the Boulevard des Batignolles from the métro station at Place de Clichy. Jennifer was for venturing into the rain. Her long, black coat was waterproof, and her wide-brimmed hat easily kept her dry. As always, I was more concerned about the cameras than our skin.

We explored under the bridge, which was a perfectly gloomy place to begin. The shadows under that bleak bridge mixed well with the cold, wet wind passing though the crypts. A handful of other tourists milled about with us, waiting out the rain. As we were learning, it never rained hard for long in Paris.

An evocative stairway enticed us from the viaduct. As soon as I spotted it, I knew it would photograph well, and I had a great opportunity to take the shot with rain falling, since I could stay under cover while Jennifer, who seemed eager to get out into the rain, could stand on the stairs for dramatic effect. She did indeed look dramatic once in place, but by then the rain had nearly stopped and I did not get the shot I had hoped to capture.

But we were in business. We began our search. And it quickly became obvious that it would not be a simple one to undertake. And the rain began to fall again.

So we missed Stendhal, passed the woman cleaning her family's crypt, and I did my best to keep the camera bag under the umbrella, with Jennifer steadfastly eying the names carved in stone as we walked the length of those wet, black avenues.

I was easily distracted. I could see the back of an emerald statue in the center of the section on our right. I left Jennifer to read headstones and picked my way across puddles and muddy paths, deciding the rain was light enough to risk unpacking my Nikon. The emerald statue was only oxidized copper, of course, a robed woman standing with her back to me. To suggest she was emerald demonstrates my romantic image of these sites. Exposed copper tends to become more pistachio than any other green. But this color reminds one of ice cream and does not sound beautiful. To reveal the woman's face, I had to circle her monument. Before I could get a full look at her, I spied the figure of a man sprawled across the top of a monument as if he had been shot and left to die. His color was a deeper green, with more mildew blacking him. The sculptor had draped a sheet or blanket over his legs. His right hand looked as if he were still gripping the edge of the crypt, though obviously he was dead. There was, in fact, a bullet hole in his forehead. This is Alphonse Baudin, a revolutionary shot dead upon the barricades in 1851. He stole my attention, and I only ended up with a picture of the woman's face in the background behind him.

I left him upon the barricade, wet from the rain, covered in glory, a scattering of dead leaves and pink tree blossoms. I also left behind the woman, who may have understood how I could ignore her, since she could not take her eyes off Baudin's sacrificial corpse for all eternity.

In the area of Degas' grave, huddled upon a tomb, was a hooded, robed figure with knees drawn to his or her chest. I am inclined to believe it was a woman; the sculptor had given his piece a delicate robe and vulnerable attitude. Still, the stone looks hard, with thick arms and a heaviness that is not always displayed on such memorial scenes. The rain wet the robe and hood; the figure's head bent forward at the drawn-up knees, as if avoiding the spray. The hooded face could not be seen so I do not know if he or she minded being photographed.

I never found Degas. Or his family crypt. My failure was due to my lack of knowledge about his name. Modern man has taken his name as one word: Degas. His family, however, knew better. Their family crypt has the family name clearly at the top of the stele: Famille de Gas. I learned this later and wondered how I could have missed it. Perhaps I did not see it, though I suspect I did, looking for a capital D while ignoring the capital G. Sometimes my American upbringing does not fill me with pride. Names are treated so lightly in the States. We do not pay proper attention to their origins, their meanings, nor the respect they deserve.

Intrigued by the many ravens we began to see, we moved on, following as they hopped and flew from headstone to crypt. An elusive black cat darted in and out of the tombs, never allowing me to capture a good photograph of him. It all seemed too perfect. As if the caretakers knew when enough tourists were in the cemetery to release the ravens and black cats. I am not a naturalist, like the travelers of old, and so I know next to nothing about flora, fauna, and species. Whether or not the birds were ravens or simply blackbirds I could not say. But there was no chance I was going to walk through the avenues of Montmartre Cemetery, above Paris, and say "Look, a blackbird!"

Jennifer continued reading names, faith in her mission beginning to falter. I had already given up, and was now just enjoying the walk, the views, and the occasional odd sight. A stone owl adorned the top of a grand crypt in the northeast corner. A rare modern headstone might stick out among a row of gothic, spired structures that could have been majestic cathedrals had their dimensions been increased exponentially. A font designer would have had a field day. I did my best to take samples, alternately working the Nikon and the Handycam.

I had been in Paris long enough to be able to read most of the French I saw. I've heard it said mastery of a foreign language can best be judged by how it is read. Does the reader translate what is seen? Or can he or she comprehend the written word without translating? I was surprised to discover how well I was doing in this regard. I had been reading French headstones without hesitation. Being surrounded by a foreign language in a foreign land, I had come to expect to see that language, and I had come to the conclusion that my own language was no longer available. When I came across a headstone written in English, I almost didn't realize it. I paused to take note of the English words chiseled upon it:

"To the memory of Vestatia the beloved wife of Ernest PENNOTTI and the only daughter of William FOSTER late of the city of Norwich. The deceased died at Paris on the 19th of July 1855."

Jennifer was nearby and I pointed it out to her. It sounded like something out of a Henry James novel. I could not help but sympathize with her family, who had to learn of her death by a letter sent across the channel. Had a trip to Paris always been her dream? One reads of this kind of thing happening often. A long trip, a sudden and short-lived illness and burial in a foreign land. Her husband is forced to bury her in such a beautiful place, leaving the record of her death in English, where few locals could read about her. Yet he wanted to leave word of her father's name, a Baron who lived until 1874, nearly two decades after his daughter. It was wise of Pennotti to do this. An online search for a Vestatia Pennotti produces zero results, which is terribly rare and a bit sad today. Her father, however, can be found, as well as her brother, nephew, and great-nephew (the last of the four Baron Fosters of Norwich, who died in 1960). It made me wonder about Pennotti. Was he Italian? Had he upset the Fosters by taking their daughter in marriage and moving her to Paris? I could not read the last line, so did not know her age though I can guess at it. Her father was born in 1798, which would suggest she could have been no older than 35 or 37. Not a child when she died, but she certainly did not live a long life.

The Pennotti headstone faces away from Avenue des Carrieres, onto the small unassuming Chemin Ledoux, which runs close to the eastern wall of the cemetery. Few people pass this way. Fewer tourists make it over this far from the spacious avenues. One can only guess at how few English readers have discovered Vestatia, especially considering that the view of her headstone is nearly covered by an overgrown boxwood. I was reminded of how fortunate we were to be traveling to Paris at a time when our health was not such an uncertain thing. At least here in these pages, in this brief space, Vestatia Pennotti, née Foster, has not been completely forgotten.

Never having found LaLaurie's temporary crypt, we continued to wander the paths of the dead, completely taken by this beautiful locale. We were in no hurry to leave.

Back under the viaduct, we began to ascend the southeastern side of the cemetery. This led to the second gate in the walls, which opened on the north end of the viaduct, level with the street. As we headed in that direction, a couple met us on the aforementioned stairs.

"Do you speak English?" asked the man. He was slim, with a head full of silver hair, and moved as if he were still in his twenties though he had to be close to fifty.

"Yes," Jennifer answered.

"Do you know where the exit is?"

That's a pretty good icebreaker to ask in a cemetery. And a practical question in that multi-leveled labyrinth.

"Back that way," I pointed, down toward the viaduct, "on the far side. But there's a gate up this way, too. That's where we were headed. I'm not sure if it's unlocked, but I don't see why it should be."

With that feeling of ease in finding someone who speaks your language, we exchanged the usual information.

"We're from California," they said. "We've been here a few days. This is really beautiful."

We replied in kind. I wasn't surprised to learn they were from California. The man certainly had that energetic health-maniac aura which led me to believe it might be wearisome to spend extensive time with him. But this also meant he was chatty and pleasant as he hurried toward the gate.

Nearing the exit—a massive iron gate that had been painted green—we could see it was closed. The energetic Californian suddenly dashed ahead. He grabbed a handle and pulled, pushed, and pulled again. The gate was locked.

To the left he spotted the door of a small gatehouse in the stone wall. He eagerly crossed and yanked open the door to peer inside. He reappeared and gave a little wave.

"It's a bathroom!" he piped excitedly, and leapt inside, snicking shut the door behind him.

That explained his nervous energy.

We bid his wife adieu and retraced our steps to the main entrance. My last triumph at Montmartre being the video capture of a black cat, who did not look happy to have been caught on camera. Perhaps he was a ghost who was not supposed to be prowling so early in the day.

We spent the rest of the afternoon climbing back to the top of Montmartre, simply as a path to our next destination, which was at the bottom of Rue de Steinkerque, where we had emerged from the métro on that first full day a week before. Jennifer had seen a duffel bag at one of the tents there with the Paris Métro map printed on it; she had not bought it, guessing that it would be available all over Paris. We'd been looking for another like it all week. She was determined to go back for it.

From Montmartre cemetery, we could have simply walked along Rue des Abbesses, which skirts Montmartre hill, and this would have saved our calves a great deal of work. However, we found a more scenic path up Rue Lepic which led us to a little square called Place Marcel Aymé. This was a wonderful surprise. I'd read Marcel Aymé's excellent short story *The Man who Walks through Walls* just before the trip, and had known about the statue that depicts his hero stuck halfway in a wall. I had no intention of looking for it during the trip and was delighted that we found it anyway.

Back up by Sacré Cœur, we stopped for coffee and pastries, then climbed down Rue Foyatier, the stairs that run beside the Funicular train. Amongst the souvenir shops and tents of Montmartre, Jennifer was thrilled to find her bag still available and we brought it home with us on the métro.

It had been a long day of walking, and we were happy to spend the remainder of the evening at rest. But we couldn't help laughing at how the day had begun.

It had not begun at Montmartre cemetery. It had begun on Rue de Rivoli where we had eaten lunch. A lunch that we won't soon forget.

It went like this:

Looking for a place to eat lunch, I talked Jennifer into trying out the bistro I'd found on Rue Saint-Antoine. And so we rode the bus to the Marais and I introduced Jennifer to l'Éléphant du Nil.

She was easily charmed by the intimate atmosphere. The host, a slick young man, spoke English easily, and seated us near the back, within arm's reach of the kitchen. A Dutch door allowed us to see a real French chef at work.

Out front, the chalkboard menu had caught Jennifer's attention. She'd seen *andouillette* as an entrée, which made her think of New Orleans. We love andouille sausage with our red beans and rice. It reminded her of a home town favorite, so Jennifer ordered the andouillette with vegetables while I stuck with the more conservative *beoff et carrot* entrée.

This was really our first French meal, and we were looking forward to it. I was facing the kitchen so I could watch the lady prepare the meals. She was a fascinating character, with a face that would have set her up in Hollywood—large, weary features with eyes that never missed a detail. If Hollywood had been in charge, they would have added a long cigarette to her lips to complete the stereotype, regardless of the recent indoor smoking ban.

When the plates were delivered to our table, Jennifer eyed the large piece of sausage on her plate and wondered aloud how unusual it was that she'd ordered sausage. She rarely eats red meat. Shrugging her shoulders, she decided not to worry about her diet. She was in Paris. She was going to enjoy it.

She took one bite and I knew something was wrong.

"How is it?" I asked with a positive inflection thrown in to encourage a similar response.

"Well, it's a little strong." She ate the vegetables, and made no further move to eat the sausage.

"Let me try it," I bravely suggested. I'm not big on sausage either, but I wouldn't mind eating it and I'd let her have my roast beef, which was excellent.

"I doubt you'll like it," she said as I speared a bite.

At this point I'd like to say that I tasted it, and even though I didn't like it I went ahead and said I did so that I could save the day for her. Instead, I told her she was right, it was too strong. I wanted to say it tasted like it smelled—and it smelled like an old outhouse.

I offered her some of my roast beef, but she declined, and just ate her vegetables. I offered to send the sausage back but she wouldn't hear of it. So we ate, and when the waitress removed the plates, she did not say a word about the sausage.

From where I was sitting, I could see the plate as it was placed on the lip of the Dutch door. The chef grabbed the plates (she was the dishwasher as well as the cook, the kitchen was so small), looked down at the uneaten sausage, then up at the waitress with a look that clearly said *what's wrong with my sausage?* The waitress shrugged; I could not hear her response.

The chef dropped the contents of the plate into a trashcan and turned away. I assumed that was the end of the andouillette storyline. We ordered crème brûlée, which I'd been bragging about since I'd had it there two days before. I kept an eye on the cook because I knew little about crème brûlée and wanted to learn a little something about it.

After prepping the custard, she poured the caramel on it, then pulled out a handheld blowtorch. That was pretty cool. Then I watched as she proceeded to burn the living hell out it. Flames shot up as if the Tuileries Palace had been rebuilt so the unhappy people of Paris could burn it to the ground again. I kept thinking, wow, I had no idea that's how they made crème brûlée!

When this tasty treat arrived at the table, I assured Jennifer she was going to love it. She tried a bite and nodded. Yes, she agreed, it's pretty good.

I grabbed the spoon I'd used to stir my cappuccino and stole a bite. The caramel crunch on top was much crunchier than the first one I'd had. It also tasted a lot like charcoal.

"Well, that's not quite what it tasted like the other day." Point of fact, it tasted like it had been forged in the first or second circle of Dante's Inferno.

We decided our imagination was playing tricks on us. What were the odds the chef would actually burn our crème brûlée in reprisal for disrespecting her andouillette sausage? We made light-hearted conversation with the waitress a little to try and smooth things over, then decided it was time to get going.

At the bar, I gave my credit card to the host, the slick young man who had seated us. He did not hesitate to ask about the meal.

"Your wife," he said in that smooth French accent, "she did not like the food?"

"It was a little strong for her," I said tactfully.

"In France, we say *yes* or we say *no*. That's all." He smiled as he said this, as if he were talking to a little child.

I'm proud to say that I refrained from replying with the

obvious comment. But if I had not refrained, I'd have said something along these lines:

"Well, in America, when a restaurant's food smells like an outhouse, we're polite enough not to say it."

There are other, more crass ways of saying this, but I refrained from these as well.

We had a good laugh about it as we stepped across Rue Saint-Antoine and spotted a Starbucks on Rue de Rivoli. By this time we'd abandoned all pretense of trying to stay away from that commercialized coffeehouse. Instead, we hurried to its door, happy to get as big a cup of coffee as they would sell.

It wasn't until we were back home that we discovered our mistake with the andouillette. There is a world of difference between it and the andouille we eat in Louisiana. What we did not know is that andouillette is the French word for what we call chitlins. And as my co-workers assured me after hearing our story, chitlins are pig intestines, and they always smell like an old outhouse.

I'd never had chitlins before, and I never will again.

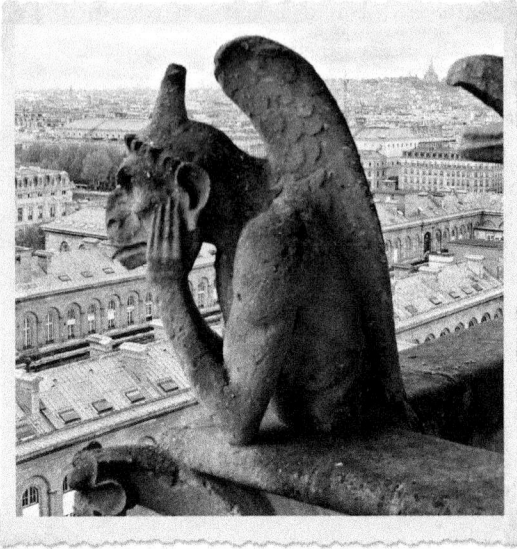

Chapter Eleven: Shakespeare and Notre Dame

Our remaining days were dwindling. We could feel the trip drawing to a close. Our emotions seemed to alternate between the joy that our trip had generated and the claustrophobic realization that we were running out of time to see everything we'd hoped to see.

Into this mix we had to add the state of our health. We were wearing down. The cold, wet weather was a problem for Jennifer, compounding chronic bronchial battles she fought every year. She also could not walk as much as I could. She'd had a childhood back injury that always nagged her when she was tired. Our walking tours had taken a toll.

To put it simply: we were tired. We were well aware that we should have taken our days of rest more seriously. But that was nearly impossible given the possibilities that surrounded us.

But there was still so much to see.

We settled on a compromise of sorts and decided to take off half a day. Versailles was the last big day we had planned, and we decided to give it a go the next day, a Thursday. But until then, we would rest, with just one little trip around lunchtime.

We had yet to tour Notre Dame Cathedral. So a little before lunch, we rode the métro to the Saint-Michel station, then cut through Rue de la Huchette as rain began to fall once more. Instead of aiming directly for the cathedral, we ducked out of the rain and into Shakespeare and Company, an English-language bookstore facing the cathedral near Square René Viviani.

Shakespeare and Company had been the name of a small bookstore on Rue de l'Odéon that operated from 1922 until the end of 1941 during the Nazi Occupation. That store was run by Sylvia Beach, a legend in the field of literature; not for her writing but for her support of writers like Ernest Hemingway and James Joyce. In fact, when Joyce could not find a publisher for his overblown *Ulysses*, Ms. Beach agreed to publish it, despite the fact that she had no publishing experience whatsoever. This explains that great mystery of the ages—how in the world did Joyce get *Ulysses* published? It still does not really explain why.

Her bookstore became a focal point for the Lost Generation, as the young group of writers (Hemingway, Fitzgerald, Eliot, and many other post-war expatriates) found Shakespeare and Company to be a linchpin for their friendships and interaction.

In *A Moveable Feast*, Hemingway credits Beach with introducing him to Scott Fitzgerald, as well as lending him as many books as he could read. Through her he became familiar with the works of Turgenev, Tolstoy, and so many other great writers from world literature.

After the war, Beach did not reopen her shop. But in

1951, George Whitman opened a bookshop by the name of *Le Mistral*. This was also an English-language shop, and it too became a hub for authors in the city. This time, the Beat Generation took advantage of Whitman's generosity.

In tribute to Beach after her death in 1964, he changed the name to Shakespeare and Company. The shop faces Notre Dame, and is in a prime location for tourists and authors alike to darken its doors. They are also widely known for providing free lodging for writers, as they have beds available in rooms above the store.

We spent an hour in the store, doing our best not to drip on the old wooden floors, though the drips coming down from the ceiling provided more water than our own rain-soaked coats and umbrellas. Books were crammed into shelves wherever we looked. We could have spent a full day perusing those titles.

While in the city, you might consider catching a poetry reading at Shakespeare and Company. You can find the same at a similar Anglo-English bookstore in the Saint-Germain district: the Village Voice, on Rue Princesse.

Upstairs there is a worn but intimate set of rooms with old couches and chairs where you are welcome to sit and read for as long as you like. Jennifer found a Baudelaire book that she had never previously seen and was thrilled to be able to get off her feet and lose herself for a time in his book.

Eventually, we bade farewell to the old bookshop and after picking through a few bouquinistes' offerings, we approached Notre Dame. Rain fell just enough to supply the gargoyles on the north side with a steady drool.

We queued up to climb the towers. Jennifer suffers from vertigo and acrophobia, but she wanted to see Paris from up high, and so we began to ascend the stone staircase that wound around the core of the north tower. (One could say I have arachnophobia, but it isn't true. There is nothing irrational about my fear of spiders.)

The stair—the center of each step noticeably worn down by millions of visitors as if they were made of soft plastic, not ancient stone—spiraled quickly upwards. Small view ports, shaped like arrow slits, allowed us to see how quickly we were progressing. Unfortunately, this triggered Jennifer's vertigo and she was forced to go back and wait for me in the sanctuary.

I had not climbed the Eiffel Tower, but I did want to see the Gallery of Chimeras between Notre Dame's towers, so I went on alone. It was still a bit rainy, but it stopped enough to enable me to pull out the camera. Though wind whipped through the towers, I ignored the cold and took in the view, enjoying the artistic works that surrounded me.

It was something of a let-down to discover that the railings had all been topped with safety fencing like that found in a science fiction movie. These cable-and-steel barriers might have been safe, but the visual effect was disappointing all the same. We are slaves to safety, it seems, going so far as to allow it to mar the beauty of something as graceful as the stone parapets of Notre Dame.

Well, at least the wind did not stand a chance at throwing

me off the ledge. I would hate to think that Jennifer and the family back home thought I died re-enacting Hugo's monumental climax.

For anyone unsure whether or not to climb the several hundred feet of steps to reach the top, let me assure you it is worth the effort. There is much to see.

Right off the bat, as soon as you exit the staircase and step out onto the parapet, you get a close up view of *Le Stryge*, that pouting, peculiar imp who is the iconic image of a Notre Dame grotesque. Of course, he is more commonly called a gargoyle, but there is a difference; gargoyles are simply rain gutter spouts, while grotesques are three-dimensional bogeymen added to churches and castles for purely speculative purposes.

After taking a picture of this rascal, and poking a little fun at him, turn to your left and take a look at his field of vision. This little monster has the best view of Paris. For over one hundred and thirty years, *Le Stryge* has been staring out over the Left Bank to the Champ de Mars. This means that he was able to see the construction of the Eiffel Tower, and has been staring at it ever since. (Which also means he saw Grace Jones parachute off the side of it to escape James Bond—or at least he saw a stuntman pull off that spectacular stunt. I would suspect he did not see Superman shove the elevator containing a nuclear bomb through the top of it and into space since that was probably just a model.)

In fact, you can see nearly every prominent site in Paris from those towers. The cathedral is centrally located. A plaque in the center of the square outside the western portals actually marks the city's geographical center. This sort of planning is usually more akin to British methods, which reminds me of an odd point. As you look over Paris, realize that since it was declared an open city during the Second World War, and therefore not defended by the French, Paris saw far less damage than London did due to the relentless

German Blitz, though I am sure the emotional scars left by the Nazi Occupation were far deeper for the Parisians.

But on that day as I surveyed the city, the only storm clouds I could see were filled with tears of rain, not rage or sorrow. (It is a curious fact that the French word for rain is *pluie*, which is also their word for *crying*. When it is raining in Paris, the sky weeps.)

Le Stryge is not the only character you'll meet here. The Gallery of Chimeras is populated with an curious menagerie: an elephant, hounds, an old man who resembles a fairy-tale wizard, and other forms eroded beyond recognition. After taking as much time as possible to film and photograph this wonderful platform, I climbed higher still to the top of the southern bell tower, then wound my way down the south tower and arrived back in the square to meet Jennifer.

When you consider that neither one of us had a cell phone, it was inevitable that we should eventually lose each other. And after thoroughly searching the square, I began to worry that this had indeed happened. So the first time I entered the cathedral nave, it was only to search for my wife.

The square was busy, but not overly crowded. The interior of the cathedral was crazy.

I had little-to-no chance of spotting Jennifer. The nave is dark, fed only by the natural light sifting through the high, stained-glass windows and the soft glow of electric chandeliers, dimmed to simulate candlelight.

I'm not the type to panic. But I can worry a bit when it comes to missing family members. This comes from years of road trips with five children. A few bad moments at the Astrodome in Houston and a shopping mall in New Orleans have demonstrated how desperate I can become.

I tried not to think about the fact that Jennifer might not know how to get back to the apartment. Or how she might not have the digital code written down that she would need to get through the main door on the street. (She not only had the code, but she had the address, and the extra door key, all of which I'd made sure before we began exploring the week before, but as I said, I tend to worry a bit when things get strange.)

After assuring myself she was not in the cathedral (which was impossible to do, though I convinced myself of the fact anyway), I pushed my way past the nuns soliciting donations at the door and came back out into the square. Still no Jennifer. I looked up at all those strange and wonderful statues over the portal and wondered if any of them had seen her. If they had, they weren't about to open their mouths or lift a finger to help. If you ask me, they were no help at all.

Of course, not long after that, Jennifer appeared at my side, her eyes red with tears as she fought to catch her breath. Had she missed me? Had she feared she'd never see me again? Were those tears of joy that had poured forth when she finally saw me again?

Hardly. She'd been in the nave, sitting in a chair, emotionally enthralled by Notre Dame. Now reunited, we reentered the cathedral properly. And please remember, as the sign says, remove your hats, no flash photography, no tripods, no cell phones, no hamburgers and shakes, and no electric razors (or no refrigerators with open doors, or no laser guns...well, I couldn't figure out that last icon on the sign).

I might not make friends with my observations on Notre Dame's interior. As much as I loved the exterior as an example of Gothic art, I have to admit that the scene inside was just a bit too circus-like to allow me to feel anything more than admiration for the art. It felt devoid of any spirituality. This may only be due to the heavy and unavoidable presence of tourists (of which we were a part), but it really did seem just a bit too much like a carnival. Sacré Cœur did not feel the same, and neither did Saint-Germain-des-Prés or Saint-Sulpice.

However, this environment may have been impossible to prevent. Notre Dame is the most visited site in all of Paris.

Again, if you were seeking an in-depth, historical account of the cathedral or a complete breakdown of its architectural design, I hope you won't be upset not to find it here. Suffice to say that Notre Dame is exceptional, should be seen in person if at all possible, and as many pictures as you have seen of it, you will still be surprised by it in person.

One little detail that I cannot pass up is on the left portal at the entrance. This portal, the Portal of the Virgin, has a number of life-sized statues. Included in them are the representations of Saint Geneviéve and Saint Denis, two of the three patron saints of Paris. (The third being Saint Marcel.) Saint Denis is depicted with his head held in his hands. His legend tells of his martyrdom at the hands of the pagan rulers over Paris in 250 AD. The traditional tale is that Denis picked up his head and carried it for ten miles, sharing the gospel as he traveled before finally falling dead. Of particular interest are the two ministering angels at his side, comforting him.

Most of these statues are reproductions from the mid-1800s restoration which was overseen by Eugéne Viollet-Le-Duc, including the work on the Gallery of Chimeras. The cathedral took heavy damage during the Revolution, when the people, tired of mistreatment by the church, took out their anger on many of the churches and the works of art within them. One can understand frustration with such treatment, but I could never understand taking out your frustrations on such wonderful works of art.

We chose to eat at another Italian restaurant for lunch at the corners of Rues Dante, Galande and du Fouarre. I discovered it during my night walk and knew Jennifer would love it. From outside you could see the Italian movie poster for *Vacanze Romaine*—Audrey Hepburn's debut film, *Roman Holiday*. La Solita Tavirna Italiana was a great place to relax.

We ate pasta, drank wine, and laughed with the waitress over the street sign that stared at us from across Rue Galande.

A red slash over an adult holding the hand of a child meant something important, we were sure of it. But what it meant was impossible to say. Were they saying that you shouldn't be holding your child's hand? No taking children? The waitress, a very hip, lively girl who did not fit the usual images of Paris café servers, agreed that it was odd, adding that it had been put up just a few days before. No one at the restaurant could figure out what it was supposed to be prohibiting.

I personally think it meant tall men should not be dating short women.

After stopping for torte normande at a nearby patisserie, we went straight home in order to be rested for the next day, when we would stand in the palace of the Sun King.

Journal Entry: April 27, morning

The variety of shapes I can see from the balcony makes for a puzzle-like scene. The little clay cylinder chimneys, tin rectangles that make up the roofs, square windows, long curving drain pipes, even a trapezoidal roof over a stairwell. There is an arc with spikes radiating out of it to keep prowlers from opening the windows in the stairwell (and climbing out onto the balcony opposite ours.) Our own spiked defense is not as well formed as an arc—too narrow, but the idea is the same.

There is a sphere on the balcony up and across from me. It is a bush, clipped just so. An old TV antennae sticks out from the roof just above it. I don't know how to describe its shape—though it looks like something from an old sci-fi movie. There are two little ship lantern lights on the balcony with the bush. They are rectangles with rounded corners, and cages over the light covers. A fat pigeon has landed on a similarly shaped fat chimney pot.

Roof lines slant at steep angles. And not steep angles. There are a few shingled roofs, where you can see checked patterns with varying degrees of darkened stains running down the roof. One roof is rounded, the slate gray metal sloping from rooftop to wall in a matter of ten or twelve feet.

Across the lower parts of the windows run cast iron railings that have fancy, delicate designs.

Below me, some sixty feet below, is the worn, muddy, checkerboard pattern of the courtyard cobblestone. A metal, spiral drain is stuck off to one side of the checkerboard.

Five or six rooftops over, white smoke streams from a cream-colored chimney and dissipates into a dishwater morning sky.

Chapter Twelve: The Palace of the Sun King

Much like the Eiffel Tower, Paris is inextricably linked to that extraordinary citadel Versailles, from whence the extravagant, astounding and ultimately destructive Louis the XIV, Louis the XV, and Louis the XVI ruled. The extravagance was designed to astound. Though astounding, it eventually infuriated, leading to the destruction of those who had designed it.

And like the Eiffel Tower, I had not rated Versailles very high on my list of things to see. Sure, it looked impressive. And of course we would make sure we saw it before leaving. But I really paid it little mind during our planning.

What little I knew of it I'd learned from an old picture guidebook that had been published back in 1984, which Jennifer had picked up at the local Goodwill store a few years ago. It had most likely been bought at Versailles by a tourist who had brought it home and never looked at it again.

The most interesting thing I'd seen in the book was a little feature on Marie Antoinette's Hamlet, which I'd never heard of before picking through the book. It seemed like an odd little place, and something that might make the trip out to Versailles worthwhile.

You see, I've never been much of a royalty buff. Kings and queens had never impressed me. Their history always seemed dull. If they were interesting at all, it was more in a soap opera style that was usually just difficult to follow. Who married whom? And who was messing around with whom? Who was his father? Who was her son? Who succeeded whom? Who cares?

It didn't help that all those kings and queens used new names once they were crowned, and the names were often repeats of kings before them, though not always the names of their fathers. This just made it harder to remember who was who. It was like trying to learn a list of Popes. Don't even try.

So we showed enough respect to Versailles to set aside a full day for it, though this may have had more to do with the fact that I knew it would take a little time to get out there and there was nothing else near it for us to see. There was not going to be a package deal on that day. Just Versailles. Well, we would just have to make the best of it.

As usual, travel plans dominated my preparations for the day. I'd read of several different ways to travel there from our apartment on the Left Bank. There is no métro that reaches all the way to Versailles. And even if it did, it would be outside the first three zones, and so would require a different ticket than the ones we were buying.

There were no buses that ran to Versailles either.

The train that ran to Versailles was an RER. There were two of these we could take. We either needed to hop a ride south to Gare Montparnasse, or we could head in the other direction and catch one at Saint-Michel Station. I mentally flipped a Euro and we headed for Saint-Michel and the RER-C train.

These large, double-decked trains are pretty impressive. We climbed aboard an empty train, took a seat on the top deck, and settled in for what was going to be about a fifteen or twenty minute ride. I immediately pulled out my Kindle and went back to Hemingway.

Hemingway spends a great deal of his time in *A Moveable Feast* poking fun at his friends Ford Maddox Ford and Scott Fitzgerald, just to name a few. Hemingway himself had warned the reader that his book could be taken as fiction, since he was describing events from memory that had occurred more than thirty or forty years in the past. I suppose this was Papa's way of telling us he was having a little fun with some of the stories. I know I was having fun with them.

There's a particularly hilarious story where Hemingway says Fitzgerald met him at a café and proceeded to express his concerns about his manhood, saying that he feared he was too small. Hemingway says "step into my office," and they go into the café's restroom to "have a look." He assures Fitzgerald he has nothing to worry about. Fitzgerald says "are you sure?" Hemingway's response is priceless. He essentially says "haven't you been to the Louvre? Haven't you seen all these naked paintings and statues of men? You look just the same!" This conversation goes on for some time, and it had me in stitches.

By now you are wondering why I'm telling you all of this. Don't worry, there's a point to it. And it has nothing to do with how big or little anything is.

I'd been keeping an eye on our stations as the train lumbered along. It stopped by the Eiffel Tower, passed over the Bir-Hakim bridge, and worked its way out of the city. In truth, I had not been keeping my good eye on the stations. It was more of a very relaxed eye.

When I finally did pay attention to where we were, we were nowhere we were supposed to be. The pretty fields with cows sort of suggested that we had taken something of a funny turn. Setting Hemingway aside, I left my seat and climbed down the stairs to the exits where a skeleton map displayed the stations.

I studied it enough to realize we were a bit off course. In fact, after crosschecking the station map with an actual roadmap, I was alarmed to see that we were heading due north, and Versailles was due south of us. And the slow, lumbering RER was picking up speed.

Sometimes you need to be patient and see what is going to happen next. At other times, you need to bail out of whatever situation you are in and undo what you did.

And that was the thing to do.

So we grabbed our coats and bags, stood by the stainless steel doors and waited for them to slide open at the next stop. By the time it did, we were about thirty minutes outside the city in the wrong direction. We hopped off, climbed the steps to cross the tracks on the pedestrian bridge, climbed back down the other steps and then had to wait for the next train. We retraced our route back to the Eiffel Tower where we caught the proper train after a dash through the station.

We'd wasted nearly an hour on a trip I hadn't even been excited to make. It was not shaping up to be a great day. And when I considered the grey clouds on the horizon, on a day that the weather man had promised to be mostly sunny, I started to wish we'd stayed back in the Latin Quarter.

To her credit, Jennifer was still excited about our day-trip. She'd been having a good time on the train, taking pictures through the windows at the passing French scenery.

I was beginning to believe we should have planned a ten-day trip instead of a two-week trip. I was ready to get Versailles over with.

We finally arrived. The RER train ended at this station. The palace is the sole purpose of this line. This train, unlike the wrong train we had taken that morning, was full of tourists. We poured off the train and out into the streets of this little suburb of Paris that did not look much different from the suburbs of Philadelphia.

The street was lined with McDonald's, Starbucks, and souvenir shops, of course. I had mapped the short walk to the Palace that morning using satellite images. This was unnecessary since the whole flood of tourists kept moving together in one direction as if we knew where we were going.

We bought tickets in a little shop near the palace stables, and proceeded down the avenue. It was only then that we finally caught a glimpse of Versailles.

The Avenue de Paris ends at what is the Royal Parade Ground, which looks like a huge, empty parking lot. In fact, that's exactly what it is on the left—a parking lot. But the Parade Ground leads to a great iron gate, painted green and gold, that leads into the Royal Courtyard. Behind all of this is the palace, with large, bulky wings coming at you on both sides, a prominent chapel to the right, and two classical Greek structures that add to a cluttered look from this perspective.

Not to criticize the builders of Versailles. This was just my initial view of it, under all of those dark, rolling clouds, after our wrong-way trip on the RER.

This appeared to be the high point of my morning, since it was right after we walked through the gate that we discovered a massive line of tourists snaking its way through the Royal Courtyard.

There's something you must know about French lines at major sites like this. Usually, back home, you queue up in a line guided by ropes connected to stanchions and everybody is forced to snake back and forth in an orderly fashion. Each turn of the snake is the same length, and everybody walks down this lane until they make a hairpin turn at the end so they can do it all over again. Back and forth, back and forth, the lines stay the same length because those in the line must follow the guide ropes.

In France, with a few exceptions, there were no guide ropes. So, here's what happens to the line:

A few soft-spoken guides show up and help everyone get into a serpentine line. All the lines are the same length, the hairpin turns are identical and so the line progresses.

However, as people walk this line, then turn to walk in the opposite direction, someone behind decides not to walk all the way. The person ahead of them is passing now, so why not just spin and follow? It makes sense, and saves a few steps. Other clever people do this. Then a bunch of clever people do this.

Soon, the lines have compressed, they are no longer the same length, many of them do not have anything that could be called *length*, and the line appears to grow shorter, which makes everyone eager for it to grow even shorter. Eventually, the lines collapse and no one knows where they ought to be, except everyone is absolutely sure the guy in front has no business being in front and should be tossed summarily from the line.

Occasionally a guide, made of one part *ennui* and one part *bonhomie*, comes and reshapes the lines, but then shows little concern in confirming that the lines remain in the shape of traditional lines.

Our line ran on the right side of the Royal Courtyard, and looked like it would stretch two miles if the soft-spoken guide had returned, become fed-up with all the line compression, and stretched the line straight with nary a bend or turn. I couldn't remember if I was in line for Versailles or if I was in line for my driver's license renewal.

The clouds continued to roll over us, wind whipped

through the courtyard, and people pushed and lolly-gagged and generally did not add charm to my day. I kept thinking of that hour wasted on the train. It was hard to get excited about standing in a massive line at the gates of a palace.

As bad as all of that seemed, the rain did not fall, the line moved along well enough, and we were able to clear through security in about an hour.

And then we stepped out from the strange, futuristic security tunnel into the Marble Courtyard and the sun came out from behind the clouds.

Everything shone with gold along the walls of the courtyard, terminating at the far end with eight pink marble columns supporting the balcony of the king.

From the far end, back at the Avenue de Paris, it all looked like a Hollywood backlot. Some of the wings seemed out of place, the whole appearance, forced. But there, within that smaller courtyard, the design was superb. We knew we were on the doorstep of a monarch.

The day was improving.

What followed was a walk through history, as we passed statues within the chateau walls—a who's who of French History. We took a peek inside the Royal Chapel. And yes, for all of you conspiracy nuts, you can see what looks like the illuminati symbol in the center of the gold décor directly over the altar. However, a closer look will reveal Hebrew letters, instead of the all-seeing eye, in the center of the pyramid, which, if I had to guess, spell out Yahweh, or something equivalent to it.

Upstairs, we found statues of kings and queens and even a young lady by the name of *Jeanne d'Arc*.

As we walked through the Hercules room, I noticed a young Asian lady trying to photograph herself in front of a massive painting. (Yet another epic Veronese, *Christ's meal in the house of Simon the Pharisee.*) I offered to take the picture for her. It seemed sad to think she was seeing such wonders alone, her only photographic memories in which she appeared taken at arm's-length. I backed up, to frame her with as much of the majestic scene as possible.

We filed through many more rooms of the chateau (an inadequate name, I thought, for such a glorious residence, as if one could walk through the Biltmore Mansion and call it a cottage), with very little to say beyond *wow* and *that's amazing*. We were, after all, seeing the State Apartment, where the king would receive members of State. Here you find the Venus, Diana, and Mars drawing-rooms, all of which look out over the North Parterre. This was our first glimpse of the gardens. By now the sun was shining brightly, the clouds had pulled back, and the grounds looked like nothing we'd ever seen.

Though the rooms were crowded, the grandeur of the surroundings kept everyone hushed and well-behaved. One can disrespect something pretentious. But when one sees the real thing—the home of the Sun King—it is easy to recognize that this is not an attempt to impress. This is, simply, impressive on a scale that has rarely been matched.

Though no one was pushing us, we were drawn from one beautiful room to the next faster than we wanted. I knew we were missing details as we went; the walls, the ceilings, everything was covered in extraordinary paintings. I imagine it would be possible to spend hours in each room, studying and appreciating each and every scene painted there. We did not linger, though, knowing that there was more to come.

The last of the rooms on that side is the War Room. Again, we could hardly take in the detail. Stepping through its entrance, you come face to face with a sculpted captive, who has been chained and holds up the great bas-relief of Louis the XIV. His somber eyes, seen where his head is pressed against the wall, are remarkable and linger in my mind, even today.

Yet it is almost impossible to linger in the War Room,

because from there it is possible to see into the Hall of Mirrors, and this room demands full attention.

This grand room, once simply an open terrace linking the two sides of the chateau and the king's chambers, was designed to use the last light of the day to fill it with golden light. Mirrors opposite the seventeen arched windows create this effect. Bronze-gilding throughout the room adds to the golden color. The entire ceiling contains paintings that tell the story of Louis the XIV.

For history buffs, it is worth noting that it was in the Hall of Mirrors that the Treaty of Versailles was signed. By all accounts, the room was in great disrepair then, and though an attempt was made to restore it after World War II, it was never really done right until just a few years ago. Had we come ten years sooner we would never have seen it so wonderfully restored.

At this point, I don't know if the grandeur became too much, or the tourists became tired and hungry, but their behavior quickly changed. We had to be careful so as not to be run over by the more agitated crowd. Perhaps we were all eager to get back outside; the view from the Hall of Mirrors over the gardens, as they slope down to the Green Carpet and the Apollo Canal, looked immaculate in the noon sun.

We toured the king's bedchambers, and then came back through the Hall of Mirrors, ending up in the queen's side of the chateau.

Here, I was reminded of the stories of Marie Antoinette. The beauty of the palace had truly become ostentatious. A few rooms like the State Apartments were fun to see, knowing that it was a way to awe visitors. But here, in the private chambers, it felt too thick, pointless.

When one considers the living conditions of the average Frenchman in the 18th century, this kind of lifestyle is hard to defend. Here, one can imagine how easy it would be to lose touch with reality. As the revolutionists stormed the palace, and Marie Antoinette fled to the King's chamber through the small door we could see in the back of her room, it was sobering to think of her fear, yet more sobering to think of the anger the throng experienced forcing its way into such opulent accommodations.

As our modern horde—wearing Bart Simpson t-shirts, blue jeans, and waving iPhones everywhere—began to push, creating a manic atmosphere, I began to side with the Royals. The idea of this mob tramping through such beauty seemed sacrilegious.

After finding and examining David's copy of his *Coronation of Napoleon*, we'd had enough. We wanted to get out on the grounds, get some fresh air, and find coffee. It was only after we'd returned to the United States that I remembered I'd wanted to see the Hall of Battles, only a few steps away from where we descended the Queen's Staircase.

It was a fitting end to our tour of the chateau, since the Parisian mob had used these steps to invade the palace, thus bringing an end to the halcyon days of the royal family.

Passing through the arches that connect the chateau to its south wing, we were thrilled to be out in the gardens of Versailles. From there we could look over the South Parterre, a highly structured flower garden full of spring flowers.

What we could not see, from our vantage point at ground level, was that beyond the edge of the parterre lay the famous Lake of the Swiss Guards, and under us was the Orangery, a large, buried gallery that houses 2,000 orange trees, one thousand oleander trees, and numerous pomegranate trees and other rare trees, during the winter months. The trees are then brought outside when the weather becomes warm enough.

On either side of the Orangery Parterre, great staircases slope down to the lake. It astounds me that we never saw any of this. For all we knew, beyond the garden was a valley, which we could not see for the near line of the garden's horizon. I keep kicking myself that we did not walk over to the edge of it.

Instead of discovering this jewel, we walked out to the Water Parterre, directly below the windows of the Hall of Mirrors overlooking the Green Carpet and the Apollo Canal. As views go, this was a pretty good substitute for the missed Orangery Parterre.

Looking out from that expanse, you can begin to gain a sense of how large the Versailles gardens really are. There are over 2,000 acres, and they've all been manicured to perfection. It made me feel lazy when I thought of my own little yard.

It was no surprise we were growing hungry. We had not eaten since we'd left the apartment. It was now well past one in the afternoon. The map promised that we would find all sorts of little eating establishments throughout the park but we were having trouble finding them. Does this surprise anyone? We couldn't see a massive tree warehouse or its companion lake when we were standing right on top of it—literally. Perhaps the food court was under the garden.

Passing by the impressive yet non-flowing Fountain of Latona, we headed off into the gardens. To our dismay, rain began to fall at the same time. And it was evident we had quite a ways to walk before finding any shelter. So instead of walking along the main passage, I guided us into a set of paths that intersected some small, manicured woods. This area was called the North Quincunx, which we were unaware of at the time. It wasn't a true maze—it was not designed to confuse and keep trespassers lost within its paths—but its angled paths left us confused as we tried deciphering the map under our umbrellas.

What we did not realize (again, remember, I'd studied very little about Versailles, which was not a very good move on my part) was that within this green labyrinth were many different fountains and grottos that would have been delightful to seek out. Instead, we pushed through, wondering how we could end up at the point on the map that had the little fork and spoon icons.

The sound of playful children drew us into a spacious avenue where we saw many young children playing soccer under the trees. Their laughter buoyed us along as we passed on our way to the easily recognizable Fountain of Apollo.

Tired, hungry, and relieved the rain had stopped, we arrived at the Grand Canal where we found an elegant restaurant, Café la Flotille. We were thrilled to rest and refuel. *Croque Monsieur* and *pommes frites* did the trick for me. Jennifer had her onion soup, with a few *pommes frites* of her own.

This was one of the few times we experienced the stereotypical rude, French waiter. Though I am inclined to say that it was only a matter of time, I think the best explanation lies in the fact that this was a high-traffic tourist zone, and either the waiter had simply developed his rude behavior as a defense against the rudeness of tourists, or maybe he put on a show for the tourists. It's possible that the answer is simpler than that. Maybe he just happens to be a jerk in his normal life and it spills over into his job. Hey, it happens in the States, why not at Versailles?

Nevertheless, we felt much better as we left the café in search of Marie Antoinette's hamlet.

At the risk of repeating myself, I want to add how amazing it was to discover the vastness of Versailles. Along the walk toward the hamlet, one has the option to visit the Grand Trianon, which happens to be a mid-sized palace added around 1700. Because if you had the Palace of Versailles, you would need another one to break up the monotony, right? Well, actually, no. You'd need two more palaces. So after you'd finished perfecting the first Trianon, you would want to go ahead and build the Small Trianon in 1750. I guess.

Then, after giving the small one to your wife, you'd let her do whatever she wanted to decorate it and the grounds around it. And when she decided she wanted her own village, you'd tell the artisans to build her one.

The grounds around the Small Trianon, known as the Queen's Domain, are a peaceful area with paths that crisscross through trees, leading to and from the domed, Greek Temple of Love. There are many benches throughout this walk, where

you can sit down and enjoy the peace and quiet. It was a nice change of pace.

When we finally found the hamlet, it was just as advertised. It reminded me of Disneyland. As if someone had wanted to build a fairytale land, which is what happened. Marie Antoinette wanted a village built that would celebrate the simplicity of peasant life. As if she knew anything about that. Or course, her artisans fulfilled her wishes, building little stone and wooden cottages.

As we walked among them, I could see how fun it would be to play there. It was simply a life-sized dollhouse/village. The Queen actually had it peopled so that she could see it in action. Imagine a leader's wife doing this today. ("Look at the cute little workers, toiling at their jobs. How cute!")

It is said that Marie Antoinette was on the grounds of the Small Trianon when she received the news of the approaching revolutionaries, forcing her to rush back to the chateau on foot. (This sounds apocryphal, but it also sounds ironic, or like justice, or simply cool karma. At any rate, I don't mind passing on this legend.) However it happened, we know for certain that this woman went from the fantasy life at Versailles to the prison cell at the Conciergerie on the Île de la Cité.

After such a long day of walking and soaking in such grandeur, we were ready for home. We caught the little tram that ran from the Grand Trianon back to the Apollo Fountain. This enabled us to rest enough for the walk back up the Green Carpet to the Latona Fountain.

We knew our time in Paris was drawing to a close. We knew our stamina was running low as well. There was little assurance that we would get out again for more sightseeing. With that in mind, we stood at the Latona Fountain and decided we wanted one last picture of the two of us together. We only had a few such photographs taken. The last had been almost a week before at the Eiffel Tower.

So I watched our fellow tourists as they too trudged back from the long walk through the gardens. I had decided to abandon all pretenses; I wasn't going to offer to take someone else's picture. I just wanted to ask someone to take ours.

I had to wait a long time before I found someone who even looked pleasant enough to ask. We were grateful to find a Frenchman who spoke English well and was happy to help. He did a great job for us, and we thanked him multiple times.

We were ready to leave. Versailles had been a major surprise. We were overwhelmed and taken in by its specifically designed charm and splendor. A cynic might suggest that we were conned, a common complaint of travel writers who have even suggested this is true for all of Paris. Brilliant artists worked and poured great effort into creating a kind of faux Paris that has become the real Paris. I must reply to such suggestions with one of my own:

If it is all a con, sit back and enjoy. If this wasn't the real

France, it has become the real France—I'm fine with that.

But I don't buy their line of reasoning. It smacks of the revisionist spirit that wants to tear down traditions and beliefs solely for the sake of tearing down. I just don't see the point.

As we walked through the Water Parterre, and into the South Parterre, Jennifer confessed that this had been her favorite day yet, though she also confessed to feeling guilty about that.

I knew what she was saying. This was the luxury and arrogance that had toppled an empire. We Americans, especially, don't truck with royalty and all its trappings. Paris is full of real artwork that certainly has more value than the pompous grandiose that was Versailles. Surely we should have felt our own disdain for the accoutrements of this regal playground.

I shrugged my shoulders and pointed out the simple truth:

"Every girl wants to be a princess for a day. Why shouldn't you? You aren't the only one."

Her little girl's smile flashed at me as she realized she wasn't alone.

We were to meet a man who would put an exclamation point on my statement. He was waiting for us just outside the Royal Courtyard at the gilded gates of Versailles.

The grounds were closing for the day. We left through the arches of the south wing, briefly hit the gift shop, and ended where we started outside the gates.

Jennifer wanted me to get a few shots of her in front of those brilliantly gilded gates, the king's chambers just as brilliant in the background. Once we were finished, and as we began to cross the Royal Parade Grounds, a Buddhist monk, in his orange robe, wearing sandals over his socks on that cold day, a brand new backpack hanging on his back, approached and asked if I would take his picture. He held out his iPhone, a smile filled his child-like face.

I was happy to help. After all, I'd asked someone else the same question not long before. So I held his iPhone and asked if I should line up the shot with the gates behind him.

"No," he said in Asian-accented, well-spoken English. "With this view, please." He pointed to what is called the Gabriel Wing of the chateau.

This short wing, which runs beside the Royal Chapel, terminates with a Greek temple façade where four Corinthian columns hold up its gabled end. Across the lintel, black letters boldly declare *À Toutes Les Gloires De La France.* "To all the Glories of France."

Across the Royal Courtyard, the Old Wing is identical on its terminus. The same words are displayed for all comers. The kings of France gathered in this place, their hands held out, pointing to the palace and its works of art, proclaiming "Behold, look upon France, see the wonders of our realm!"

It was this backdrop the Buddhist monk wanted for his portrait. He almost did not get it. He had to explain to me how the iPhone worked. I'd never used one, I had it facing the wrong way. He firmly turned it around in my hand and at the same time, explained that I should tap the screen where I wanted it to focus.

He smiled broadly as I snapped the shot. He made little bows and thanked me, greatly pleased with my help. After we left him, I turned, to take a last look. He was standing before the gates, that big smile still on his face, as he paged through the pictures on his phone. Like everyone we'd seen during those weeks, not only did he want a picture of himself in front of these majestic sites, but he also had to immediately look at the picture; to be sure it was right, and also to see himself—to see himself in front of all the glories of France. To be sure he could prove that he had been a prince for a day.

Whether we were oversaturated with all the extravagance, or we were just tired and hungry after our full day on the vast grounds of Versailles, we hit the McDonald's with enthusiasm, not feeling the least bit of guilt at indulging our American tastes. Full of this good "home" cooking, we boarded the train and rode home, our heads full of the amazing visions that we found at the Palace of the Sun King.

We were now certain we'd seen the best Paris had to offer. With only a few days left, we planned to rest on our laurels and relax for a day before we began to pack and say goodbye.

All that Jennifer asked was that we take a little time during the next day to walk along the Champs-Élysées.

It didn't sound exciting to me, but by then, I should have known better.

Journal Entry: April 27, evening

I cannot stop wondering about the Buddhist Monk at Versailles. I first noticed him at the gates, as we were leaving. He was looking at the people passing, his face open, looking for help. He just wanted someone to take his picture. He was being ignored. Perhaps people thought he wanted to preach to them—or he was begging for money. I knew right away what he wanted. We had been seeking the same thing only minutes before—someone to take our picture together. But he was alone. When he asked if I would take his picture, I was happy to do it. I thought he would want his picture with the golden gates of the palace behind him. He shook his head, and pointed to the cathedral. Over the face of that wing it says in French—To All the Glories of France. That is what I wonder about. Not the fact that he owned an iPhone and had to teach me how to frame and snap the picture. I wonder instead why this Buddhist Monk wanted a picture of himself in front of that vain scene? Versailles is, after all, one of the great morality tales of our time. Like Caesar fiddling while Rome burned, the French Royalty played as if they were on Mount Olympus, until the mortals climbed up and dragged them off the mountain and decapitated them. To All the Glories of France.

Did the Monk think about this? Or was he simply caught up in the grandeur, as we all were, on that sunny afternoon when the wind blew hard, the smell of Spring made us feel young and beautiful, and the golden gilded palace shone like it really was Olympus, and we were allowed to stand on its summit for a few hours? I don't know which to hope for.

As we walked away, I snapped a picture of the Monk. He was standing in his robe and sandals, looking intently at his phone, examining the picture I had taken, I suppose. Because in the end, though he knew the Palace looked perfect, like all of us, he wanted to know how he looked in front of it. We might get to stand on Olympus once in our lives, but we really want to see ourselves standing on Olympus. Even the Buddhist Monk.

Chapter Thirteen: The Most Beautiful Stroll in the World

Jennifer sat next to me on the stone steps, shivering in the night air. I offered her my sweater, but she bravely turned me down. Night was falling all around us and we were miles from the apartment. We were exhausted. Our day of rest had been anything but. Jennifer was having trouble walking. Her feet refused to cooperate anymore. My own feet hurt as well.

A beer bottle broke below us on the steps. People on the steps around us were getting restless as the last of the daylight retreated beyond the horizon.

Somehow, we'd done it again. I'd done it again. I had turned a small outing into something else. So there we were, tired, cold, wishing we could magically snap our fingers and find ourselves back in the apartment.

But there would be none of that.

It had all started because of a bookstore.

We had little-to-no plan beyond taking a walk along the Champs-Élysées later in the day. I was fiddling with the video files and photographs we had accumulated. Jennifer was writing again, and I even pulled out my journal for some note-taking. It was a nice, quiet, relaxing morning.

After reading more of Hemingway's memoir, I became curious about his famous lodgings on Rue Cardinal Lemoine. I knew the general area it was in, and had an idea I could find it. I was getting cocky about navigating around Paris. I'd conquered the métro and the RATP buses. Somehow this gave me the confidence to think I could find my way through the streets without a hitch.

So I grabbed the video camera, left my camera bag behind, and headed out to find Papa's former digs.

In a bit of defiance, I decided to go ahead and wear my tennis shoes, which was something of a cultural no-no, we'd been told. It tags you as a tourist, since Europeans don't wear tennis shoes unless they're playing sports. But at this point, I no longer cared if anyone knew I was a tourist. Besides, I'd learned early that I had fooled nobody. (Unless you count the few tourists who stopped me to ask directions.)

I only mention this because the major travel advisors touch on this topic, and I want to weigh in with my own opinion.

It is true that I saw few Parisians wearing tennis shoes. A few teenagers wore them, with one or two other exceptions. But beyond this, unless they were jogging, I did not see tennis shoes on Parisian feet.

This was not an issue for Jennifer, since she rarely wears tennis shoes. However, I had to change my habits. I did have some walking shoes which I wear to church and other casual/formal situations, so I was used to walking in them. However, they just don't have the padded heels found on running shoes, so after a week and a half of walking all over

Paris, my dogs were barking, to use a southern phrase.

I will add one thought. Why the French would mind what I wore baffles me. If a Frenchman were to show up in the States wearing a beret, we would love it. It would fit the image we have of Frenchmen. And so we might remark on it, make a joke or two about it, but in the end we would be most impressed by it. So if a ball cap and tennis shoes marked me as American, I really couldn't see the downside to that.

But I'd happily played along for most of the trip. This included wearing slacks, not jeans. On the day I headed out for Hemingway's place, I was in jeans and tennis shoes. A double sin. For those of you planning a trip, I can tell you no one treated me differently dressed like this.

With rain drizzling off and on, I walked the now familiar streets of the Latin Quarter, heading in the direction of Cardinal Lemoine. I didn't make it past Rue Saint-Michel.

Nothing catches my eye quicker than a table full of discounted books. And that was what I'd found. Several tables of books sat waiting for me outside a large bookstore. This was Gibert-Joseph, the French equivalent of Barnes and Noble.

I think Ernest Hemingway would forgive me if I confess that I forgot all about him when I saw the books lined up on the tables. All of these books were obviously marked down, just like the bargain book table at Books-a-Million. These were mostly divided into 2 and 3 Euro sections.

I quickly found a few slim paperbacks I could not pass up. All of them were in French, of course, which was great. I found a small soup recipe book for Jennifer, complete with pictures, that I knew she would love. *Soupe à l'oignon* was in there, as were many others she would love to try out.

Stepping inside the store, I discovered this bookstore extended to the floors above. There were four floors all together, including the basement. I knew I would need to bring Jennifer.

After perusing the paperback sections, I found the graphic novels and comic books. It was easy to snatch up some Star Wars comics for the kids. Just the thing for a fun French lesson.

Having piqued my interest in gifts, I walked along Rue des Écoles, browsing a shop dedicated to Middle Ages armor and die cast figures, and a game/toy shop. I was able to pick up some unique decks of playing cards at both.

On a whim I stepped inside one of the many antique bookstores that line these University streets. It is said that these stores are a researchers delight, full of the arcane. I'd been looking for any Baudelaire that was unusual for Jennifer.

The shop I entered was tended by a thin, bespeckled lady who eyed me with wariness—perhaps she disdained me for my shoes and jeans—and we exchanged *bonjours*. I'm sure she knew I was an American tourist, and she would not have been expecting me to buy something. Maybe I would just look around and put my grubby hands on her books for a while before dashing back out the door. I did my best to dispel such notions by keeping my hands to myself and specifically asking her in my limited French if she could point out her poetry section.

She came out from behind her desk and politely guided me to the shelves containing verse by Rimbaud, Valéry, and other well-known Frenchmen. It was a small section, and it did not take long to find what I was looking for. Incredibly, it was a book of essays written about Baudelaire back in the 1950s. I knew I'd struck gold. This was a volume Jennifer had never seen, perhaps one that no one in present day poetics even knew existed. I hope the shopkeeper could see how pleased I was to be able to hand her the six or seven Euros required to purchase it.

I decided I should go back and let Jennifer know about

Gibert-Joseph. We could check it out together and then take our little walk on the Champs-Élysées. I walked back across the Latin Quarter eager to share my news.

Despite her fatigue, she loved the idea of browsing through a French bookstore. So off we went, down our steps, and out into the grey, wet streets of Paris.

After a quick tour of a small curiosities shop on Rue Bonaparte, we grabbed a bus on Rue de Four and it dropped us off at Rue Saint-Michel and Avenue Saint-Germain. We ordered large coffees at a Starbucks on that corner, and then we entered the Gibert-Joseph a little further down the street.

One of our little habits at home is to visit our local bookstore and drink coffee as we browse the shelves. It is a way for us to relax, the way some couples walk the banks of a lake or sit on a blanket at the beach. So this was a perfect way to spend an hour or more in Paris.

By the time we left, Jennifer had picked out a few paperbacks (we were still worried about weight limits on the luggage), including Baudelaire's *La Spleen de Paris,* in the original French, which she had never read.

From there, a short walk brought us out to the *bouquinistes* on the Seine outside Notre Dame. This was a Friday, and nearly all of them were now open. We could feel the difference in the atmosphere. Traffic along the quays was heavier than usual, and the sidewalks were filling quickly. It was a Friday afternoon, and much like the French Quarter in New Orleans at the same time of the week, the place was beginning to hop with an influx of tourists.

After marveling at many of the antique offerings found within the green boxes of the *bouquinistes*, we took a table at Café la Notre Dame, catty-corner to Notre Dame Cathedral, where we indulged in some coffee before heading off for Jennifer's stroll up that famous avenue. It was a fun place to people-watch.

Fortified with caffeine, we rode the number 24 bus along the Seine, getting off at Pont du Carrousel so that Jennifer could see the Hotel du Quai Voltaire, which is a Baudelaire landmark, being one of his temporary homes where it is said he wrote some of his more famous poems. A large brass plaque outside the front entrance proudly displays a quote from his poem *Le Crepuscule du Matin*. Jean Sibelius, Richard Wagner, and Oscar Wilde are also on their famous guest list.

Way off topic here: it is thought that catty-corner and all of the slang variations thereof derive from the French term catre-corner which literally means four-cornered, as in an intersection. So anyway...

Now here is where I could have hailed yet another bus, for the sake of our feet. But as you know by now, I knew better; I had another surprise for Jennifer. In all the hustle and bustle of our Paris visit, she'd sort of forgotten about something which I felt certain we would regret missing. So under the pretense of leading her toward the Champs-Élysées, we walked across the Pont Royal and into the Tuileries Gardens.

Paris is like that. You can stumble over magnificent landmarks without trying very hard. We'd been in the city for twelve days, had come close to the Tuileries on two separate occasions, but had not yet been inside it. And had we chosen instead to visit the Place de Vosges, or Place de la Bastille, or if I had redoubled my efforts to find the rest of Palais-Royal, or Les Halles—I guess you get the point—we would have missed the Tuileries. But I knew we shouldn't. And I was right.

This park, much like the Champ de Mars, is a precious sanctuary for the people of Paris, with playgrounds hidden in the trees, benches everywhere, and some of the most beautiful works of statuary art we'd seen yet. We slowed down, as Jennifer delighted in its profusion of flowers and I captured pictures of the white marble statues, with their numerous companions, those purple-black ravens.

This being Paris, it also had a small café where one could purchase a glass of wine to drink at your leisure in the park. We were tempted to indulge, but we kept moving.

At the edge of the gardens, where it meets up with Place de la Concorde, we met a particularly memorable clerk at a little snack/soda stand. He was a lot of fun, and a slight misunderstanding led to a great show of kindness on his part, proving yet again that the French were not the curmudgeons we'd been told to expect.

Now, I have to go into a little detail here about our next purchase. You see, at all of these patisseries, and sandwich stands, and crêperies, I kept seeing what looked like a baguette with cheese on it. It was about a foot long, and the cheese was baked into the top. I had initially thought it was some kind of pizza boat, like those delicious disgusting things we were fed in school cafeterias. But here, at Place de la Concorde, I finally realized what it was.

A big mobile sandwich vendor, in what we would affectionately call a *roach coach* back home, was selling this, along with crêpes and other fried delicacies. Written in big English letters for the tourists were these words: *Hot Dogs*.

Of course! This was France's idea of how to serve a hot dog. Put a foot-long hot dog inside a piece of French Bread, cover it in cheese, of course, and bake it. *Voila!* Considering my state of hunger (we'd only eaten a little lunch back at the apartment) I suddenly felt like I had to have this French delicacy. After all, the signs and the servers' shirt proudly proclaimed this to be a product of the *Paris Gourmandises*. So, against my better judgment, I ordered one, sat down on the curb, and with the Eiffel Tower and Place de la Concorde as my dining view, I ate it.

Jennifer was amused at my choice, since I did not often eat this sort of State Fair food. I couldn't eat the whole thing, and tore off the remaining bits of bread to give to the birds. We had a bit of fun with the pigeons and sparrows, then crossed the traffic-frenzied circle to reach the beginning of our destination.

Champs-Élysées. This is one of those singular French phrases that evokes images of ladies in great sweeping dresses accompanied by men in top hats and black frock coats while holding walking canes topped with brass knobs. This is the domain of Maurice Chevalier and Edith Piaf. This is Paris.

We politely refused the pedicab's offer of a ride. Jennifer was determined, despite her blisters, to walk that famous avenue. The good news for her was the fact that we could see the *Arc de Triomphe* just ahead. We would walk until we reached the Arch, and then we'd call it a day. Jennifer felt sure she could handle that much.

That Friday afternoon, the Champs-Élysées was alive with the pulse of tourists mixed in with the hurrying figures of Parisians heading home for the day, their arms full of groceries or shopping bags with prominent clothing brands splayed across them. Five o'clock approached; the weather cleared up, as we were coming to expect. Wind blew along the avenue, we were still a bit chilled, but the traffic circle at Avenue Franklin Delano Roosevelt was in full bloom and this cheered Jennifer and gave us the energy to keep going.

And we needed it, since the Arch was apparently bigger than we'd thought, which meant it was a lot farther away than we had thought, too.

Passing the flower beds, we entered the upscale shopping district that is most identified with today's Champs-Élysées. It looked much like Chicago's Miracle Mile, or New York's Times Square. Most of the stores were common to us: The Gap, The Disney Store, Addidas, Sephora, LaCoste, Toyota, Virgin Records. In the middle of them, we decided to stop at a massive McDonald's. I know, I know, we'd just been to one the day before. Let me explain.

In the village of Versailles, we discovered that French McDonald's have the McBaguette. This is a great looking hamburger, with a baguette taking the place of the traditional hamburger bun. Jennifer had declined to eat one at Versailles, but she'd been thinking about it that whole day. I wasn't sure, but she was. Her eating one of those was as incongruous as me eating that great big hot dog. Even more so. Her diet is far healthier than mine. But she had earned one with all of the walking we'd done, so we pulled open the doors and stepped into a riot.

This McDonald's was stuffed with people, and Jennifer soon found that they were out of most menu items, including the McBaguette. However, they did have a separate McCafé where she could buy a cappuccino and a croissant.

Unfortunately, though the line was short, the service was almost none existent. One poor girl was trying to fill orders and she was unable to do so since the oversized espresso machine was not working properly.

Enter the manager.

A bedraggled man with a pronounced slump in his bearing appeared behind the counter. The girl, a fast talker, gave him a piece of her mind about the equipment, or the weather, or the state of fashion for young girls as imposed by the moronic designers of the day—who knows what she was saying?—but the manager just nodded, shrugged his shoulders, and trudged over to the big, stainless steel machine.

Jennifer ordered her coffee, and moved over to allow others to order. She watched the man shake his head at the broken down, mechanical wonder, as if he were a doctor, examining a chronically ill patient.

"How are you today, Sir?" she asked in French, her voice full of cheer in this dismal setting.

"Well," he shrugged again, and began his tale of woe. He was sorry about the mess. Sorry for everything. Employees had not shown up. Supplies had not arrived. Jennifer expressed her sympathies, to which he just sighed and said it would all work out. He smiled a little as he handed her the coffee. The girl added the croissant, and gave her own view of how the day was going. It was a day they would rather forget. We wished them well, and climbed the stairs to the upper dining room where we sat at a countertop by the windows overlooking that grand avenue. It was a day we hoped always to remember.

I didn't eat anything. That hot dog was killing me. I wanted to find H.G Wells' Time Machine so that we could go back to the point where I made that horrible choice to buy a French hot dog, but this was the land of Jules Verne, not H.G. Wells. That was the other side of the channel. I was out of luck.

We took our time, Jennifer recharged, and once we started off again we felt great and were excited to arrive at the *Arc De Triomphe*. It was chaotic there as we took the obligatory pictures of each other with the Arch behind us. We were surprised and pleased when a couple offered to take our picture. I wasn't sure of their nationality, since they spoke English with mixed accents, but we were happy to reciprocate and take their picture once they had captured ours.

The man had used my own ploy, which was perfectly fine with me.

As crowded as it was, we moved to one side and actually

found an empty spot which provided a large field of vision to photograph the Arch. Jennifer urged me to step into the middle of it so she could get me in the picture. As soon as I took my place and turned to look at her—this is not a joke, I promise—a tour bus pulled up beside me, the doors hissed open, and seventy-five camera-toting Japanese poured out around me.

Well, we had enough pictures, so we decided it was time to go.

The métro station Charles de Gaulle–Étoile was right there at the end of the avenue. All we had to do was go down the steps, jump on Line 1, take it to Saint-Michel Station, transfer to Line 4, and we would be home at Saint-Sulpice in about ten minutes.

We would climb the stairs, pour a glass of wine, and watch the lights come on over the rooftops as we relaxed on our second-to-last night in Paris.

But that's not how this chapter began, and it's not how it will end.

I had a better idea.

Our little stroll had taken far longer than I had anticipated. It was now about a quarter to seven in the evening. The one thing we really had not seen yet in the City of Light was the city at night with all of its lights.

And I had a plan.

So down into the métro we went. I worked a little misdirection on Jennifer, indicating that we were going to follow that sensible plan I'd outlined above—the one that involved Line 1 and Line 4. Instead, I put us on Line 2 without a word that would lead her to think we were going anywhere but home.

Basically, I lied.

When we stepped off the train and began to ascend the steps, Jennifer eyed the métro station with tired but not so stupid eyes. As we emerged onto the street, she knew right where we were.

"Why are we back at Montmartre?"

We were indeed at Montmartre, at the base of Rue de Steinkerque.

Before she could cast a veto, I quickly outlined my plan: our last free night in Paris, a chance to see the lights come up over the city as we sat on the steps of Sacré Cœur. (Isn't that the most romantic thing you ever heard, ladies?)

To her ever increasing credit, Jennifer agreed it sounded wonderful, though she also agreed she would never have gone for it if I had asked earlier. So far, the plan was going perfectly. (And my lie had been justified!)

Jennifer was actually happy to get a last chance to browse the souvenir shops and she took her time as we worked our way up the vertical street. Once we reached Place Saint-Pierre, I cheered Jennifer with the news that we would be riding the funicular up the rest of the way. This incline railway has been a famous landmark of Montmartre ever since it was built in 1900.

It turns out that many people think sitting on the steps of Sacré Cœur to watch the lights come on across the city is a romantic or just-plain-fun idea. The steps weren't packed, but they were certainly boisterous. We found a spot to one side, about a third of the way up, and we settled in to wait for the sun to set.

It was about 7:30 pm. The sky was still full of light, though clouds kept a continual cover high above. As a group of young men carried around boxes of Heineken, selling individual bottles, and as more young men stood near blankets spread out on the pavement with dozens of tiny Eiffel Towers, Venus De Milos and other such wares on display, Jennifer pulled out one of her new Baudelaire books and read it aloud, translating as she went.

I have to consider myself lucky. A great many people enjoy reading Jennifer's Baudelaire translations. I'm the only man in the world who has been privileged enough to hear her translate Baudelaire as she read his *Paris Spleen* for the first time as we sat overlooking Paris. It's okay to be jealous, guys. You have a right to be.

As the crowd continued to grow, an American with a guitar took center stage on the steps with a microphone and an amplifier and began to sing for the crowd. He was a funny sight. He was not hip, wore a tourist's fedora, much like mine, only his was all white. He looked like some teenage girl's father who was doing his best to embarrass her. But for some reason, it seemed to work, and the crowd encouraged him.

He picked his way through a few modern hits, most of which he slowed to resemble folk songs. As he played a hit song from a Nineties boy band, I was struck by how universal music can be. Behind us, on the steps, four or five girls, speaking in a rapid Scandinavian language, briefly stopped their conversation to sing the background vocals to the song, all in English. They immediately switched back to Swedish, or Norwegian, or whatever it was they had been speaking, once the chorus was over.

The Scandinavians eventually left, rain fell for a while, and we huddled under our umbrella. A Spanish couple sat behind us and asked us to take their picture once the rain shower had ended. I took the picture, and asked the man where he was from.

"Spain," he said. His smile reminded me of the actor Erik Estrada's.

"Okay, but where did you live before that? Your English is too good." Seriously, he had less of an accent than the Harlem-born Erik Estrada.

"Boston," he admitted with an even bigger smile. "I lived there as a teenager."

We continued to wait for darkness as the guitarist played *Hotel California*. There we were in Paris, listening to an American street-performer play an Eagles song. Where were the Parisian guys with the berets and black and white striped shirts, hugging accordions as cigarettes dangled from their open mouths while playing *La Vie En Rose*?

It's a wonderful and strange world.

Even stranger was the fact that it was getting close to nine o'clock and the sky still was not dark. I could not figure this out. There were precious few lights on over the city and it was nearly nine o'clock. The wind kept blowing and the temperature was dropping. Jennifer was ready to go home.

But this was the City of Light. Where were the lights?

I knew that Paris was higher on the lines of latitude than we were. I'd forgotten that it is even higher than Michigan. It is more like Canada. But this still didn't make sense to me. Shouldn't it have been darker due to the higher latitude? I'm no scientist, but I wish someone would explain it.

We finally decided to go. The cold was too much, and the crowd was getting rowdy. The bottle that rolled down the steps and broke just below us was the last straw.

It had finally grown dark enough, after nine, for the Eiffel Tower to turn on its lights. We walked to the other side of the hill and looked down on the Champ De Mars and the Tower, and then rode the funicular back down the hill.

This was the latest we'd ridden the métro. It was around ten o'clock, and the trains were packed. Jennifer managed to get a seat. I watched an older woman with several children as she taught them the names of the station. This was grandma, I assumed, making sure the grandkids learned how to get around without becoming lost.

Limping the last of the way, my steadfast bride made it back to Rue de Vieux Colombier. She never complained about my deception or my detour. She had enjoyed our stroll immensely, no matter how difficult it had become. Our quick walk along the Champs-Élysées had turned into a seven hour trek, and once again, she claimed it might have been the best day we'd spent in Paris yet.

Journal Entry: April 28, morning

At Saint-Sulpice fountain again. I am supposed to go up to the Pantheon, in search of Hemingway's Rue du Cardinal Lemoine. But I had to stop. It may be the last time I see it. It is crowded today. I share my bench with an older French lady. We do not speak. She is smoking a cigarette, and watching the people and the fountain. She can come here every Saturday. I may never be able to come again. I don't mind it is crowded. I had a few moments when the square was mine. As it once was for Hemingway. Perhaps it was never mine, or Hemingway's. Maybe it has always been the old French woman's, and I am the intruder. If so, "désolé"—I am going. "Merci" for the brief time I was allowed to live here. I'm just a kid from Illinois, who had a brief chance to live in Paris.

Chapter Fourteen: Saturday in the Park

It is difficult to be practical as you wake up in Paris, knowing it is your last day and you may never see her again. There was much to do—packing, arranging the cab to the airport, deciding what last minute gifts we could afford to stash in the luggage—the sort of things that stole time away from what I really wanted to be doing; exploring Paris.

Yes, after thirteen days, I still wanted to get out and wander. Who wouldn't? We had missed whole swaths of the city. How could I stay in and not attempt to see more?

Jennifer had an easy answer. She might have wanted to go somewhere that day, but she was physically unable. She had nothing left. Her only plans were to do a little packing and relax as much as possible.

The good news was the weather. It had warmed sufficiently for us to open the French windows along the apartment wall, allowing fresh air and light into the rooms. It was enough for Jennifer just to enjoy Paris from the view out the windows. She wasn't going anywhere.

But I couldn't. I had to go. After a few promises to be back in time to help clean and pack, I grabbed the cameras and went in search of breakfast. Shortly after leaving the apartment, on Rue de Rennes, I stopped to help a couple looking for Boulevard Saint-Germain. They looked relieved to hear my American voice. Perhaps I had looked like a local. By this time, my beard had filled in pretty well, and even my father, after seeing pictures with my beard, hat, and pullover sweater (I never wear sweaters!) had called me "Frenchy." I'm sure the *real* locals would not have been amused.

On Boulevard Saint-Germain, I found La Croissanterie Café, one of the few places open that early. It is a modern coffee shop, with light fare: yogurt, fruit cups, quiches, and of course croissants.

Before waiting on me, the lady behind the counter had to climb down into the basement for supplies. I watched a little thief come in through the open doors and sneak behind the counter to steal a croissant. This little guy was clever enough to hide behind the rolling racks of croissants as the young lady returned to view. She did not notice the imp as she passed, took her place at the counter, and waited for my order.

I ordered, keeping an eye on the bread thief. He finally gathered enough courage to grab at a croissant again and made a break for the door as she turned her back to fill my order. She never noticed him fly by.

Having ordered a croissant, I was glad she pulled one from under the front glass and not from the tray where that bird had been stealing bites from the croissants cooling on their racks.

Returning to the apartment with breakfast, I downed a cup of coffee then dashed back out. This time, I meant to explore.

I had the whole of Paris. I could have ducked into the métro and gone to any of the twenty *arrondissements*, but I chose to stay on the Left Bank. My first destination was the Luxembourg Gardens.

We had visited them on our third full day in Paris, though in reality, we were just passing through in the rain. We had peeked through the gates the evening before that, after the park had closed. For my last morning, I was determined to spend some time in the gardens. The sun had not come out, and an occasional drizzle wet the pavement. but I was not going to give up on exploring those wonderful grounds.

Before entering the gates, I stopped at a pâtisserie (why not?) and ordered a cappuccino and a brioche *à emporter.* Coffee and sweetbread in hand, I stepped through the gates on Rue de Vaugirard and found a seat beside the basin fountain in the center of the garden, under the southern façade of the palace.

This palace, built in the 1620's by Henry the IV's widow Marie de Medici, then regent of France, now houses the French Senate. It is a stately edifice, built on the Italian design of the Florentine Palazzo Pitti. It is not as large and grand as Versailles, but it has great lines and solid dignity.

The fountain is surrounded by alabaster-white statues, most of which depict former Queens of France. In all, there are over one hundred statues throughout the gardens. They are not always easy to see, many of them are tucked in beside or even behind bushes and tree branches.

As I drank my coffee, I enjoyed watching families who had come out to enjoy the warmer weather in their park. Again, like the Champ de Mars, here were the people of Paris enjoying their city. Most of them seemed to be joggers, padding along on the crunchy gravel paths that wove through the trees of the park. Many children played around the fountain, or rode little bicycles as their fathers jogged beside them. A constant thrum filled the gardens on that late Saturday morning.

Though the sun was still hidden by clouds, its warmth

could not be ignored. The air was not actually warm, but temperatures were certainly warmer than they had been. Those barren flowerbeds we'd seen just over a week before were now bursting with yellows, reds, pinks, blues, purples and whites. No matter where I wandered in the park I found statues with their bases surrounded by flowers.

Finished with my brioche (look for this when you go to Paris—it is a sweet roll with large granules of sugar sticking all over its top), I pulled out my camera and proceeded to circle the park, taking pictures of statues and Parisians in equal numbers for the next hour and a half. I was mesmerized by what I found.

My goal for that walk was to find Paul Verlaine's bust, somewhere in the trees. I had read about it in a book on the literary history of Paris. Verlaine, a famous poet from the early 1900s, was known to spend most of his time in cafés, drinking absinthe and bumming francs off admiring tourists who were thrilled to have seen him in person. He was a very rough character, and had infamously whined about his bust in the Luxembourg gardens because he felt the bust on his bust was too exaggerated. His rather crass remark left no doubt just how much he hated it.

But this was Paris, and no one was going to remove the man's bust because he didn't like it. In fact, the more controversy, the better. And maybe they had been right; there I was, eighty years later, walking through the gardens looking for the blasted thing simply *because* it was notoriously hated by Verlaine.

So off I went, taking my time, enjoying the day. I had the long lens on the camera. This was my people-watcher, and I often took pictures of interesting people (I'm a writer, so my job is to observe and glean what I can from everything) from a distance. I figured it would look like I was taking shots of the scenery around them, since there is hardly an angle or view unworthy of being photographed.

I was particularly intrigued by an older couple walking near the orangery. They must have been in their late seventies, if not their eighties. He was slightly stooped, wearing a Greek fisherman's cap, an oversized wind-breaker, baggy pants and a pair of workman's boots. She walked with a cane, her neck bent forward while wrapped in a white wool scarf; an old, gray fur coat covered her shoulders; a small-print, flowered skirt reached just below her knees. She wore soft, comfortable tennis shoes.

The cane was actually an aluminum crutch, held in place at her elbow by a black plastic brace. He was on her left; his arm crooked to allow her to hold on. As she spoke, hand gestures added emphasis to her words. Their pace, amidst all those joggers and children, was charmingly tender. She jabbered to him as he watched me warily. Somehow, though I was at least twenty or thirty yards away, he seemed to guess that I was invading their space.

Would I could have! If I'd known French, I would have approached, and asked (politely, ever so politely) if I could speak with them. If they might tell me their story. Had they been children during the war? Had they lived in fear of the Soviet threat? Or had they just ignored it, and raised a family without giving such worries a second thought? And how long had they been coming to the Luxembourg Gardens? Did they realize how special and unique their little neighborhood park was?

But I'm getting carried away. I did not know French, and I did not wish to start a conversation with those perfectly hideous words "Do you speak English?"

I came upon an old marionette theater. There, lined along the wall by the entrance, were dozens of little strollers. From inside I could hear the raucous laughter of children. Not far from there, I found an old monument with a sculpted relief of a woman performing a marionette show for children, entitled *La Comedie Enfantine.* It seems this has been going on for a very long time.

Then I found two ladies (who will forever live within my memory) exercising on that damp, cool morning.

These two beautiful ladies were playing badminton. At first, I was merely intrigued at their skill in keeping the shuttlecock off the ground. They stood only ten or twelve feet apart, there was no net. They played on the apron of the park's perimeter walking/jogging path. Their game consisted of flicking the shuttlecock high in the air for the other to hit in return.

They were very good. In fact, they never chased the shuttlecock. This might have been unremarkable if these were two young women in the peak of health. But they weren't.

One lady, probably in her forties, stood leaning back against a concrete stanchion. If you didn't notice the empty wheelchair next to her, you might not notice that she never moved her feet. She kept one hand back on the top of the three-foot high stanchion to maintain her balance.

The second lady stood on the path in a full-length, quilted winter coat. A tight scarf around her head, she wore dark glasses, with dark plastic shields on each side, as if she were wearing goggles. This lady must have been seventy-five or eighty years old. Maybe older. She was slight, with paper-thin hands that firmly clasped the handle of the racket. She took a step or two every other shot, flicking the racket with ease and grace.

Twice, during the six or seven minutes I observed them, the birdie hit the ground. Each time, the younger woman would take a long white stick that she kept on the stanchion behind her, using it to spear the birdie. Then they would start again.

I guessed that this was a mother and daughter, getting

some fresh air in the local park. How long had this caring woman pushed her daughter to the park and helped her stand against that stanchion so that she might get a little exercise and have a little fun? Judging by their skill with the rackets, it was possible they'd been doing it for many years. It is one of the most endearing images from our trip.

Just a few yards from the badminton players I finally found a bust of a poet. To my surprise it was not Paul Verlaine but was, in fact, Charles Baudelaire. Knowing Jennifer would be sorry to have missed it, I dutifully shot him from various angles so that she might not feel so left out.

There was a never-ending parade of children, families, joggers, tennis players, lovers and even a pétanque player practicing his toss. I noticed a few tourists, most of them like myself, snapping pictures of the statuary. But the majority were locals, out in their park. I've seen Central Park in New York City, and it too was full of locals exercising or just goofing off, but in the Luxembourg gardens, a smaller park, there is a perfectly astonishing mix of intimacy and grandeur.

I know where I would spend my free mornings in Paris, if I were ever to have the privilege to live there.

One of the more extraordinary scenes in the Luxembourg is a grotto that stands at the head of a long reflecting pool. The design is impressive. This rectangular pool is flanked by an iron fence and stone vases. The Medici Fountain frames the far end of the pool. This elegant, highly intricate stone edifice was built under the direction of Marie de' Medici around 1630.

After her death, the palace and grotto underwent several changes in ownership. Eventually, the grotto became rundown and in need of much repair. During the reign of Napoleon Bonaparte, the fountain was restored, and a statue of Venus replaced the original statues of water nymphs at the center of the fountain.

Later, under Baron Haussmann, the fountain had to be moved thirty meters for the construction of the Avenue de Medicis. Before this, the fountain stood against a wall, but it was now freestanding, and another fountain, from the nearby Rue Vaugirard, was added behind the grotto. This fountain, the Fountain of Leda, can still be seen today by walking around to the back.

During this move, the Venus statue was removed and a massive bronze statue of the monster Polyphemus was placed above a white marble statue of Acis and Galatea, reclining in each other's arms. The scene is exquisitely dramatic.

I found an over-the-top monument to the painter Delacroix. A modernist distorted monument to the Resistance Fighters. I even found a very busy and wild statue of Bacchus. But I never found Paul Verlaine. Perhaps after all these years, his ghost had finally found a way to manipulate stone and had ground it to dust.

Maybe I just missed it.

There was one other famous statue in the gardens; another copy of the Statue of Liberty, from 1870. Its base, however, was empty. It had been removed for cleaning. Back in the States, I learned that it has been permanently installed at the Orsay Museum, where it will be safe from cameras, as we well know. Just forget about it, and go see the bigger one on Swan

Island.

By the time I had given up on Verlaine, it was past lunchtime and I walked to Rue de Rennes and found a pâtisserie that was selling vegetable quiches. I brought one back for Jennifer (yep, my second trip up those stairs), ate lunch with her, then headed right back out for my second destination.

I was determined to find Hemingway's old neighborhood on Rue du Cardinal Lemoine. I cheated, locating it online. I had precious time left to waste in Paris.

A brisk walk across the Latin Quarter, down Rue des Écoles, then up Boulevard Saint-Michel (pausing to study the entrance to the Sorbonne). I eventually reached the Pantheon. From there, it was only a short walk around the back, where I found the white plaque announcing that during the years 1922 and 1923, Ernest Hemingway had rented rooms overlooking these streets.

Specifically, his rooms overlooked the Contrescarpe; a square tucked between the streets Lacepede, Mouffetard, Blainville and du Cardinal Lemoine. A modest fountain gurgles freely in the middle of the square. I had to seek shelter under the awning of La Contrescarpe Café as more rain fell. I took a table facing the square and drank coffee amidst a sidewalk crowded with tables and customers. The waitress, cute and perky, did not want to let me use my credit card until she realized I was buying more than coffee. I ordered an ice cream sundae that combined coffee ice cream, coffee beans in the bottom, coffee syrup, chocolate syrup, and graham cracker sticks, all topped with whipped cream.

What a wonderful city.

On my way back, I stumbled across the remains of a fruit and vegetable market. These roving markets appear on Saturdays and Wednesdays around town and this one was on Boulevard Saint-Germain. I had just missed it; all that was left was ice spilled across the wet pavement, scraps of lettuce, and carrots and many other bits of produce scattered around. Big refrigerated trucks sat idling, their noisy compressors running as the last of the unsold goods were sealed in for a trip to another market.

I knew it was getting near the time I should head home. There was still packing to be done, and the apartment to clean. I really had intended to help Jennifer with all of that.

Nagging at me was the thought of skipping out on her for a blonde I'd seen the day before. She was, in fact, one of the most famous blondes of all time. I was thinking of spending the rest of the afternoon with Marilyn Monroe.

The day before, while shopping along Rue des Écoles, I'd come across another old theater that was advertising its line-up of classic movies. The *Cinemas Action Écoles* was showing *Bus Stop*, or as the French call it, *Arrett D'Autobus*. It was showing all weekend, every two hours. I just had time to catch the three o'clock showing.

I'm not the biggest Marilyn fan, but a chance to see one of her films in Paris—one I'd never seen—was nearly impossible to pass up. I lingered at the corner of Rue des Écoles and Rue de la Montagne Sainte-Geneviève. Right would take me to the theater. Left, back to the apartment.

If you had any idea of how much I love old movies, you would understand my pain.

But it was our last night in Paris, and I didn't want Jennifer to spend it alone, though she's such a good sport, she would have understood. In fact, she later told me I should have gone to the movie. But I wouldn't have enjoyed it, knowing she was waiting for me.

I took my last walk through the streets of the Left Bank. The rain couldn't make up its mind whether it should stay or go. I did not have such a luxury of choices. I had to go. There would be no staying for us.

Along Rue Lobineau I noticed a beautiful old Citroen 2CV parked outside a little café. I realized this scene could have come straight out of 1955. I grabbed my camera. As I lifted it to my eye, I noticed a white-haired gentleman doing the same thing not ten feet away from me. He was shooting the 2CV as well.

When we were done, he had to pass me, as we were heading in opposite directions. Once we'd passed, we both stopped again, to take pictures from our new angles. I knew he was not French.

"It's beautiful, isn't it?" I pointed at the car.

"Oh yes, it's marvelous." His British accent confirmed my conviction that he, too, was visiting Paris. I had not noticed that a woman was steps away from him, waiting. She came near when she saw we were talking.

"We're on vacation, from Hong Kong," she said. Sprinkles wet our coats and she raised her umbrella. "Isn't this weather awful?"

"Well, my wife and I are from Louisiana, where we're used to a lot of hot weather. We've been enjoying the cold. And we're used to wet weather. It doesn't bother us."

"Oh, I can see how you wouldn't mind all of this. But it's *cold* in Hong Kong, and we were hoping to get warm weather here. This isn't what we were hoping for at all!"

Though she was bemoaning the weather, she seemed to be more amused than angry. We chatted a little more. They had not been in Paris long, and I wished them well, and hoped that the weather would improve for them. We said goodbye. I noticed that he took another long look at the Citroen before they turned and left.

I had to turn and leave, too. I walked to Saint-Sulpice, and sat on a bench to watch the fountain. No more cameras, no more videos. I just wanted to sit and enjoy that last moment in a corner of the world that I'd previously never known existed.

A corner of the world that fit me perfectly.

Back at the bottom of our stairs, I ran into Shirley, a newly-arrived temporary resident, like us. We'd met her two days before. She was with her husband and son.

The evening we'd returned from Versailles, as we approached the street entrance to our courtyard, I saw a mini-van cab sitting by the curb. Next to the door was a pile of luggage that could not have possibly fit in that van. Beside the luggage stood an older man, next to him was a younger man in a high-backed wheelchair.

When our door opens, which it does when you punch in the proper code, you must step over a four-inch metal lip. It is made of solid iron, and if you want to enter, you must drag anything you are carrying over it.

Once Jennifer and I were through the door, and it automatically swung shut, I realized this older man would have trouble getting the wheelchair through the door. I asked Jennifer to wait as I went back to the street.

I introduced myself and asked if I could help. The man nodded in the direction of the cab—"my wife handles all of the details," he said. "She's paying the driver right now. "

"Well, let's get you through the door. You'll want some help with that." I keyed in the door code, the door swung open, and the man saw the obstacle. I began snatching luggage and setting it inside the door. After we'd moved it all, we then carefully lifted the wheelchair over the iron frame. By then, the man's wife had paid the cab driver and she came over to introduce herself.

They were Bob and Shirley of Colorado. They had brought their son Steven to Paris. He had multiple sclerosis, and despite the cool temperatures in the shade of the courtyard, Stephen's smile was as big as the *Arc de Triomphe*. Shirley, clearly the one in charge, was full of energy and talked a mile a minute.

Their apartment was on the ground floor of our staircase. I was able to help them get through the digital lock, and we chatted about Paris. They were worried about the weather. I made sure they were aware that they needed to buy everything they would need Saturday since everything would be closed on Sunday. Once they were settled in with their bags we left them alone, knowing how tired they had to be from their flight.

We saw them only once more, when I ran into Shirley coming back to the apartment. She told me they'd taken Stephen to Notre Dame and that he had enjoyed it immensely. I was relieved to hear that they were managing just fine with him. I had the feeling that Shirley never let anything get in her way. Navigating through Paris with her wheelchair-bound son would be no problem.

It was as easy as a game of badminton.

Epilogue: Leaving Paris Behind

In the French language, the base for *rain* is the same as the base for *cry*: *pleu*. We'd seen plenty of rain, at least a small shower every day, but it had rarely rained enough to slow us down. On that last morning in Paris, rain threatened from heavy, gray clouds, as we drove through the now familiar streets of Saint-Germain-des-Prés. Only a few drops fell; just enough to force our cabdriver to employ his wipers. In the same way, tears gathered in Jennifer's eyes, with only a few staining her cheeks.

We were saying goodbye to Paris.

"This rain, it is terrible." Our cabdriver, shaking his head, leaned forward and eyed the skies through his windshield.

"Oh no," Jennifer assured him. "We like the rain. It's been wonderful."

"No, no." His English was not the best, but I could

understand him easily. "Two weeks of rain, this is catastrophe. It's no good."

He continued to murmur, switching to French. I sat back and settled in for the long ride to Charles de Gaulle Airport, watching the last images of Notre Dame pass to our left as we crossed the Pont Sully on our way to the *Périphérique*, the expressway that circles the city. For this last trip through the Paris streets, I chose not to pay attention. I'd had enough navigating. I was happy to let the drive take over.

The big question for that last day had centered on our transportation to the airport. Again, I'd read all the advice, and the one thing I knew for certain was that we did not want to use the métro one last time. We'd barely made the short trip from Gare Montparnasse to Saint-Sulpice while we were still reasonably fresh. I was not about to ask Jennifer to do it again.

I considered taking a cab to the train station to catch the AirFrance shuttle but I'd decided that if I was going to go to the trouble of ordering a cab, and if he showed up on time, and we loaded all our luggage into it, I did not want to get right back out of it a few minutes later.

I'd decided that no matter the cost, even if the driver took the long way and charged me more than necessary, we were going to stay in the cab the whole way to the airport.

We were up early; the cab was to meet us at six-fifteen in the morning. I had no idea how long everything would take: the ride to the airport, the flight check-in, the customs and security process. I left plenty of time. If all went well, we'd have several hours of sitting at the gate.

As long as we didn't miss the flight.

I'd arranged for a taxi the day before through G7, a popular and highly-recommended service. I did my best to quietly portage the luggage down the stairs. This was not easy, considering we knew how easy it was to hear people in the stairwell. One night, we had listened as one individual slowly climbed the stairs, each step on the wooden stairs echoing with increased force as he approached our floor. Upon reaching our landing, the climber stopped, paused, then let out a single, lengthy breath that nearly had us bursting with laughter, though we did our best to hold in our giggles, since we knew the climber would be able to hear us as easily as we had heard him.

With the luggage down the stairs and out through the door, we stood at the curb and waited.

I was restless, pacing, wondering what I would do if the driver did not show up. Walking about, I came upon a homeless man who was sleeping against the side of our building, behind a piece of cardboard. I'd been talking to Jennifer, and my voice woke the man, who promptly sat up, staring wide-eyed at me, startling the both of us.

I quickly murmured *pardon, pardon*, and backed away, but the damage was done. He was awake and too disturbed to go back to sleep.

Later, I was amused to see a trail of smoke drifting from the other side of the cardboard; a morning cigarette for breakfast.

When our driver arrived, he tossed our luggage into the back of the cab, and off we went.

The discussion about the rain moved on to other things. Jennifer took the opportunity to speak French and she and the driver found plenty to talk about. He showed off the picture of his four-month-old girl, bragging about her in ways even I could understand.

Jennifer asked about the election, and he switched to English, complaining about Sarkozy. Things are alike all over.

"You are from the United States?" he asked us. "Where in the United States?"

We explained that we were from Louisiana. He nodded,

then began to speak.

"For me, America is this great place, I want one day to live there. To go to America. All of it."

Jennifer told him of her love for Paris, and her pain at leaving; he shared a different perspective.

"Paris is so expensive," he said, "a man cannot raise his family but his wife must work. Two people must work. My father worked, just one job, my mother did not work, they raised a family like this. But it cannot be done now. This is not right."

I did not have the heart to tell him that this was true for too many people in the United States as well.

At the airport, as he unloaded our luggage, Jennifer asked him his name.

"Slim," he proudly announced.

Ah yes, I thought, a good American Cowboy name.

At the check-in counter, I was horrified to see the weight of our luggage. We were *under* weight. By *a lot*. I thought of all the books I could have bought and tried not to shed a tear.

If you are looking for a traveling tip, here's one you should take seriously. Buy a portable scale (they have plenty of them in the luggage section of Wal-Mart). It will be well worth it. It is the one accessory I wish I had brought along. If I had been able to weigh our luggage I would have known how much room we had left.

On second thought, it might have been a good thing I did not bring a scale. There's no telling how much money it saved me.

My plan had succeeded all too well, and we had many hours to wait in the terminal; plenty of time for Jennifer to dwell on what we were leaving behind, plenty of time to cry. In a souvenir shop, as Jennifer collected goodies to bring home to our kids, she could not stop crying. A sales clerk became distressed, sure that Jennifer was upset over something in the store. I do not know if she ever understood.

I was unable to sleep on the flight across the Atlantic. I watched movies, read, and thought about Paris. I could tell Jennifer was thinking about it too. Every once in a while, rain would fall upon her cheek.

There is no way to know if we will ever make it back to Paris. From the beginning we had treated this as a once-in-a-lifetime event and we made the most of it. There might be other trips—perhaps to St. Petersburg, Russia, or Rome, or London—though we cannot even be sure such an adventure will happen again. But if it does, I feel fairly certain we'll pass on those other cities and make plans for Paris once again.

I'm sure that we annoyed many of our friends and family with our photographs and stories and praise of everything Paris, yet we received repeated encouragements to share more pictures and more stories even after our lives had returned to normal. This book is for those who wanted to hear more.

During the course of the summer after our trip, I began to write down my recollections of our visit. In such a short time I'd begun to forget details that I thought I would never forget. Thanks to the magic of the Internet, mixed in with pictures from two cameras, video from our Sony Handycam, and my journal notes and blog entries, I was able to slowly (in some cases *painstakingly*) recreate this adventure.

It is amazing what one can do with Google Earth and Wikipedia these days. Mixed with our own photos, I was even able to retrace our steps on the days we were lost in the Montparnasse and Palais-Royal neighborhoods. A cell-phone with a data plan might have been worth it, but then we might have never have had the fun of wandering those streets.

My goal writing this book was two-fold. It is, of course, a record of our trip, which I will be glad to have in a few years when my memory is not as sharp as it once was. This is not a trip I want to forget.

Secondly, I wanted to provide a little help for anyone thinking of striking out for the City of Light. There is a lot of confusing advice out there about Paris, and I don't see why I shouldn't add to the confusion.

Mainly I want people to know that a trip like this is not so difficult. And once you finally decide to go, I want to make sure you have an idea of what you could do when you get there.

And as you might guess, I suggest you start at a little fountain beside an old church known as Saint-Sulpice. After that, you should be able to figure out the rest on your own.

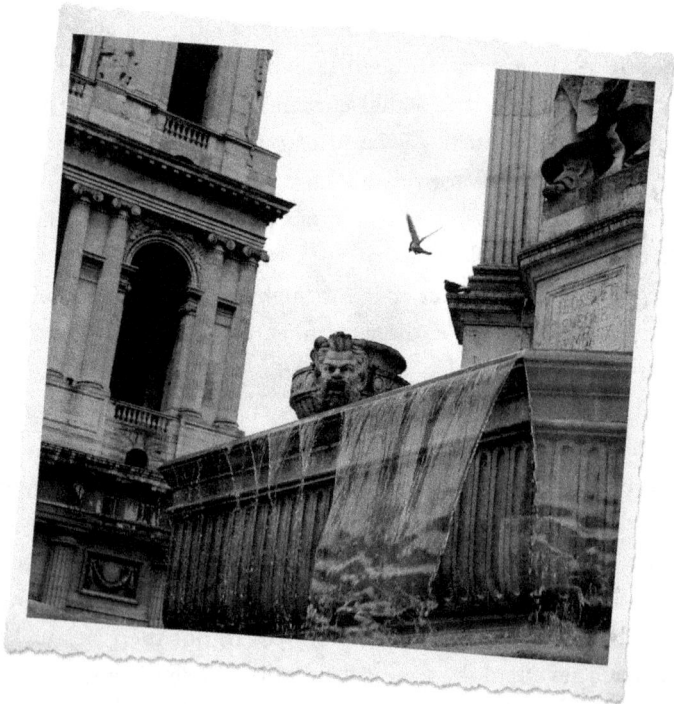

Travel Advice from yours truly:

Adapt or Convert: A dilemma in Faith

You can read all the advice you want about whether you should buy converters for your electronic devices or adaptors. However, at the end of the day, you have to choose one, and have faith as you plug your expensive do-hickeys into a European 220 socket. Even if you buy both, you still have to choose one to plug in the first time. After much reading and hand-wringing, I decided on the adapter, armed with the knowledge that I'd examined my laptop and camera cords and somehow deciphered the itsy-bitsy writing stamped on the black plastic. All of my equipment was fairly new, and so I had read in several different places that the newer cords only needed an adapter. Sparks notwithstanding, the adapter worked just fine.

The chord for your device should say it is rated for up to 240V. DO NOT take my word as the last word on the subject. Read up on this. I've seen too many stories of people burning up their cameras, cellphones, and laptops because they had the wrong equipment. So take your time on this and get it right.

Euro'kay, I'm okay: The crazy truth about Euros in America.

This story may sound apocryphal, but every word is true. This is really weird.

I went to my local bank to buy Euros before our trip. I didn't want to try exchanging cash in the airport after our arrival. Besides, I was excited, and wanted to get some Euros in my hands. It sounded pretty cool! Right?

So into the bank I go.

"I'd like to buy some Euros," says I.

Blank stare from the teller.

"You know," says I, "those funny little Monopoly-money looking bills that a massive portion of the world's population uses?"

"Oh," she says, "we can do that. Tell us the amount you want and you'll get it next week."

"Hmm, okay. I'd like some fives, tens, twenties, and a handful of ones and twos in coins."

"Oh, no sir, you cannot choose which denominations you get, and you certainly can't get any coins."

"Pardon?"

"You don't get to choose the currency denominations. And you cannot get coins anywhere in the United States."

Undaunted, I go home and call the main number for my bank, in New York City, asking to speak to someone who handles foreign currencies. (That's the way I roll, sometimes. Go right to the head of the class.) After the call is transferred, I hear this calm, slightly hesitant voice say:

"Hello?" This guy sounds as if he's just received the first phone call in the history of the world. He sounds confused, and amazed.

"Yes, I'm trying to find out how to buy some Euro coins before my trip to Paris in the spring. Can you help me?"

"I think you have the wrong department," he says, still reluctant to speak. But now, his curiosity is piqued. "What were you wanting to do?"

I explain in detail. His answer was classic.

"That must be a different department. Here at my department, if you're talking to me, it usually means some not very good things for you. I deal with money that is suspected of being tied to certain organizations that are not..." he hesitates here, unsure of how much he can tell me, "...well let's just say if I'm talking to you, there are bad things in your future."

"There are bad things from the bank?"

"Well, for those who are involved in illegal activity."

"Oh, I see."

"But hold on," he says, before I can hang up, "I may be able to help you. I've done a little traveling, and know a little about Euros. Can you hold one second?"

"Sure," I say, wondering if a black SUV is going to show up outside my door in under ten minutes. I'm trying to decide if I have any illegally copied CDs I need to flush down the toilet before the men with the dark sunglasses and wingtip shoes knock down my door. The man comes back on the line:

"Okay, I think I've found what you want to know. Your local bank *can* order specific denominations of Euros. This requires a certain form that needs to be filled out. Now, the tellers at your bank may not know this, because, well..." he stumbles here, and I fill in the blank.

"They're sort of *provincial* in their experience?"

"Yeah, that's a good way to put it. Now as to the coins, they are right. I know this, because I found out the hard way after returning from abroad. Not only can you not buy Euro coins in the US, unless it is from a coin collector, but you cannot exchange ones you have when you get back. The bank will not touch them."

We had a pleasant discussion about the absurdity of banks not being able to touch legal forms of currency, and I thanked him profusely when we were done. Really, I think he was bored. And he enjoyed the novelty of someone calling his phone number. I got the idea *no one* ever calls him. He's like the Grim Reaper at a birthday party. I think most people avoid him.

I ordered the cash just like he said I could. And I was fortunate enough to have a friend/co-worker who is originally from the Azores. He gets back home a few times a year, so he was able to sell me a pocketful of Euro coins. They were useful to have in the airport. There were many coin operated machines, and they tend to require the one or two Euro coins.

When we returned, I kept the coins I had left, but when I went to the bank to sell the cash I still had, a teller at the bank wanted them for herself, so she bought them from me privately.

Fly the French Skies: That big flight across the Pond.

As I mentioned, flights from the United States generally take off in the afternoon, so that they arrive in the morning. The idea is, you get aboard, eat a nice little meal (and with AirFrance, the little bottles of wine are *very* good), you relax as the plane heads into the night sky, then they lower the lights, everyone snuggles against their seat partner with little pillows, blankets, and even eye-masks, all provided by the airline, then everyone awakes refreshed as the plane is landing at Charles De Gaulle Airport.

That's the *idea*, anyway. If you're like me, you might not sleep well, and you'll sit there and play with the little video screen in the back of the seat in front of you. This goes on for a long time. A very long time. A really long time. Like seven or eight days long time. Like my back is killing me and my legs no longer are a part of the great mystery that is the body's circulation system. But then again, I'm nearly six foot three inches tall, which feels more like seven feet fourteen inches tall, in economy.

Fortunately, Jennifer was able to sleep nearly the whole time, so she wasn't inconvenienced by my discomfort. And that's all that really mattered, right?

I have little advice on the trip through the vastness of the CDC Airport. You won't get lost. Everyone is going the same way. Just follow along. You'll go down halls, take escalators, cool little trains, escalators, halls, lines, passport dudes who do not look amused, and it will all work out for the good, since you will eventually realize you are just moments away from Paris. Keep this in mind!

This One's on the Tip of My Table:

A real simple guide to tipping in Paris; tips are already figured into your bill. Simply drop one or two Euros on the table, maybe a one and a two together, as a sign of respect to your waiter as you leave. That was the advice I'd read, and I have no idea if the waiters were happy or not since I rarely went back to the same place. So follow my advice and you too can be blissfully unaware if you've offended the local servers or not.

Actually, one time, I forgot to leave my usual tiny oblation to the server-gods after lunch on the Rue Galande. This was at the little Italian place I mentioned earlier. I remembered after we'd walked off, and I went back, after Jennifer schooled me in the correct way to say "Pardon me, I forgot to leave this." The waitress, who was very friendly with us while we were there, was quick to shake her head and say it was okay, there was no need. At least I think she said that. And who knows what she thought I was saying? For all I know when I came back through the door alone with the money in my hand she thought I was saying I wanted to hire her for some shocking and nefarious designs and she was quickly waving me off because she was not that kind of a girl. Who could say?

You Can't Say it Enough: Because they can't either.

For all of you who grew up in the less friendlier confines of the United States (excepting those in the South, who are used to making eye-contact and saying "hey" and "how's it goin'?" to *complete* strangers), make an effort to be friendly! Parisians are nuts about saying "*Bonjour!*" to everyone. It is a little odd at first, but you'll get used to it. Even to the point that you'll miss it when you get back to the grumpy United States.

At one point, as we were walking along a semi-darkened street, we passed a foreboding figure leaning against a wall smoking a cigarette. In New Orleans or New York City we would have sped up a little, not made eye contact, and hoped the man wouldn't turn out to be a nefarious member of the underworld. However, this man pulled the cigarette from his lips, looked us in the eye, and—you guessed it—greeted us with a solid "*bonsoir*".

Oh yeah, and you'll know it is five o'clock or later in the evening, because without any visible signal, Parisians will switch from *bonjour* to *bonsoir* at 5 pm. On the dot. You can set your watch by it. It's a little strange, to be honest.

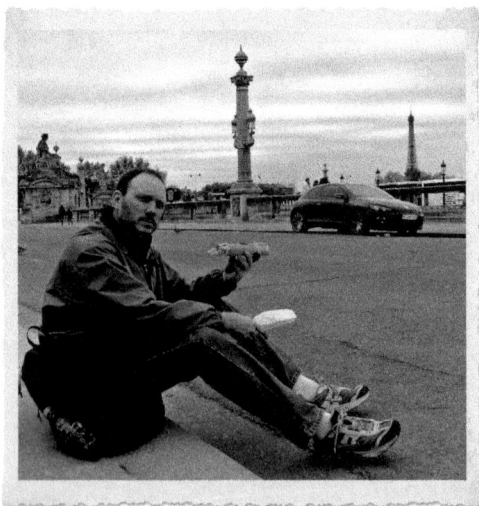

Selected Bibliography

The following is a list of publications I used in preparation for our trip. Some of them may help those who would like to plan their own Paris excursion. All of it can be read for fun (and a little education).

The Greater Journey: Americans in Paris
by David McCullough, 2011
This exhaustive look at the history of Americans visiting and or moving to Paris (including artists, doctors, politicians and others) came out the summer before our trip. What an exciting and inspirational book to get me in the proper frame of mind for Paris! It really enabled me to see beyond the tourist veneer of the city and encouraged me to dip into its creative influences. I would have missed so much without this historical guidebook.

Walks Through Lost Paris: A Journey Into the Heart of Historic Paris
by Leonard Pitt, 2006
I devoured this book just a month before our trip. It details the changes wrought by Baron Haussmann on the Left and Right Banks during the redesign of the city in the mid-1800s. Before this book, I'd never even heard of Haussmann, who is both vilified and highly esteemed for his work in the city. Yes, he knocked through the old quarters of the city like a bull in a china shop, but what he left in their place is the image of the city we know today. And what an image! In this book, Pitt takes the reader on several virtual *walking tours* in which he matches up old photographs with current views of the streets and houses to detail the history of such lost gems as the *Cour du Dragon*, and the intricate maze of streets that once ran right

up to the front steps of Notre Dame Cathedral. Serious lovers of Paris history can use the maps included to tour the city and examine the historical flotsam and jetsam that remains throughout the modern city. My walks through the city were benefited immensely by this more intimate look at the streets of Paris.

Writers in Paris: Literary Lives in the City of Light
by David Burke, 2008

Okay, time for me to admit that my knowledge of the writers in Paris was sorely lacking until I read this book just weeks prior to our visit. As I mentioned before, I was never interested in Hemingway when I was younger, so I found a way as a writer and lover of books to grow up completely ignorant of him and his "lost generation". Sylvia Beach? I'd never heard of her. Gertrude Stein? I was pretty sure she was either a 1920's Nightclub dancer or one of Hitler's mistresses from his pre-Nazi days. (And there's no proof that I'm wrong on either one of those, okay?) It was in this book that I discovered that our apartment was on the same street as the legendary headquarters of the Musketeers. Author David Burke takes a literary tour of each neighborhood geographically instead of chronologically, and it leaves one nearly out of breath while reading the section on the Left Bank.

France, the magazine.

Every two months I would grab the next issue of this excellent magazine off the shelves of our local Books-A-Million and *devour* it. Perfect for planning a trip to France. It is written toward a British audience, but it still has plenty of useful articles and resources for your trip. If you can, get an issue that was put out the season in which you plan to visit. It will have a list of local events that will clue you in to what will be happening during your trip.

Practical Paris [Kindle Edition]
by Karen Henrich, 2011

This great little compilation includes truly practical sections like "Some Good Public Washrooms" and "How Not to Come Across as an Ugly Tourist". The public washrooms bit was actually the place where I discovered the information about the live jazz performances at the Hotel D'Aubusson, without which I would never have found the Cinema Christine. Missing out on both of those would have been a shame and I have Ms. Henrich's well-researched Kindle book to thank for it. Since it is on Kindle, it is a resource you can take with you to either read on your laptop while in Paris for quick reference, or if you have a Kindle or Smart Phone, you can actually have it with you while out in the city.

Travel Paris, France 2012- Illustrated Guide, Phrasebook & Maps (Mobi Travel) [Kindle Edition]
by MobileReference, 2012

Another useful Kindle book that I kept handy as we traveled about the city. The maps are not very easy to read with the Kindle, but there is great information here on transit, currency, and other details of foreign travel. Something like this is a must for rookie World-Travelers.

The Unofficial Guide to Paris
by David Applefield, May 2010 edition

This was our Paris Bible. It was the first resource I bought and if I had never found the other books I could have successfully made the trip with just this one book. The advice in this book was more than practical, it was unvarnished, it was not full of the over-hyped, fear-mongering/whining common to foreign travel books. It was in these pages I learned about the possibility of renting an apartment, and how safe and practical it can be. I wish I still had the book. However, in a weak moment of sentimentality, spurred on by a fear that our luggage would be overweight, I left it on the bookshelves of our apartment for the next guests. I hope someone gets some use out of it. It was full of highlights and dog-eared pages. To be honest, I miss the darn thing. And it would have helped to have had it while I was writing this book!

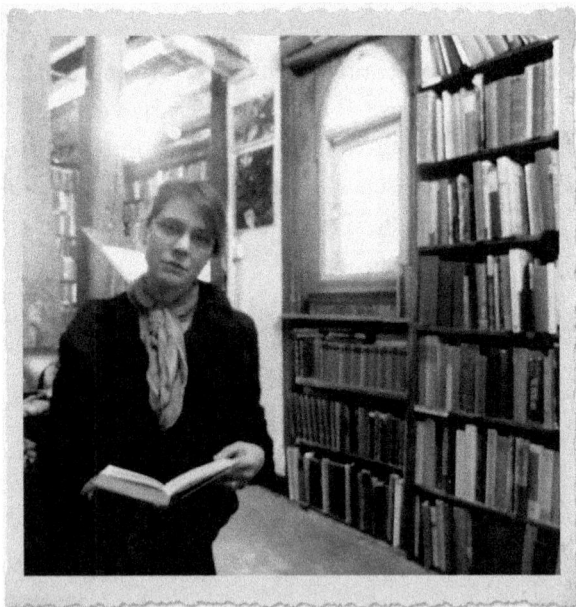

Paris in Print and Film

I'm including a small list of what I consider a fun way to "visit" Paris without actually going there. These can be used to educate yourself on the city before a trip, or to experience a little of it if you cannot get there in the near future.

Paris in Classic Fiction:

The Hunchback of Notre Dame, and *Les Miserables*, by Victor Hugo. Must reads for a Paris education. This is non-negotiable.

The Belly of Paris, by Emile Zola. A delightful look at *Les Halles*, the historic food market that dominated the Right Bank before it was torn down and replaced with a shopping mall.

L'Assommoir, by Emile Zola. Though this is not an uplifting storyline, it is a very detailed look at life in 19th century Paris. Zola was a mad-dog researcher and I can attest to some of it. His details are so exact, I saw many of the same things over one-hundred years later. A testament to both his excellent research and the constancy of Paris. His chapter on the wedding party mirrors some of our same wanderings down the streets of the Right Bank as well as our tour of the Louvre.

A Tale of Two Cities, by Charles Dickens. I was in the middle of reading this on our trip. A sobering look at the Revolution from an outsider's viewpoint. I'm pretty sure Dickens was as unhappy with all the destruction heaped upon the city by the rabble as I was. He does not portray them sympathetically.

Paris in Non-Fiction

A Moveable Feast, by Earnest Hemingway. No matter your opinion of Hemingway's fiction, I would strongly urge anyone with an interest in Paris to read this memoir. He admits that it should be taken as fiction, since his memories were as aged and fermented as a good French wine at that point. But his descriptions of the city are dead on. And his admittedly embellished memories are quite fun to read.

Death in the City of Light: The Serial Killer of Nazi-Occupied Paris, by David King (2012). This book is not for the faint of heart. (Or weak of stomach.) However, it gives a harrowing and sad look at Paris during the years of the Nazi occupation. This is difficult to read if you love the city, but it will certainly change your perspective on what those in the city endured during this tragic time. The story of the serial killer is astounding in its own right.

Paris, Paris: Journey into the City of Light, by David Downie (2011). A native San Franciscan, David Downie moved to Paris in the 1980s and while living and working there began to write about the city. His book is a collection of articles and essays he's written on the city. His familiarity with the city flavored the book with a slightly jaded view of Paris. But the book that is full of information and there are many moments of poignant observation.

Paris in Film:

*Paris 36 (*original title *Faubourg 36),* 2008. This is a stunning musical that gives us a thrilling look at Paris in the 1930s, at a musical theater. The sets and special effects would make the movie worthwhile if it didn't have an exciting and compelling story filled with memorable characters. But it has both, so it is really a complete package. Don't miss this one.

Midnight in Paris, 2011. If you have even the slightest interest in Paris, you've already seen this movie. Woody Allen offers what I consider to be his best movie ever as he gives us a glimpse at the Paris of Hemingway and Gertrude Stein. Mixed with a modern love story, the viewer is treated to scenes from present-day Paris as well as a look into the past and the days of Picasso, T.S. Eliot, and Salvador Dalí. It was a special treat to see this movie just before we left for Paris. And equally special to watch it after we returned. Allen captures Paris perfectly.

French Kiss, 1995. Full of fun location shots, this touching romantic comedy is chock full of what makes Paris a great visual city. It may be the best romantic comedy set in Paris, if you don't count Cary Grant and Audrey Hepburn's *Charade*, which you really shouldn't, since it is more of a thriller than a romantic comedy.

Charade, 1963. One of the best pairings in a Paris movie (how could you get better than Grant and Hepburn?). The nice touch here is how they spend their time traipsing all over Paris, never paying attention to the great sites in the background.

Frantic, 1988. This gritty, *noir* thriller has some of the most realistic, pedestrian location shooting you'll see in modern day Paris. Added to that is one of the best thriller scripts ever and it becomes a movie you cannot pass up. If you missed this then, look it up now. It is where Harrison Ford developed his "someone's taken my wife and I'm *really mad* about it" character. I'll admit it. I cry at the end.

A View to a Kill, 1985. One of the lesser Roger Moore Bond movies, it does have the classic scene in which Grace Jones' Mayday character dives off the Eiffel Tower. That gets this movie a place on my list.

The Bourne Identity, 2002. An action thriller that gets the feel of Paris just right. One of the best chase scenes ever filmed takes place in the city. Three words: Ready, steady, go!

Rififi, (original French title: *Du Rififi Chez les Hommes*), 1955. This rough, dark *film noir* has some of the greatest location shooting from the fifties I've ever seen. And the story is top-notch. Jean Servais plays of the toughest noir heroes you'll ever see. The ending is flat out *unforgettable*.

Paris, 2008. This French film, with an ensemble cast including Juliette Binoche, captures Parisian life amongst the working class. It may be a bit too odd for American audiences, but there are ample scenes of Paris for anyone looking for a Paris fix.

A Monster in Paris, 2011. I include this animated film not only because it is a fun, silly,

● ● ●
There are many more movies shot in Paris; more than I could list. This was but a short list of the ones that helped to inspire our interest in this trip. (Or helped to remind us of what we left behind.)

● ● ●

thrilling movie set in Paris of the early 20th Century, but also because we watched it on the flight back to the States. Jennifer and I loved it.

About the Authors

Jason Phillip Reeser is the author of the short story collection *Cities of the Dead,* as well as the novel *Jury Rig.* His novel *Lady in the Lazaretto,* which will be published the summer of 2013, is the second book in his Space Noir trilogy based on his 2012 novel *The Lazaretto.*

Jennifer Reeser is the author of *Sonnets from the Dark Lady and Other Poems, Winterproof,* and *An Alabaster Flask.* Her epic poem *The LaLaurie Horror* will be published in the Fall of 2013.

They live with their children in Louisiana.

Saint James Infirmary Books is a small publishing company. If you enjoyed this book, we would appreciate your willingness to mention it to friends who might also enjoy it. If you are active online, at sites like Facebook, Goodreads, Amazon, Shelfari, or similar sites, we ask that you remember us when reviewing and recommending titles. For more information, look for us at saintjamesinfirmarybooks.com, as well as our Facebook page:

Facebook.com/SaintJamesInfirmaryBooks.

Thank you in advance.

SJIB

Now Available from Saint James Infirmary Books. Look for these books on our website or check with your local bookseller. Also available for Kindle at Amazon.com.

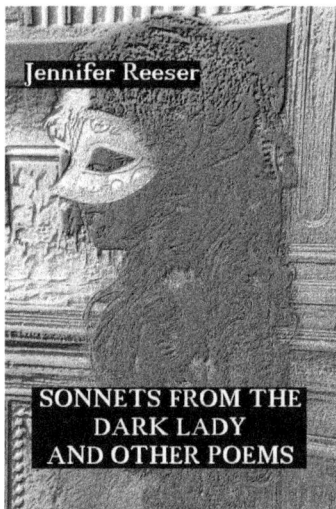

"...a stunning collection of top-notch poetry..."
— Joseph S. Salemi, Editor, *TRINACRIA*

"I love these sculpted and energetic poems, full of drama and wit."
—Michael Potemra, Literary Editor, *National Review*

Watch for Jennifer's epic poem *The LaLaurie Horror*, coming, Fall of 2013!

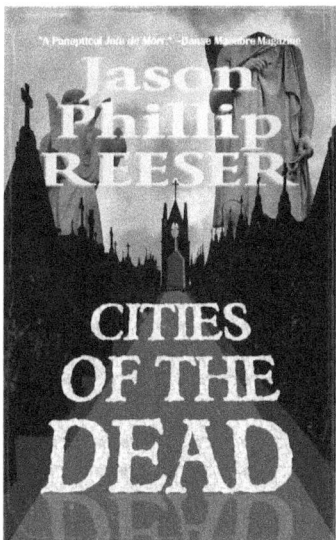

In New Orleans, Louisiana, the dead refuse to be buried.

"...a skilled and entertaining Louisiana storyteller."
—*Lake Charles American Press*

"...powerful and compelling."
—Neal Connelly, author of *St. Michael's Scales*